Thomas Adolphus Trollope

**A Lenten Journey in Umbria and the Marches**

Thomas Adolphus Trollope

**A Lenten Journey in Umbria and the Marches**

ISBN/EAN: 9783742814555

Manufactured in Europe, USA, Canada, Australia, Japa

Cover: Foto ©Andreas Hilbeck / pixelio.de

Manufactured and distributed by brebook publishing software (www.brebook.com)

Thomas Adolphus Trollope

**A Lenten Journey in Umbria and the Marches**

# A LENTEN JOURNEY

## IN UMBRIA

AND

## THE MARCHES.

BY THOMAS ADOLPHUS TROLLOPE,

AUTHOR OF

"A RAMBLE IN BRITANNY," "A SUMMER IN WESTERN FRANCE,"
"LA BEATA," "MARIETTA," ETC.

LONDON:
CHAPMAN & HALL, 193, PICCADILLY,
1862.

# CONTENTS.

## CHAPTER I.
Introductory .................................................................... 1

## CHAPTER II.
From Arezzo to Città di Castello—The Cerfone—Monterchi—Valley of the Tiber—First appearance of Città di Castello—The Vitelli—Days of Prosperity and Days of Decay in Italy—The Cannoniera   14

## CHAPTER III.
Other Vitelli Palaces—Earthquake in Città di Castello—Paolo Vitelli, the Architect—Remarkable Picture—Neglected Gardens—Remarkable Frescoes of Gherardi—Pliny's Villa—Wine of the Valley of the Tiber—Its Qualities—Italian Local Historians—Their Scarceness—Their Value—Those of Città di Castello—Specimens of Municipal Records .................................................. 29

## CHAPTER IV.
Route from Città di Castello to Gubbio—Difficulties—Valley of the Tiber from Città di Castello to Fratta—Ferry of the Tiber—Fratta—New Road to Gubbio—Picture at Fratta by Signorelli—Monastery of Monte Corona—Legislation respecting the Regular Clergy in Umbria—Pepoli—Civitella Raineri—Subterranean Passage—Difficulties of the new Road—Specimen of Italian Character—Valley of the Assino—Solitary Monastery—Castello di Danno—Well-Head of the River Assino .......................................... 44

## CHAPTER V.
Position of Gubbio—Hotel there—Italian Innkeeping—An Italian Reception—Monte Calvo—Palazzo Pubblico—Former Population of the City—Curious Anecdote—How the Dynasty of Montefeltro became Lords of Gubbio.................................................. 59

## CHAPTER VI.
The residence of the Dukes of Urbino at Gubbio—The Duke's Cabinet—The Palace of the Municipality—Destroyed Loggia—Mauro Sarti's Description of the Palazzo Pubblico—Cost of the Building—Public Library—Remains of a Roman Theatre—The "Bottaccione"—Aqueduct—Soulage Collection—" Momo Nicchi "—Statue by Maestro Giorgio—Pictures at Gubbio—Picture by Damiani—Fresco by Nelli—Local Historians—Italian Society ................ 76

## CHAPTER VII.

Route from Gubbio to Perugia—Limits of the ancient Picenum—No Guide to be had—Vallugegno—Fratticciola, a Robber Town—Approaching to Perugia—Political Changes—Perugia deserted by Travellers, and Why—An Italian Juryman—The Fortress after the Expulsion of the Papal Government—Its Demolition—Former Prisoner—The Swiss in the Benedictine Convent—Political Feeling—Old Carbonaro—Curious Anecdote, showing the Isolation of the Papal Provinces from one another................................................. 101

## CHAPTER VIII.

Drive to Assisi—St. Francis—the Great Convent—The Church Services—Sermon by one of the Friars—Scene in the Church—Bell of Santa Lucia—The great Refectory—The Kitchen—The No Library—The Ambulatories—Excursion to Le Carceri—Mountain Subasio—Convent at the Carceri—The Superior—Legends............................................ 115

## CHAPTER IX.

From Assisi to Foligno—Basin of Assisi—Spelto—Foligno—Making Bargains at Inns—Foligno to Camerino—Belfiore—Scepoli—Colflorito—Serravalle—District of Camerino—Situation of the City—Theatrical Ciceroni—Wanderings in Search of a Rare Book—Ravages of Earthquake at Camerino—Palace of the Varani—Wealth of the City under their Rule—Decadence under the Papal Government—History of the Varani—Dennistoun's Memoirs of the Dukes of Urbino—Passages from the History of the Varani—Fratricide, and Extermination of the Family—Escape and Adventures of Giulio Cesare Varani—A good Aunt—The Chiavelli Family at Fabriano—Second Escape of Giulio—Finally murdered by Cesare Borgia—Religious Experiences of Camilla Varani—Beauty of the Camerino Women—Quotation from a Poem of the Fifteenth Century on this Subject—Legend of St. Ansinus—History of Camerino, by Camillo Lilli................................................................................. 126

## CHAPTER X.

Route from Camerino—Castle of Varano—Origin of the Family—Tolentino—Mediæval politics—Remarkable report to Alexander the Sixth—The Accorambini Family—A Sentence on Treason—St. Nicholas—Castello di Rancia—Great Battle in 1815..................... 157

## CHAPTER XI.

Macerata—Its Points of Similitude and Contrast to Camerino—Origin of Macerata—Its Mediæval History—Prosperity—Terraces around the Walls—Views from them—Divisions and Hatreds between City and City—Literary Quarrels—Remarkable one between Macerata and Camerino—Origin and Progress of the Dispute—Real bitterness of feeling attending such Disputations—Macerata and Recanati—Origin of Ricina—Work of Fra Brandimarte—Absenteeism

CONTENTS. vii

PAGE

at Macerata—Brick Palaces—Bramante's Church of La Madonna Delle Vergini—Enormous Ball Court—Probable Future Destiny of Macerata .................................................................. 171

## CHAPTER XII.

Route from Macerata to Fermo—Montolmo—Pausulæ—Difficulty of assigning Localities to the Names of destroyed Cities—Ancient Picenian Cities built in the Plain—St. Giusto—Curious Treaty between a number of Picenian Cities—Monte Granaro—St. Elpidio—Lete Morta — Turnpikes v. Non-Turnpikes — Difficulty of distinguishing these Hill-towns from each other—Long Ascent to Fermo—The Streets of the City—The Appearance of it from without the Walls—Dalmatia visible from Fermo—Situation of the Cathedral .................................................................. 186

## CHAPTER XIII.

Expressions of Fermo—The Picturesque v. the Prosperous — Deteriorated Aspect of the Country—Wealth of the Church at Fermo—Its proportion to that of the Country in General—Inn at Fermo—A Brigand Host and Hostess—Clean Sheets and Garlic—Architectural Features of the City—The Cathedral and the "Girone"—Former Military Importance of the Spot—Tyrants in Fermo—Destruction of the Castle—Tura da Imola—The Euffreducci Family—Oliveronto Euffreducci—His Story, as moralised by Macchiavelli—Ludovico Euffreducci—His Death Scene—Papal Rule in Fermo—The three Martyrs of Fermo—A Story of Papal Justice ... 199

## CHAPTER XIV.

From Fermo to Loretto—Porto di Fermo—Why no Fish are to be had at Fermo—Unattractive Coast Scenery—Soil brought down by the Rivers—Railway Works—Sites of Ancient Cities—Cupra Marittima—Cluentum—Potenza—St. Elpidio—Brandimarte's Work on Picenum—The Hill of Loreto—Legend of the Santa Casa—Dalmatians at the Shrine of Loreto—Belief in the Legend .................. 223

## CHAPTER XV.

Commencement of the Religion of the Santa Casa, St. Francis di Assisi, at Loreto—St. Carlo Borromeo at Loreto—First Church built there—Second Church—Third Church built by Guiliano da Maiano—Altered by Picconi da St. Gallo—Little to admire in the Church as it now is, except the Sculptures enclosing the Santa Casa itself—Measures of the Santa Casa—Description of the Interior—Mode of blessing Articles—Santa Scodella—The officiating Priest—The Treasury—Robbery of it by the French—Its present Contents—Majolica Vases—Main Industry of the town of Loreto—An Esprit Fort—Battle of Castel Fidardo took place under the eyes of the Canons of Loreto .................................................................. 236

## CHAPTER XVI.

Recanati—Its Situation—And Form—A mad gallop thither—Appearance of Recanati within the walls—Curious ancient Law—Former History, and political Constitution—Montefano, and its direct subjection to the Holy See—Ughelli's Libel on Recanati—Typographical Enterprise at Recanati in these days—The "Great Rebellion" at Recanati—Specimen of a Papal Bull in the fifteenth century—Remarkable charge of Idolatry—Friar Andrew and his Fortunes—Crusade against Recanati—Terrible Fate of the City—Return to Loreto .......................................................................... 258

## CHAPTER XVII.

From Loreto to Osimo—Position of Osimo—Classical Authors who mention it—Besieged by Belisarius—Maintained its Independence—Its resistance to the Popes—Succeeds in causing its Fortress to be destroyed—The Citizens take cognizance of the disorders of a nunnery; and succeed in having it abolished—The Cathedral of Osimo—Remarkable series of portraits—Storm of wind at Osimo—Walk round the walls—From Osimo to Ancona—Monte Conero—Position of Ancona—Apparent discrepancy between Strabo and Pomponius Mela—Entrance to Ancona—First Impressions made by the City—Contrast between it and the Cities around it—Inconvenience of the "Free Port"—Memorial of an Inquiry—The Cathedral—Its Situation—Its Dangers from the Encroachments of the Sea—Military strength of Ancona—The Port ..................... 277

## CHAPTER XVIII.

From Ancona to Rimini by rail—Rimini to San Marino—Difficulty of the Journey—Position of the Town—Its Elevation—Means of reaching it—Appearance of the Town on approaching it—Life at San Marino—Postal Arrangements—Territory of the Republic—The "Borgo"—Ascent thence to the City—Manufacture of Gunpowder—Of Playing-cards—Solitude of the Town—Its Aspect—Church—Water Supply—The Fortress—Its Guardian—Its Position—Ancient Name of San Marino—View from the Fortress—Inmates of it—Administration of Justice—Meeting of the Council—Sunrise Visit to the Castle—Knocking up the City—Sunrise from the Castle Battlements—Coast of Dalmatia—Preservation of its Independence by San Marino—Return to Rimini—Thence to Florence—Conclusion .......................................................... 300

# A LENTEN JOURNEY.

## CHAPTER I.

#### INTRODUCTORY.

THERE is no square mile of Italian soil, that does not merit our curiosity and examination. It may possibly be said, in reply, that the same remark may be made of the entirety of the earth's surface. And if the objector be as much interested in the facts and annals of Nature as in those of the human race, it would be perhaps difficult to gainsay him. But at all events, and especially with reference to all that man has done and has been on earth, the above assertion is true of Italy to a degree far superior to that in which the same may be said of any other portion of the globe. And a very cursory reflection on the part, or rather on the various successive parts that Italy has played in the history of the world, will suffice to show how and why this should be the case. The soil is rich in different strata of memorials and reminiscences superimposed one on the other, as they have been deposited by the diverse human tide-streams which have passed over it, after the manner of geological successions in the formation of the crust of the globe.

That part of this strangely-storied land with which these pages are concerned, has witnessed the rise and progress of *at least* four different social systems and widely-differing civilizations,—the Etruscan, the Roman, the Mediæval, the Modern. And although it may seem to us that the two latter are divided and distinguished from each other by a less well-marked boundary line, than that which to our eyes wholly cuts off each of the two older civilizations from that which succeeded it, it is probable that this seeming is only due to the greater remoteness of the time and our consequent smaller knowledge of the details of its history. It may be well believed, that the Roman civilization was quite as largely a debtor to the Etruscan, and the Christian Mediæval to the Pagan Roman, as was that which arose at the period of the, somewhat misleadingly so called, *rénaissance*, to the life of the centuries which preceded it.

During two at least of these four periods, the first that is to say, and the third, the districts visited in the journey here described were among the most cultivated, the most socially and artistically important, and in every respect the most interesting of Italy. But they have not hitherto received from travellers a fairly proportioned share of attention. No land was ever visited by nearly so great a number of foreign travellers as Italy; yet no European country, not even Spain, has remained so wholly unknown and neglected in certain parts. No stream of foreign travel ever flowed in so undeviating a channel as that of the visitors from the northern side of the Alps to Rome and Naples, unless perhaps that of the caravan of the faithful to Mecca. Generation after generation the thousands come every year, and all tread with the utmost exactitude in the footsteps of their predecessors. The French and Russians do not look to the right or the left as they pass on their way to the great capitals. The English and the Americans do look out to right and left as they journey along the beaten track, and see as much as can be seen by such means. But they very rarely do much more than this. The reasons why this should be so are very obvious. The great objects of an Italian journey, Venice, Florence, Rome, Naples, are so paramount, and so sufficient in themselves to occupy all the time, that the great bulk of pleasure-travellers can give to their tour, that this cause alone has ensured the neglect of objects of secondary interest. But the mere force of routine, and the sheep-like tendency men have to follow, nose to tail, their path through the gap made by those who have gone before them, has perhaps contributed still more to the result. And the habit of course tends to perpetuate itself. The more wheels pass in the same ruts, the deeper the ruts become; and the deeper the ruts, the more difficult is it, and the more decided the effort required, to pull the coach out of them and find a new track.

And in Italian travel these well-worn ruts consist of every kind of facility provided, and preparation made for moving on in the wonted path, together with the absence of all such facilities for the adoption of any other, making the difficulty of doing so appear the greater by contrast. It is difficult for any one who has not tried it, to imagine the amount of active resistance requisite for the quitting of these deep old ruts, and warring against the prescription which ordains that they shall be followed. Everybody with whom the traveller comes in contact, from his banker in one of the great capitals, to the horse-boy who stands loitering ready to lend confirmatory testimony to the horse-master's assertion, that this or that route is impracticable, is in a conspiracy to force him into the beaten track. Everybody in his own sphere and line has made his preparations for forwarding the traveller along the accustomed track. The banker has his correspondents in the capitals in their due order, the innkeeper his ca'-me-ca'-thee friends in the towns along the route; the postmaster his relays at the appointed stations; the *vetturino* his wonted stopping-houses along the road.

And all the reasons with which each of these persons assails you in favour of keeping to the old ways are by no means fictitious and void of foundation. Travel in Italy out of the beaten track is, and to a far greater degree has hitherto been, a very different thing from travel in it. For very many generations, foreign and mainly English travellers have passed through Italy by means of a system of appliances and facilities organized and kept up for their special behoof; and of course this system is confined to the great lines, trodden smooth by the annual stampedo of northern travellers. The extraordinary perfection to which this system has been brought is evidenced in a curious manner by the complete separation of the mass of foreign travellers from the life around them. An Englishman, especially one of station

## INTRODUCTORY. 5

and wealth, passes from one end of Italy to the other, without having come in contact with genuine Italian life at any one point in his career. All that he uses, all that he eats, all that he drinks, is provided expressly for him. All who minister to his wants, from the English physician who understands northern constitutions, to the laundress broken in to British methods in the getting up of linen,—are there expressly to serve him differently from the manner in which the natives of the country are served in similar matters, and to prevent him from coming into real contact with the ordinary Italian world around him.

And all this does tend to make travelling easy and luxurious; and although those who provide it all, of course estimate the necessity of it far more highly than those for whom it is provided, yet the sudden absence of it all, as soon as the beaten track is left, does tend to keep the wheels in the old ruts.

But all this is rather descriptive of what has been the case hitherto, than of what will be the case henceforward. The rapid progress which is being made in the amelioration of the means of internal communication in Italy is daily making access to districts hitherto rarely visited by foreigners more easy; and, what is contributing, perhaps, still more powerfully to the same result, the great increased facility of reaching Italy is very rapidly increasing the number of English visitors to the southern side of the Alps, and bringing thither a large class of travellers, of a kind less likely to submit to the ordinances of routine in the direction of their movements. Englishmen, it is true, have for some years past been, with more or less success, rebelling against these prescriptions and vested interests. And perhaps as much may be said of the increasing crowd of American travellers. The Russians are exclusively persons of rank and wealth, who come to drive handsome carriages and horses in fashionable malls, to give and frequent balls, and be seen in opera-boxes. The French, of whatever class, seem to care for nothing but the large cities. Seeing Italy means with those of higher station among them, frequenting the drawing-rooms of diplomates and the houses of the very restricted number of native nobles in the habit of receiving foreigners; and is understood, by those of a less distinguished class, to be accomplished by haunting the cafés and theatres. And accordingly they write and print, when they return to Paris, "*spropositi*," as gross as those to which we are so accustomed in the works of French visitors to England. As for the Germans, they contribute very few to the yearly crowd of travellers; and those few are for the most part men with some special object in view,—very generally men of science or of learning, bound on some errand of inquiry or investigation. And your German bent on such an object is not the man to be stopped by any want of horses or fear of bad inns, or other minor inconveniences. If there be in some remote and very inaccessible mountain townlet among the Apennines any neglected and almost unknown vestige of antiquity or memorial illustrative of any one of the bygone centuries, it is probable that the only extant account of it may be found in a monograph, printed on whitey-brown paper, at the 1000th page of the 99th volume of the memoirs of some third-class German university city. German travellers certainly cannot be accused of seeking their ease by servilely following in the beaten track. And Englishmen have manifested a sufficient amount of impatience at being confined to it, to justify the hope that, for the future, they will not be content to limit their acquaintance with Italy to the leading capitals, and the main routes that lead to them.

Some little amount of inconvenience must be encountered at first, mainly in the kitchen department. Italy is not the land of good eating, nor of good cooks. The temperate, sober, and thrifty habits of the people lead them, especially when travelling, which is always a disagreeable necessity, and never a pleasure to them, to be content with very frugal fare at their inns; and the traveller who is persuaded to follow the route I am about to recommend to him, may perhaps find the journey rather a *lenten* one in another sense than that intended by the title I have prefixed to my volume. Decent lodging and clean beds he will find throughout the district. And the means and facilities for locomotion will be carefully noted, as we proceed on our way.

It was not, as I have said, by way of any allusion to the meagreness of fare to be expected from the Umbrian hostelries, that I have called this a Lenten journey; but from the time of year at which it was made, and at which any one who may be induced to follow the same route may conveniently and advantageously do so. It is true the following pages are the result of more than one visit to the districts in question. But the most recent and most complete tour through them was made during the Lent of the year 1862; and, flattering myself that any traveller purposing to go over the same ground would find his path made easier for him and his time saved by the use of this volume, I think that the forty days of Lent would be found sufficient for the object in view; supposing, that is to say, the starting-point to be that of the present writer,—Florence, or any other not much more distant city.

In general, the early spring is a very pleasant time for travelling in Italy. It is true that you have only twelve hours of light; but they are all available and enjoyable; which is not the case in the longer days of summer, and the early autumn. Then, for those who have been spending the winter in Italy, the time is convenient also in other respects. The winter gaieties and the carnival fun are over in the cities; and the stranger has probably had fully enough, for the present at least, of balls and concerts, and galleries and studios, and city life in general. Those, who are driven to the southern side of the Alps by the rigour of a northern winter, dare not yet return to face March winds at home; and for those nomad tribes, who will be found spending the summer months in dalliance at some Mediterranean sea-side bathing place, or favourite resort among the valleys of the Apennines, the time for that *dolce farniente* has not yet come.

What then, under such circumstances, can the fortunate possessor of a few weeks' leisure, health, and a very moderate rouleau of Napoleons, do better than spend the first and third, while increasing the second of these possessions, in adding to his real knowledge of Italy, by a ramble through a little visited though highly interesting part of it.

*Orsu! Andiamo!*

The start may be made—from Florence, we will suppose—in the most impromptu and unpremeditated manner. No need to trouble oneself about passports, or any such obsolete impediments. There are no frontiers to be passed, thank Heaven! We may be off on the morrow of an overnight decision, to make the trip. There is a diligence at 6 A.M. to Arezzo, which will be the best mode of commencing the route; nay, there are two starting from two rival offices within an hundred yards of each other, just behind the *Palazzo Vecchio;* and a place will be sure to be found in one or the other of them. They are not very diligent diligences, it must be confessed; taking nine hours—from 6 A.M. till 3 P.M.—with a bit over to do the distance,—some forty English miles. And it is provoking, that the bitter rivalry which exists between them, never by any chance exhibits itself in stimulating either of them to pass the other on the road, or to see the slightest gratification or credit in arriving first at the journey's end.

The drive from Florence to Arezzo is quite sufficiently pleasant and interesting to make patience during the loitering journey an easy virtue, and the composition of a chapter or two on the details of it a not difficult task. Nevertheless, I do not purpose attempting it.

The author of "Un voyage autour de ma Chambre," would have written a charming book full of suggestive matter on a journey from London to Highgate. But as I have no pretension to emulate any such *tour de force,* I do not mean to dwell on the details of the route from Florence to Arezzo, which is almost equally beaten ground. Not that there is no temptation to do otherwise. There was the magnificent sunrise view over the Valdarno and queen-like Florence in the midst of it, from the top of that spur of the Chianti Hills, so celebrated by Redi, which the road reaches about nine miles from the city gate. There is the grand old Rinuccini Villa, Torre a Poni, with its immense terraces and cypress groves, a little beyond the crest of the hill; Rinuccini no longer,—that fine old name having become extinct a few years since, and this portion of the property having passed to the Corsini, in the person of the last Rinuccini's son-in-law, that much lamented Marchese Lajatico, who died in London, when on an embassy from the Provisional Government, which succeeded that of the late Grand Duke. There are things untold as yet in any guide-book or tourist's volume, to be written of this historical villa, the earliest records of which date from the year 1072.\*

Then again, it was market-day as we passed through the thriving little country town of Figline; and the large market-place was thronged with a crowd of Upper Valdarno Tuscan faces, of a characteristically different type from those of the city race of Florentine cockneys. The political sentiments of these country-bred Tuscans too, as expressed in inscriptions in colossal letters on every available inch of wall, of "*Abasso il Papa Re!*"—"Down with the Pope King!"—were worth noting.

\* V. Ricordi storici della Famiglia Rinuccini Di G. Aiazzi. p. 30. Firenze, 1840.

At St. Giovanni again, a few miles further, there is that wonderful mummied figure, discovered some half a century since, built up in the wall of the church. This strange spectacle has, in all probability, been made booty of by some former tourist. But has he or she solved the mystery? How did the dead find so strange a tomb, implying so fearfully strange a fate? I think some documents, throwing light at least of probability on the matter, might be found.

Then we come to Montevarchi, where some three hundred years ago, Benedetto Varchi, the historian, was beneficed. Does not that entitle one to say something—and how much might well be said?—of the genial, simple-minded, honest, Montaigne-like old writer? But still I refrain.

Arezzo itself, though half the yearly tourist-tide flowing Rome-wards has slept there for generations past, is full of temptations. Half the tide, I say, because the other half always went the other road by Sienna. And recently, since the rail has brought the latter city to within three hours from Florence, a far larger portion than half have taken that route. So much so, that I find the great inn at Arezzo, once one of the best in Italy, is no more! He, who would now rest him in the little upland city of Tarlati, the fighting bishop, who bearded the Republic of Florence, of Vasari, and of jolly Redi, the medico-poet, author of the "Bacco in Toscana," must now content him with such an hostelry as contents Italian travellers. The above-mentioned worthies are but a very few among the citizens of Arezzo who have achieved fame in one walk or another. The inhabitants maintain that there is something in the air especially favourable to the sharpening of the wits. And the good people seem bent on proving the truth of their theory by making the most of their celebrities. Never was saying so notably contradicted, as is at Arezzo that of a prophet being honourless in his own country. The whole city is full of marble tablets, drawing the attention of strangers to the fact, that in this, that, and the other house, lived and died some celebrated poet, philosopher, or warrior. The practice, which is an excellent and laudable one, may be observed at Florence, and in other Italian cities; but nowhere is it so prominent a feature in the aspect of the place as at Arezzo; evidently, the Aretini would say, because in no other city have there been so many men worthy of commemoration! But perhaps, as others might hint, because a slenderer amount of celebrity has sufficed to merit such honour at the hands of the Aretini. It must be admitted that some of the great captains and poets so recorded, will in all probability be thus heard of for the first time by most people ; as for instance, a certain general— I already have forgotten his name—who is thus introduced to the notice of the passing stranger by a remarkably *voyant* slab of marble in the main street, now called the "Corso Vittorio Emanuele:" "Here lived and died the terror of the Turks!"

But not even the desire to introduce this terrible notability to the British public, nor the singularly interesting records contained in a small publication entitled "The Public Calamities of Arezzo," which I found in my inn, and in which, on opening it at hazard, I read: "In this year many dogs went mad in Arezzo!"—not any of all these interesting matters shall induce me to break my determination of beginning this Lenten journey from the time of quitting the beaten track of English travellers; and this was on starting from Arezzo for Città di Castello.

## CHAPTER II.

FROM AREZZO TO CITTÀ DI CASTELLO—THE CERFONE—MONTERCHI—VALLEY OF THE TIBER—FIRST APPEARANCE OF CITTÀ DI CASTELLO—THE VITELLI—DAYS OF PROSPERITY AND DAYS OF DECAY IN ITALY—THE CANONNIERA.

ALL the world, playing at "follow-my-leader," as is the world's custom, goes on its appointed way, the second stage of its route from Florence to Rome, following the post-road from Arezzo to Perugia. We—I and my companion, that is to say—went forth from the former city by a far less used gate directly facing the mountains, which, as soon as we had crossed the small extent of flat and fertile fields lying around the knoll crowned by Arezzo, we began at once to climb. They are outlying spurs of the Apennines, buttresses of the main range, which seems to have more need of buttresses than any other of the great mountain systems of Europe,—so friable is the soil, and so rapidly is it being carried away to form along the coasts of the Adriatic and Tuscan seas, first malaria-smitten *Maremme* and swamps, and then in Nature's good time, rich, corn-bearing alluvial plains like that now around Pisa.

In the first instance this process does not produce anything pleasant either in the locality to which the water-borne soil is being transported, or in that from which it is removed. Nothing can present an appearance of more hopeless and blasted looking barrenness, than those portions of the naked, scarred and seamed flanks of the Apennines where the waters are most active in this work of washing down the great dorsal bone of the Italian Peninsula! And the road to Città di Castello, winding in admirably engineered zigzags up the mountain, passes at first through a few miles of such country.

Here and there was a bleak and dreary looking farm-house, with its usual dove-cot on the top of it, and a half-dozen or so of doves painted on the white walls around the pigeon-holes, for the purpose, I suppose, of showing the real birds the way in. It seemed difficult to imagine what business farm-houses could have in such situations, till a more minute examination of the surrounding hill-sides discovered here and there a few isolated patches of painfully cultivated and ungrateful soil, which constituted the mountain farm. And the specimens of the population of this hill country, who were coming down to the city as we were climbing the hill, and leaving it behind us, seemed quite in character with the physiognomy of their country. A young priest, who could hardly have been guessed to be such, save for the indispensable little linen collar, which had sometime towards the early part of the current year apparently been white, came trudging down the hillside brandishing a stout cudgel as he walked. He was dressed in a ragged and threadbare blue cloth coat, which came down to his heels, and a sadly battered and shapeless chimney-pot hat; he had a stubble black beard a week old, and a lean, hungry, gaunt look, which told the poverty-stricken state of his cure among these barren hills, more eloquently than aught else could have done. What must the poverty of the flock be when such was the shepherd!

Then, at the next turn of the winding road, came a solitary charcoal-burner, with his half-score of black sacks closed at the mouth with twigs of arbutus, laden on a very miserable-looking, lean little pony, whose meek head peered out from beneath his overhanging load. Charcoal-burners share by prescription the picturesqueness of brigands. I hardly know why, unless it be that their out-of-door and solitary life among the forests lends a similar air of *farouche* freedom to their movements and bearing;—to which may be added the strange look imparted to their eyes by the blackened skin of their faces. The solitary figure which met me—for I was walking up the hill far in advance of the carriage—as I came to a sudden turn in the bleak road winding cornice-wise round the flank of the Apennines, was a gaunt, stalwart-looking fellow, over six feet high, stepping along at a swinging pace, with a huge branch of a tree by way of walking stick.

There is a very striking view of Arezzo with the upper valley of the Arno, stretching away behind it from a spot in the road a little below the summit of the pass. And although the old frontier of Tuscany is in fact not passed till several miles further, the traveller may consider that from this hill-top he is taking his last view of Tuscan scenery and Tuscan life. There is no longer any frontier to pass. No loathsome Papal officials—filthy, insolent, and cringing—come out to bully you and be bribed. But the moral frontier line between the land, which has been for so many generations poisoned by its subjection to Papal rule, and that of more fortunately circumstanced Tuscany, is still, and for many a year yet must be strongly marked and very visible.

The ridge which we were crossing forms the watershed between the valley of the Arno and that of the Tiber. We were therefore when we had passed it, still on the Tuscan side of the main chain of the Apennines. But the style of scenery is entirely different. A steep descent brought us down to the margin of a rapid stream, which finds its winding way through a series of wooded gorges to the Tiber. Cerfone is its name; and it deserves to be mentioned by it; for the combinations of rock, wood, water, and mountain, through which the road winds as it follows the banks of the stream, passing once or twice beneath the grey ruins of a mediæval fortress tower, would have been cited ere now as equal to much of the vaunted scenery of the Moselle, if they had not laboured under the same disadvantage as the heroes who lived before Agamemnon, and died unpraised, "*caruerunt quia vate sacro.*"

The route follows this charming valley of the Cerfone till it opens into the wide basin of the Tiber, about seven miles above Città di Castello. Just at the opening of the smaller valley into that of the Tiber there is a singularly situated isolated knoll, with the little walled town of Monterchi on its summit. The road winds round this rising ground, closely skirting its base, before it takes its course down the valley of the Tiber; and thus gives the traveller a series of views of this strikingly picturesque little hill-town, seen from different sides, and with varied backgrounds.

This "Mountain of Hercules," for "Monterchi" is but a modernized corruption of " Mons Herculis" —has been, situated as it is at the confluence of two valleys, a place of some importance in the good old fighting days. Possessed and ruled in the twelfth and thirteenth centuries by a family of " Marchesi" of its own, the little lordship fell in the fourteenth century into the power of that masterful mitred man of war, Bishop Guido Tarlati of Arezzo, in obedience to that continually operative law of agglomeration, which has at last formed a new kingdom of Italy of the minute fragments into which the old Roman world was shivered by the irruption of the barbarian.

The Tarlati held the town, partly as sovereigns and partly as feudatories and dependants of the rising and growing Republic of Florence, till in 1440 we find the lady Anfrosina, the widow of Bartolommeo Tarlati, and her three daughters, driven forth from their home and stronghold, "for rebellion against the Republic of Florence,"—the noble lady having, on the occasion of the quarrel of the haughty burghers with the Duke of Milan, shown her sympathies with the latter, as naturally as any dame of old cavalier stock would have preferred the cause of Charles to that of the Parliament.

The Tiber has its source in Monte Falterona, the same Monarch of the Tuscan Apennines that gives birth to the Arno. But the Tuscan river springs from one flank, and the Roman stream from the opposite one. The latter comes down, a little mountain torrent from the hills, and first assumes the dignity and bearing of a river at a little Tuscan town, called Pieve Santo Stefano, about twenty miles above the spot at which it is joined by the Cerfone. The valley, or rather the wide basin, through which the Tiber flows at this point of its course, is of extreme richness and fertility. There can be no doubt that the whole of this flat extent from hill-side to hill-side was at one time, probably long within the historical period, a lake. The grey tints, to which the traveller has become accustomed in the Valdarno, are changed for a prevailing tone of the richest and deepest green. It cannot be said of these fields, as of those around the Tuscan Athens, that the same land produces corn, wine, and oil; for the latter product is here wanting. But the harvest of the two former is of the richest. And in the place of the olive there is the oak; which to those who are more concerned with that which the country offers to the eye of the traveller, than with what it gives to the pocket of the owner, is by far the more valuable product. Possibly when we come to our salad at supper-time, within the walls of Città di Castello, we may feel the absence of the grey olive-coloured hill-sides of Valdarno. But for the present, while we are seeking delight for the eye only, the oak is assuredly the more desirable growth.

A drive of about five miles through this world of greenery brings us to Città di Castello. Neither the river or the town are to be seen till the traveller is close upon them. The bottom of the valley through which he is passing is too flat to show him the latter, and the richness of the vegetation is too abundant to allow to him catch a glimpse of the former, although it is flowing within a few paces of him. At length the shabby, dilapidated looking little city, and "Flavus Tiber" flowing beneath its walls, disclose themselves to his eyes at the same moment. "Flavus Tiber" eminently deserved its classical epithet, as it appeared on this occasion. To the angler it suggested no possibility save that of eels. And characteristically it welcomed us to Papal territory—or at least to that which so recently was such—by a scene of ruin. For the old bridge had been thrown down by Father Tiber in one of those mischievous moods to which he is still subject. He had recently been seen by the people of Città, "*retortis, Littore Etrusco violenter undis;*" and we had in consequence to enter the city by a very far from reassuring temporary bridge, built as surely bridge never was, save in Pope's land!

But I am sinning against the proverb, that bids one speak well of the bridge which has carried one over; for, miserable and tumbled down as it looked, the make-shift bridge of Città di Castello *did* unquestionably carry us over the Tiber, and land us safely in the midst of the congeries of lanes which constitute that historical city.

The appearance of Città di Castello is not calculated to engender love at first sight. Like most of the other old-world cities of this part of Italy, it has no principal and main street, but seems, as has been said, a congeries of by no means inviting lanes. On entering the town by an old tumble-down gate, —now happily unguarded by soldiers,—one fancies that for some unknown reason or other the driver

has chosen to make his entry by some little used
postern; and that the part of the town on which it
opens, is some miserable quarter, inhabited only by
the poorest classes. One is jolted round corner
after corner of squalid lanes, so narrow as to make
the turning from one into the other a feat requiring
some skill of coachmanship, expecting at every
minute to emerge on the busy, decent part of
the city. But second-rate Papal cities have no
busy and no decent part! And gradually one comes
to the disappointing conclusion, that the first view
disclosed a fair sample of the whole.

And yet this miserable squalid mass of dilapidated,
rotten-looking buildings was once the birthplace of
genius, the home of art, and wealth, and splendour;
the scene, on which were enacted passages of history
which the world still deems among the most
memorable it has recorded, one of the abiding places
of a civilization, from which the comfortable Englishman, who is now revolted by its decay, was
once fain to take lessons in everything that em-
bellishes life!

A series of apparently aimless turnings round
sharp corners, among buildings that looked as if
they had been "in Chancery" for the last half
century, brought us at last to our inn—*the* inn
—"*La Cannoniera!*" and all the misgivings which
the appearance of the city was calculated to suggest
as to the character of the accommodation it was likely
to afford, were dispelled. The "*Cannoniera*" is as
good an inn as a tired traveller need wish to meet
with. But what is the meaning of its strange
name? The answer to this question plunges us

at once into the midst of the history and antiquities of Città di Castello.

Every reader knows, in a general way, that the Papal territory on the Adriatic side of the chain of the Apennines was acquired piecemeal by the Popes by a long series of usurpations, more or less violent, more or less plausible, more or less justifiable by the quarrels, the crimes, the incapacities of the numerous princely families who more or less despotically ruled in the different cities. Every page of mediæval Italian history is filled with the often revolting, sometimes picturesque details of the atrocities, extravagances, and misrule of most of these petty tyrants. And it cannot be denied that in many instances the population welcomed the advent of priestly government as a decided improvement on that of their native lords. Nevertheless it is the fact,—and it is a remarkably suggestive and instructive fact,—that in every case the turbulent days of the petty native princes were for each city the palmy days of prosperity, to which they still look back with pride, and to the visible remains of which they still point, as constituting their only title to claim an ascertained and recognized place in the history of the world's civilization. When we read the details of municipal history, which in the case of these little once independent states, is the history of a national life, it seems impossible that anything like prosperity, and almost that anything like culture, should have existed under such social circumstances. And yet it was amid the turmoil and confusion and violences of the centuries previous to the commencement of Papal rule, that genius was produced, that art throve, that wealth was created, and population increased in these cities and the small districts of surrounding territory subjected to each of them. And it was after the commencement of the comparatively regularized, and legalized system of the Pontifical Government, that universal death and decay began. The noisy, roaring, rattling, struggling iron age passed away; and a sullen, silent, noiseless age of lead succeeded. And the superior healthfulness of the former arose probably mainly from the fact that it *was* an age of *struggling*. The reader, who from the constant use of the word "tyrant," applied by the old historians to the lords of the mediæval municipalities, and from the accounts of the various acts of despotism committed by them, should be led to picture to himself these communities as living under recognized and regularized despotisms, would form a very erroneous conception of mediæval Italian history. These despotisms were despotisms tempered by constant rebellion and resistance in every shape. They were in every case usurpations, more or less tolerated, more or less audacious or concealed, more or less submitted to as really beneficent, more or less short-lived as they were more or less tolerable to their subjects. The life in them was in short, as has been said, a life of *struggle*. It was *life* and not *death*. And the rich Italian nature, and the rich Italian soil *did* produce great men and great things under the rough energy-generating influence of those stormy times. It was under the "orderly" rule of the cassock that the nation reached the perfection described by the celebrated formula of the Company of Jesus, and became "*utpote cadaver.*"

In Città di Castello, as in her sister cities, the stormy times were her best times. And they were, it should seem, especially stormy times. For we find an old author, Benedetto Dei,* thus writing in 1470: "I say, and will say, and will always stick to it, that the City of Venice has made more changes and revolutions, and shed more blood than the four most bellicose and fighting cities in all Italy; that is to say, Genoa, Bologna, Perugia, and Città di Castello!" Poor little Città di Castello may well be surprised nowadays to find herself marshalled on equal terms as one in such a goodly company! But there are many evidences that ancient Tifernum, for that was the original name of the Roman colony and *municipium* founded on the site of an ancient Etruscan city on the banks of the Tiber in the midst of this rich valley, was a place of much greater relative importance in old times. Tifernum was founded, we are assured, by Caius Tifernius Sabinus, in the year 3242 from the creation of the world, was destroyed by Totila, King of the Goths, and rebuilt by Saint Florido, its quondam Bishop and present patron. Then it set up for itself; became a republic, and showed much ingratitude to its episcopal benefactor. For we find a successor of his in 1270 dragged by the hair of his head through the streets for prohibiting a certain friar from saying mass in a private house. †

As usual however one of the noble families of the

---

* Cited in the "Memorie di Città di Castello; da M. G. M. V. di C. di C.," which means "Monsignore G. Muzzi, Bishop of Città di Castello." Vol. IV., p. 10.

† Istruzione Storico-pittorica di Città di Castello. Dul Cavre. Giacomo Mancini. 2 vols. 8vo. *See* V. I., p. 224.

city, having become more powerful, richer, and influential than any other in the town, gradually made themselves lords of the little commonwealth. These were the Vitelli; and all that the city still retains, that is remarkable, consists of traces and memorials of their wealth and greatness.

And this brings us back to the question; whence did the excellent hostelry of the "Canonniera" get its strange appellation? and prepares the way for an answer to it.

"The mania for superfluous building," writes Mancini, in the History of Città di Castello above cited, "excited by wealth, extended itself to all the individuals of this illustrious family,—the Vitelli,—who within a short space of time built for themselves no less than five large palaces in this city."

Of these the "*Canonniera*," so called from the owners having established there one of the earliest cannon foundries in Italy, was one.

And what palaces they were! In these days every house that is, or that professes to be the residence of a gentleman, is in Italy called by courtesy a palace. But the five palaces of the Vitelli were palaces indeed! And there they are now! the stones of them preaching not only sermons on the trite text of "*Sic transit gloria mundi*," but also the most eloquent lectures on "the Art of Government," on all the laws of political economy, and the principles which rule the rise and fall of nations. A more melancholy sight than these squalid wrecks of splendour can hardly be conceived. And the splendour was no mere vulgar display of material wealth. These Vitelli, in their remote little city amid the vineyards and cornfields of the high valley of the Tiber must have been lovers of art, and bountiful patrons of a school of artists, who flourished under their rule, and died out when it was over. And here on mildewing, crumbling walls are the traces of their works—in some cases much more than the traces—sharing in the doom of universal decay and neglect.

A portion only of the huge edifice of the whilome "Canonniera" is occupied by the present inn, itself at least four times more spacious than all the needs of its business can require. This part of the building has been modernized, its repair cared for, and it is in decent habitable condition. But the remainder of the vast palace is exactly as it was when its ancient lords abandoned it, with the exception of the busy work done on it by the hand of time.

The innkeeper took down a bunch of huge rusty keys from a nail, and proceeded to show me the uninhabited part of the building, which seemed to be all—it can hardly be said in his occupation, but at least—in his keeping. It is known from still existing records in the custody of the municipality of Città di Castello, that this palace was built in the first quarter of the sixteenth century. But despite the labour bestowed on the adornment of it by several of the most esteemed artists of the day, it appears to have been soon abandoned by its owners, ambitious of lodging themselves yet more magnificently. The vault of the grand staircase was painted by Cristofero Gherardi, as well as several of the friezes in the state apartments. The paintings on the staircase, and several of those in the rooms are yet, though rapidly perishing, sufficiently preserved to bear witness to the truth of Vasari's remarks on their author. Towards the end of his biography of Gherardi, Vasari says that he himself furnished some designs for the ornamentation of this palace. But with his usual careless inexactitude, he does not afford us the means of identifying them. Around the walls of the grand saloon, opening off the staircase, there are a series of frescoes by that Niccolo della Matrice of whom Vasari speaks at the conclusion of his biography of Marco Calavrese. Notwithstanding the miserable state in which they are, enough remains to show that this little-known artist had merit that might have taken a first place in any country and age, in which the first places were not occupied by such names as filled them in Italy at that period.

It is extraordinary that these frescoes have not perished more entirely than has been the case. The windowless rooms, closed only by rough makeshift shutters, are open to damp, and dust, and vermin. Many of them seemed to be used as places of storage for forage, or firewood, or timber. Yet the people seemed to have a sense of the beauty of the handiwork that was perishing under their eyes, and to feel a pride in pointing out these evidences of what their city had once been.

One large room of magnificent proportions on an upper floor, which still showed traces of having been highly decorated, and which was admirably lighted, had been assigned, I was told, to a young native painter, as his studio. Several of his works were pointed out to me in different houses in the city, and they all bore unmistakable marks of a rich and strong imagination, and a hand of no mean skill. Here he had laboured among the perishing works of the masters of the palmy days of art, with scant recognition and no encouragement, till one day he flung himself from the window of this decay-smitten room into the street some hundred feet below!

"That was the picture he left unfinished on his easel, *poverino!*" said an acquaintance of mine in the city, pointing to a couple of heads, male and female, facing each other on a small canvas. "The man looks as mad as he was, and the woman as sad as his mother, after his ending!" added the speaker with a shrug.

# CHAPTER III.

OTHER VITELLI PALACES—EARTHQUAKE IN CITTÀ DI CASTELLO—PAOLO VITTELI, THE ARCHITECT—REMARKABLE PICTURE—NEGLECTED GARDENS—REMARKABLE FRESCOES OF GHERARDI—PLINY'S VILLA—WINE OF THE VALLEY OF THE TIBER—ITS QUALITIES—ITALIAN LOCAL HISTORIANS—THEIR SCARCENESS—THEIR VALUE—THOSE OF CITTÀ DI CASTELLO—SPECIMENS OF MUNICIPAL RECORDS.

CERTAINLY the Vitelli were Marquises of Carabas at Città di Castello. Their names are repeated in answer to every question, and the remains of their greatness meet the visitor at every turn. A second vast building in the centre of the town, still habitable and inhabited, and now the property of the Marchese Bufalini, is pointed out as the original and earliest dwelling of the Vitelli. But in this case Nature has interfered by means of one of her more exceptional operations with the slow work of time and social change. The inner quadrangle must have been a very magnificent specimen of the domestic architecture of the *rénaissance* period. The stumps of the square pillars of cut stone which supported the colonnade around it are there to declare what the manner and style of the building must have been. But all is ruin—just as the earthquake which visited the city on the 30th of

September, 1789, left it. The pillars are all snapt off at an equal height of about two feet from the ground; and huge chasms opened by the rending of the vaults of the cellars below, yawn in different parts of the court.

Nearly all the churches in the city were so shaken by this earthquake, that they had to be rebuilt. And there is consequently no church architecture of any value in the town. Many frescoes also were destroyed at the same time; especially those on the walls of the Bufalini Villa, at San Giustino, about four or five miles from the city, in the direction of San Sepolcro, the work of Cristofero Gherardi, and specially cited by Vasari in his life of that artist. Works by Signorelli, Raphael, Pietro Perugino, and Pomarancio, were also destroyed at the same time.

In another part of the city another still larger Vitelli Palace has absolutely begun to show signs of the renewed vitality, which is beginning to rouse Italy from her lethargy of three hundred years. A spirited and enterprizing merchant has purchased one half of the building for an incredibly small sum, and has repaired the magnificent stables, with the intention of turning them into a storehouse for the purposes of his trade. These stables consisted of a noble hall, about one hundred and twenty feet in length, divided lengthwise into three equal naves, by two ranges of stone pillars. Few dealers in the great commercial centres of modern Europe have such a warehouse for their goods, as has this ambitious citizen of little Città di Castello for his few bags of rice, hogsheads of sugar, and bales of spices. And still fewer horses are nowadays lodged as those were, which carried the free lances, who constituted the Vitelli's stock-in-trade, and were maintained by them, ready for the call of any of the larger and wealthier States of the Peninsula, which might need their services, and those of their soldier-leader and master. For these Vitelli were among the most famous of those Captains of " Venturieri," or Free Bands of Adventurers, who were always ready to sell their military skill and prowess to the best bidder.

Over these superb stables is an equally large hall —a " ritter-saal," as it would be called in Germany— for the entertainment of the riders of the steeds below. This is being turned into a sort of club, partaking of the nature of a reading-room and a café. But it forms no part of the spirited owner's plan to preserve the very fine frescoed arabesques, which run round the upper part of the walls, in a band about six feet wide. For it was whispered to me, as I stood straining my eyes to trace the half-obliterated design, that these remnants of the wealth and art of the sixteenth century might all be mine for the sum of three hundred francs, *plus* the expense of cutting them from the walls!

The most magnificent of the remains of the Vitteli splendour, however, consists of another palace still in a much better condition than either of those that have been spoken of; and now the property of an absentee Florentine family, which inherited it by marriage from the last of the Vitelli race. This truly splendid mansion was erected about the year 1540 by Paolo Vitelli; of whom we are told, that besides making himself master of the military studies which especially pertained to his position in life, he pursued that of civil architecture with all the energy of a master passion. We are told also\* that this palace was the result of his artistic studies. But if so, he must have found, prince as he was, a truly royal road to excellence. For he was born in 1520, just twenty years before this very creditable specimen of his architectural talent was built. Doubtless, some long since forgotten clerk of the works held the same position in respect to this sumptuous building, that many a first lieutenant has held in the winning of victories which have made captains famous.

The vaults of the grand hall, of the staircase, and of the principal apartments, were painted by that same Cristofero Gherardi, better known in the history of art by his nickname of Il Doceno, whose fantastic brush may be almost said to have painted Città di Castello; so vast was the extent of wall covered by his quaint imaginations in the different buildings of the city. Lanzi says that *all* the ceilings of the palace in question were painted by him. But here also the earthquake of 1789 was a ruthless destroyer; and very many of the frescoes then perished.

On the first floor a grand hall of truly magnificent proportions was painted throughout, by Prospero Fontana, who came from Bologna in 1574 expressly to execute this work, with historical subjects from the lives of the worthies of the Vitelli family. But the beautiful proportions of the hall have been destroyed by running a partition across it to adapt it to some meaner need of a meaner generation; and

---

\* Mancini. Op. cit., V. II., p. 95.

damp, dust, and neglect have done their work upon the paintings.

The amount of art-produce which modern Europe has inherited from the Italy of those wonderful fourteenth, fifteenth, and sixteenth centuries, is matter of ever-increasing amazement to those whose inquiries lead them to form any accurate idea of the facts. But a detailed examination of what may in truth almost be called the ruins of this and other similarly circumstanced third-rate cities, forces upon the observer a conviction, that we have received but a small portion of the incredibly abundant store of wealth bequeathed by those generations to their posterity;—that the part which has perished in the barbarism of Italy's second "lower Empire," has been in every kind infinitely larger than the fragments which have been saved from the wreck.

A considerable number of old portraits of the family still hang on the walls of the various rooms of the long and magnificent suite, which runs from end to end of the entire first floor of the palace; and among them one attracted my attention from the singularity of the subject, and from the circumstance of my having seen another but much inferior representation of the same, hanging on the walls of an abandoned villa a few miles distant from the city. The picture represented a young and beautiful girl, in a magnificent gala dress, lying prone on the ground with a large and gaping wound in the back of the neck. There can be little doubt that this was the pictured record of some domestic tragedy, of which the city, if not the house, in which the picture yet hangs, was the scene. I asked if it were known whether there were any record connected with it, and was told in reply that my informant believed there was a history in the family archives connected with the subject of the picture; but that all the contents of the muniment room had been carried away by the present owners to Florence.

The gardens attached to this princely residence were very famous in their day, having been laid out, as a recent historian of Città di Castello informs us, in that regular and stately fashion, which was in vogue " before the Chinese taste was introduced by the Englishman Whately." They were full of all those waterwork contrivances, which were so much admired by the seventeenth century gardeners; and had been abundantly supplied with water brought at an enormous cost from the hills bounding the wide valley of the Tiber to the eastward. They were long celebrated also for their noble plane-trees, said to have been many centuries old. But the water conduits have been broken, and the trees cut down; and, as the historian already cited writes, " all in short lies in the most utter squalor, to the inexpressible grief of the citizens and the amazement of strangers."

But in these neglected gardens, there still remains a monument of sixteenth century art, which is perhaps what Città di Castello has yet left most worthy of a stranger's attention. This is a large open *loggia* at the further end of the garden, the vault of which is entirely painted by the hand of Doceno. Vasari, in his life of Cristofero Gherardi, speaks specially of his skill in painting birds and other animals. And these frescoes abundantly justify the praise. The ceiling of this *loggia* is covered with the most extraordinary and fantastically grouped assemblage of birds, beasts, fishes, fruits, and flowers, that it is possible to imagine; painted all of them with a truthfulness and vigour that is most striking. But the most extraordinary part of the thing is, that all these frescoes, with the exception of two or three spots locally injured, are literally as fresh as if they were painted yesterday! They are, as I have said, exposed to the action of the atmosphere in an open *loggia*, looking eastward. Yet the condition of them is incomparably superior to that of any of those in the city, which have been protected by doors and windows. Indeed, the frescoes in the garden loggia are in a better state of preservation than any I have ever seen of equal age. Can it be that they owe this to the fact that they *are* open? The people in the city, to whom I spoke on the subject, said that it had always been asserted that Il Doceno had some special secret for rendering the colours of his frescoes imperishable. But it may be replied to this, that if so, he assuredly did not apply his secret process to the many other frescoes by him on the walls of this city. In any case this garden-house in the garden of the palace of Paolo Vitelli is well worthy of a visit; and the very remarkable freshness of these paintings, which are, it may be remarked, entirely free from restoration, is worth the examination of some competent person, capable of forming a probable opinion on the cause of the truly singular phenomenon.

On the lowest slopes of the chain of hills, which shuts in the basin of the Tiber on the eastern side, about three miles from the city up the stream, there is a spot, which is worth visiting at the cost of the pleasant walk which leads to it. The present name of the place is Passerino; and there is every reason to believe that it is the site of that Villa of Pliny of which he gives such a detailed description in one of his letters. It is the sixth epistle of the fifth book, written to Apollinaris to reassure his doubts as to the salubrity of the air in this his friend's favourite summer retirement. The description of the villa thus given is so elaborate and minute that English, French, and German, as well as Italian authors, have attempted to base on it complete descriptions of the house and its dependencies. Felibien, in 1698, published the letter in question, and absolutely gave a regular ground plan of the villa as an illustration. Robert Castet, in his work entitled, "The Villas of the Ancients Illustrated" (London, 1728), gave a less pretentious and more really accurate description of it. The passage from Pliny is too long and prolix to be reprinted here. But if any traveller curious on such matters would refer to it on the spot, he would be struck by the exactitude of the applicability of it to the locality I have named.

Passerino is the name not of a village, but of an isolated farm, situated on the lowest slope of the hill. The greater part, almost the entirety of the cultivated ground belonging to it, lies below the site of the present farm-house; in a position, to which the words of Pliny apply most accurately. "The Villa," he says, "situated on the lowest part of the hill, has as complete a prospect of the valley, as if it were at the top of it; and the ascent is so gradual and insensible that you become aware of having reached an elevation before you are conscious that you are climbing."

The ancient proprietor of the spot goes on to describe the extreme fertility of the soil, and says that in many parts it would be impossible to find a stone in the tilled ground if you looked for it. This certainly is not the case now. Yellow Tiber has been made yellow during all the centuries since by the soil which it has washed away from these and similarly situated hill-sides. There are stones enough now; but mingled with them in the sloping fields immediately below the present dwelling may be seen an immense quantity of fragments of Roman brick. In one spot of these same fields the peasants found a few years ago a piece of leaden pipe apparently as far as I could learn from talking to the men who had found it, *in situ*. There is a strong spring of water in the hill-side, a little above the site of the farm-house; and this fragment of pipe was just in the position which it would have occupied, had it been placed there to convey the water of this spring to the gardens, if the precise site of the villa were, as it seemed to me probable, that of the modern dwelling.

Immediately by the side of, and a very little below the farm-house are the grey stone fragments of ancient walls, evidently mediæval work, and probably the remains of one of the fortress towers, of which several are known to have existed in the vicinity of the city. Now it seems to me very probable, that when the mediæval builders of this edifice, let it have been what it may, were choosing a spot for the purpose, they would take advantage of any older foundations, which may have saved them the trouble of constructing new ones. And a very small amount of labour would suffice so far to remove the remains of the mediæval masonry as to enable a competent judge to discover, whether they rested on the work of Roman builders.

Pliny describes the clipped hedges and closed walks, and the animals cut out of box-trees, "so to the life that they seem looking at each other," which adorned his gardens, in a manner that indicates curiously how little taste has changed in Italy in this respect from his day to the present. With us the fancy for garden work of this sort, was borrowed from Italy, had its day, and became obsolete, as the national taste became changed in conformity with a new stage of general mental culture. But in more stationary Italy the same puerile fancies which delighted Pliny, are still in fashion more than seventeen hundred years after his time.

In another matter of somewhat more importance some of the observations of Pliny apply to the present aspect and productions of the country. It is still a great wine district. Not that it is famous as such. The want of communications, and perhaps also defects in the method of preserving the wine, have prevented it from becoming so. But it should have been so; and the time may yet come, when the wines of this upper valley of the Tiber may be heard of in the English wine market. Both white and red wine of excellent quality are produced on the lower slopes of these hills, very far superior in body and flavour to the cheaper wines of Bordeaux and of Burgundy. The red wine is fruity without being luscious, and generous without being heady. The white wine, as light in colour as the palest Amontillado sherry, is much drier than the red, quite as strong, and will, say the farmers of the district, bear age better. But it is stated that none of these wines will bear transport; and that the red cannot be kept for a second, or at all events not for a third year. But I very much doubt the accuracy of these statements. Or at all events if such be the case now, I am very strongly of opinion that it would be so no longer, if the wine were made with a little more science and care. I drank some of the red wine, which is stated to be more perishable than the white, which had been three years in bottle, and which was all the better for its age. But this had been made and bottled by an intelligent and careful man off his own vineyard for his own drinking. His opinion was that all that was needed to make the wines of this district both keep and bear travel, is to take care that the process of fermentation is fully completed. The wine in question is at present—*i. e.* after a series of short crops, due to the grape disease—worth about fourpence a bottle in Città di Castello. And I am very much persuaded that if it could be had in London for, say, about three or four times that price, it might command a large sale.

There is a class of books, large in most of the countries of our old and storied Europe, but larger probably in Italy than any other, of which I purpose giving some notices in connection with the districts spoken of in the present volume—I mean the local historians and chroniclers of the municipalities. These form a branch of literature, still almost wholly unknown beyond the Alps, save in Germany, where nothing is unknown; and, till very recently, equally unknown in Italy. They are mostly scarce books, many of them exceedingly so. They have for some time past been sought for exportation to Germany, chiefly to Berlin. And, quite latterly, they have come into great requisition in Italy. The newly awakened attention to the history of the Peninsula, and especially to those centuries of it, during which the municipal liberties grew and were consolidated, have very necessarily directed attention to these works. The largely increased attention also, which has for some years past been given in Italy as well as in the north of Europe to the history of Art, has contributed to the same result. And for this purpose, as well as in a far greater degree for the study of the political history of the country, works of the class in question are far more valuable in Italy than they would be in any other country. The most superficial glance at the general course of Italian history will suffice to make it clear why such should be the case. The local chroniclers of all the crowd of cities that stud Italy so thickly from end to end, are not mere topographers, antiquarians, or genealogists, but are the historians of little nations, and, what is more important in most cases of more or less *free* nations.

In most of these books a mass of curious, often very interesting, and sometimes exceedingly amusing reading may be found. And as it is only by their aid that a curious and intelligent traveller can obtain a full and accurate idea of that past, which has made the cities and countries he is traversing what he sees them, and of the intimate connection between the

## LOCAL HISTORIES. 41

monuments of all sorts around him and the political and social life of the people who raised them; and as almost in every case, a stranger on application to the communal librarian will meet with the most courteous and obliging attention, and with every facility for referring to the works on the " Storia patria " of the locality, I think that it may be useful to furnish the reader with a few notes, as I go, of the best books of this class to be consulted in the different towns.

To the home-keeping student of Italian political, artistic, and social history, the indication of precious sources of information not to be found elsewhere, and in all probability new to him, can hardly be other than acceptable.

What has been said in this and the preceding chapter will have in some degree, but perhaps inadequately, given the reader to understand that not only the positive, but in a still greater measure the relative, importance of Città di Castello was much greater in the centuries that preceded its definitive subjection to the church, and probably also in those which preceded the fall of the Western Empire than at the present day. The following two works may be consulted with advantage, the first for its political, ecclesiastical and social history; the second more especially for its artistic and biographical details:—

" Memorie ecclesiastiche e civili di Città di Castello. Raccolte da M. G. M. V. di C. di C." (Monsignore Giorgio Muzi; Bishop of Città di Castello). In seven volumes, 8vo., 1842-4.

2ndly. " Istruzione Storico-Pittorica per visitare

Città di Castello. Dal Cav^(re.) Giacomo Arr, Mancini. 2 vols. 8vo. Perugia. 1832."

The former of these works gives with great detail a long series of records taken from the rolls of the municipality, from which a great many notices might be culled, throwing an interesting light on the manners and life in the Italian miniature republics of the Middle Ages.

Here are a few specimens :—

On the 13th of January, 1498, the city " confirmed the election of two masters of grammar and poetry, inasmuch as one was found to be not sufficient. They were Bernardino Carleoni of Cremona, to whom was given seventy florins a year and a dwelling, and Maestro Angelo Passerini."

On the 26th of July, 1499, Master Vincenzo, son of Antonio of Valenza, arrived in Città di Castello. He was a sugar-refiner; and the city offered him fifteen florins and the privilege of free import and export of sugar and all else needed for his business, on condition that he should settle with his family in the city, and abide there until he had instructed "at least one person" in his trade. As soon as he had accomplished this, he was to receive a premium of twenty-five large ducats; but was not to be allowed to quit the city without having given notice six months previously.

In the year 1500 the city made an agreement in twenty-six conditions with thirteen Jewish families, who made application to be permitted to open a pawnbroking establishment.

On the 3rd of April, 1503, the municipality "gave to St. Antony Costantino di Lucca, who had murdered his wife, and obliged him to serve for life in the hospital of the above-named saint. The rectors and confraternity of the Company of St. Antony had made a supplication to that effect."

These few specimens may suffice to show the sort of light thrown by some of the entries in almost every page of these old municipal memoranda, upon the social condition of the times to which they refer.

# CHAPTER IV.

ROUTE FROM CITTÀ DI CASTELLO TO GUBBIO—DIFFICULTIES—VALLEY OF THE TIBER FROM CITTÀ DI CASTELLO TO FRATTA—FERRY OF THE TIBER—FRATTA—NEW ROAD TO GUBBIO—PICTURE AT FRATTA BY SIGNORELLI—MONASTERY OF MONTE CORONA—LEGISLATION RESPECTING THE REGULAR CLERGY IN UMBRIA—PEPOLI — CIVITELLA RANIERI — SUBTERRANEAN PASSAGE — DIFFICULTIES OF THE NEW ROAD — SPECIMEN OF ITALIAN CHARACTER—VALLEY OF THE ASSINO—SOLITARY MONASTERY—CASTELLO DI DANNO—WELL-HEAD OF THE RIVER ASSINO.

It had been our intention to go from Città di Castello to Gubbio, which to ideas formed only from study of the map seems to be a very simple matter. The distance in a direct line may be some sixteen or eighteen miles; certainly not more. But a very short conference on the subject with the authorities of the stable sufficed to dispel from our minds all such agreeable illusions.

Go to Gubbio! In the first place, what business could any one have to go to Gubbio at all? Everybody went from Città di Castello to Perugia! That was the regular course of things, and the law of nature! After that they might go to Gubbio, or whithersoever else might seem good to them. There was no road to Gubbio! Nobody had ever attempted such a thing. At all events it was necessary to follow the road to Perugia to within a very short distance of that city, and then diverge into the road thence to Gubbio.

It turned out on more closely pressed inquiry, that there *was* indeed a new road to Gubbio scarcely finished as yet, from a town called Fratta, twelve miles on the way to Perugia. This was at all events much better than going some two and thirty miles to Perugia, to come back again seven and twenty to Gubbio. The distance by the new road from Fratta to Gubbio is about sixteen miles. But was it passable? That was the question. And it was debated at great length in the principal café of Città di Castello, with all that participation in the dispute by everybody then and there present, which is so characteristic of Italian manners on similar occasions. The owner of the little carriage in which we purposed making the attempt, was unfortunately strong on the "*non possumus*" side of the question. He knew what could be done, and what could not! All that could become a *vetturino*, he dared! He that dared more was none—only an ignoramus! Finally it was determined by the united wisdom of the parliament assembled *ad hoc*, that the question should be left to the decision of the weather, which was threatening. If it should be fine, why then the arduous attempt should be made. If the night were wet, then we must knock under to *Jupiter pluviosus*, and consent to go round by the old road.

Jupiter was against us! "*Nocte pluit totâ, redeunt spectacula mane.*" The diligence, which was to start at the same hour with ourselves, *i. e.* at 6 A.M., declined setting out at all, alleging that after such a night the Tiber would be in a flood, and that the boat-ferry over it, some four miles before reaching Fratta, would be impracticable. Our *vetturino* would fain have followed the lead of so imposing an authority. He strongly urged that we should in Città di Castello—

> "Rest awhile,
> Nor tempt the stormy flood to-day."

But this we would not hear of. We had used up Città di Castello, and were bent on flying to fresh fields and pastures new. So we started in the rain, leaving the lily-livered diligence behind us, prophesying with all its voices our defeat and ignominious return.

The rain continued perseveringly, and destroyed the pleasure of what would otherwise have been an extremely pretty drive. A more exuberantly fertile valley than this part of the stream of Tiber runs through, it would be difficult to conceive. Instead of corn, wine, and oil, as in the Valdarno, the landscape is here composed of corn, wine, and oaks; very greatly to the improvement of the scenery. And the low hills which enclose it, together with the innumerable tempting-looking ravines between them, are almost entirely covered with oak-woods. Here and there we saw a few sticks of timber lying by the road-side squared, ready for removal, which sufficed to prove that the soil could produce trees of a very magnificent size. We saw also several villas in charming positions on the hill-sides, overlooking this richness of foliage, equally magnificent in point of size, but of a very different style and taste from those of Tuscany, and especially of the Valdarno. They had, for the most part, a decided tendency to run to frontage; were built more with a view to show, were less solid, less picturesque, less castellated in style, and evidently of a more recent period—of the seventeenth and eighteenth centuries probably. More picturesque remains of the habitations of an earlier period were to be seen here and there, not on the sides, but on the tops of the hills, and almost in every instance in ruins.

But all this was seen athwart the thick-falling rain; and we could only say to each other, "How lovely this *would be* in fine weather!" Our observations were made too to the constant accompaniment of the driver's forebodings, that we should find the river impassable. And in truth whenever we caught a sight of the swollen stream through the trees, there was a turbulent and angry look about it, which seemed very defiant.

At length the road made a sudden steep dip down the bank; and the river, and the ferry-house, and the huge, crazy-looking boat, doubly moored to the rope, which was stretched across the stream, were before us.

I jumped from the carriage, determined to have the genuine opinion of the ferryman, before the driver should have an opportunity of warping it to the confirmation of his own judgment. The Tiber ferryman was a huge, jolly-looking fellow, six feet high, and more than broad in proportion;—a goodly specimen of the Umbrian race, which is a larger and heavier one than the Tuscan, as the other products of this richer and deeper soil are also larger and more abundant.

The soil which will grow big oaks, will generally grow big men. He was evidently a man in authority, this Tiber king, having sundry ferrymen under him; and he spoke as such.

"*Si passerà, ma malamente.*"

Such was the sentence of the oracle. "The passage can be made, but with difficulty." So we triumphed over the *vetturino*, who was fain to console himself by dwelling on the latter clause of the sentence.

But why "*malamente?*" What was the nature of the difficulty? The turbid stream, of the colour and apparently of almost the consistency of pea-soup, was running, it is true, at a tremendous pace, and the waters were a good deal higher than the ordinary embarking place. But the rope, which passing out from an aperture in the ashlar wall of the upper story of the ferry-house, made for the purpose, crossed the river, and was fastened to a ring well fixed in the opposite bank, was at least two inches in diameter, and seemed strong enough to defy any force of the stream to break it. Was there any fear that the rope might give way, or the chain and running wheel, by which the boat was attached to it, be found too weak for the strain upon them?

"*Che! che!* The rope was sure enough; otherwise he should not be mad enough to put off."

But might the force of the water against the side of the boat swamp it, despite the rope?

The water would swamp it, sure enough, if the side of the boat were exposed to it; but we should pass showing only our stern to the stream. He should go over himself, and see to it.

But, once again, where then was the difficulty?

"*Si passerà malamente, caro mio Signore!* and half an hour hence, you would not be able to pass at all. From minute to minute the flood is increasing. Last year we could wash our hands in the river out of that first-floor window, see you. *Si passerà malamente.*"

And that was all the explanation I could get And there did seem to be some little difficulty in getting the carriage in and out of the boat. But, though the turbid water rushed past us with a velocity, which made one's head swim to look at it, it seemed to me that we swung across with no difficulty save that; and once launched from the bank, it was all done in less than five minutes.

This ferry is an old and venerable institution, and the jolly ferryman has his vested interest in the bridgelessness of the river. Nevertheless the days of him and his ferry are numbered; and any one who would try the adventure of crossing Tiber in flood must not delay the exploit. For a few hundred yards below the old crossing place the piers of a fine stone bridge are already standing in the stream; and in a few months the ferryman's place will know him no more.

About another hour's drive through the rain brought us to the extremely picturesque bridge and gateway of Fratta, with its town-wall of weather-stained brick, descending sheer into the river. Here our steed was to have his mid-day rest and feed; and we were glad to get shelter and a cup of hot chicory-water and goat's-milk, *alias* coffee, in a little café, which seemed to be the only place of public entertainment in the town.

And it was fortunate that we did not disdain the hospitality offered by it. For it so happened that the master of the café had himself recently made the journey from Gubbio by the short road. And when this circumstance led to a re-debate before the *Senatus Populusque* of Fratta respecting our route, there arose from a dark corner of the café a thick and husky but very authoritative voice, from one whom all seemed to acknowledge as a supreme authority on the subject. He was a very stout elderly man, the father, as he said, of all the *vetturini* in the country.

"The new road to Gubbio was not a good one; he was not the man to say it was; indeed, it was premature to call it a road at all; for it was by no means finished yet. Nevertheless, it might be traversed by a driver, who knew his trade."

This of course put our *vetturino* on his mettle. Whatever another could do, he could do. But after such rains as had been falling?

The stout father of the profession stuck to his opinion, that the thing might be done. There was a certain spot where the mud was very deep; but by making the "*trapelo*"—*i. e.* the additional horse to be taken to help up a steep hill;—by making the *trapelo* continue a little beyond the normal place for parting with him, we could get pulled through the mud.

"And then," said I, "we shall be quite willing to walk over any specially bad bit of road."

"Ay!" said the stout man; "but you would find it difficult to get through on foot!"

"I won't try it without horns!" cried our *vetturino*, suiting his action to the word by elevating a forefinger on either side of his forehead. What he meant was, that he must have, not a horse, but a yoke of oxen to help him. Eventually however this plan was overruled; and we left Fratta tandem-wise, the driver and proprietor of the second horse walking by his side.

The sole "lion" at Fratta besides its pretty and picturesque situation on the banks of the Tiber is a really fine picture,—a Descent from the Cross,—by Luca Signorelli in the little Church of the Santa Croce. Attempts had been made, it seemed, to purchase this picture from the confraternity to which it belongs; and I was struck by the remarks made on these unsuccessful offers by one of the principal inhabitants of the little town in speaking on the subject. "It would be a great pity," he said, "to part with the only thing of value the town contained, because then there would be absolutely nothing to call foreigners thither!" He had no thought whatsoever for any pleasure or advantage to be derived from the sight of the picture by the inhabitants themselves! Its whole and sole value, in his eyes, consisted in the possibility that it might be the means of causing *his* little town also to share in the gold-deposit left by the tide of travellers that is continually passing over Italy.

The hills which bound the valley of the Tiber to the right of one descending the valley, rise in the neighbourhood of Fratta to a considerable height, and are well wooded. And at about two miles from the town, on an isolated hill, nestling among the rich oak-woods, is the Camaldolese monastery of Monte Corona. We had originally purposed visiting this convent and passing the night there, in accordance with the hospitable habitudes of all the monasteries of this Order. But it was a little too late in the history of the world for the execution of any such plan. Throughout Umbria the monks have been turned out of their convents; and there is no more hospitality to be had on Monte Corona. We consoled ourselves for our disappointment, partly by reflecting on the great desirability of the measure, and partly by the fact that it would have availed little to go scenery-hunting in such weather.

The sentence of banishment against the monks passed and executed throughout Umbria by the Provisional Governor Pepoli, has given rise to much discontent and hostile criticism on the part of the Umbrian population. Not that there is any feeling in favour of the monks, or that any doubt was felt as to the absolute necessity of their ultimate extirpation. But the Provisional Government did not meddle with the friars. And it is remarked that the Government was in a very great hurry to expropriate the monastic Orders, who had property to be confiscated; but were by no means eager to suppress the mendicants, from whom nothing was to be got. But an exactly contrary order of proceeding, it is argued, should have been pursued. The friars, who in every point of view are the most mischievous, and who live by preying on the scanty means of the labouring population, should have been turned out at once; and the monks, who to a certain degree assisted the poor by the alms distributed at their gates, should have been left to become extinct by the natural operation of time.

## CIVITELLA RANIERI.           53

"But Pepoli,* you see," as it was remarked to me more than once or twice in Umbria, "was the Emperor's man; and acted in that and various other matters expressly with a view to disgust the people with their new governors, and indispose them towards union with Piedmont."

We entered on the difficulties of the threatened pass immediately after leaving Fratta; quitting at once the valley of the Tiber by a stony track traced in a direct line up the mountain side in days when inaccessibility was deemed for good reasons a greater advantage than accessibility, and long before engineering zigzags were dreamed of. For we were to enter on the newly traced road only at the top of the hill. This steep track had been made to render just possible the approach to a fine old castle in a singularly commanding situation at the top of the hill. It is called Civitella Ranieri, and belonged to a race of *Marchesi* of that name. Just above Fratta the little river Nicone falls into the Tiber from the west, flowing through a narrow valley of great beauty, green with emerald-coloured meadows along the margin of the stream, at its narrow bottom, and green with infinitely varied tints of forest verdure on its now widening, now narrowing sides. Almost opposite to it, coming in from the east, is the wider valley and somewhat larger stream of the Carpina. And this position at the meeting of the valleys must have rendered the site of Civitella Ranieri an important one once upon a time. At present its only value consists in its beauty.

* The Provisional Governor of Umbria after the annexation.

The building as usual is dilapidated; though not to such a degree as to be uninhabitable. But it has descended to the rank and functions of a farm-house, the life in which probably beats only in some one very small corner of the huge pile. There is a grand terrace on the western and northern sides of the castle, commanding complete and very charming views of the three valleys beneath it. The interior court is as feudal and grim-looking as ever with its dark-grey battlements, and carved stone armorial bearings on the walls, as long as the eye is cast upwards. But when it returns to earth, the present living occupants of the space,—a gaunt, arch-backed pig or two grubbing among the herbage which in the course of centuries of neglect has substituted itself for stones, a few cocks and hens similarly employed, a couple of great, lazy hounds, and as many still lazier masters of them lounging on the steps of the main doorway,—serve to bring the imagination back to the realm of "actualities." The people here have a story that there exists a secret subterraneous passage from this castle to Perugia, to which city the Ranieri belonged. It is quite out of the question that such a communication should ever have existed; and the tradition is only worth mentioning from the curious ubiquity of similar stories. In an hundred such cases the people tell you similar tales; and in some cases, of very much shorter distances than that here spoken of, they are probably true. And they afford at all events a curious evidence of the traditional notions held by the populace of the present time of the needs and habits of their "*Signoroni*" of other days.

While we stood on the terrace of Civitella Ranieri the rain ceased, and the sun somewhat dubiously and shyly showed himself. There is no more happy moment for looking over a wide and varied landscape of wooded hills, green valleys, and distant townlets than that of such a change. But to us, with the terrors of the doubtfully practicable road before us, this timely change of weather was yet more welcome.

Passing round behind the castle, we entered at once upon our troubles; and we were more than once inclined to think that our *vetturino* had shown the better part of valour, and that the fat "father of the road" by whose advice we had decided on attempting the adventure, would possibly have been less enterprising, if he had been called upon to perform the task himself. The road was not of a nature, except at one or two points, to cause any serious danger beyond that of sticking fast from absolute impossibility of proceeding. And this would assuredly have befallen us, if we had not profited by the hint of the father of the profession, and retained our leader, as a permanent institution, instead of a mere assistance up the first hill. But in the midst of all these difficulties the good side of the Italian nature shone forth. Though the thing had been attempted in opposition to his own judgment, and though the work tried his own really good horse, and his carriage terribly, when he was once in for it, our driver never lost his cheerfulness and good temper for a minute. There was no "I told you so!" only a little boasting as to the triumphs of himself, his horse, and his carriage, when we succeeded in reaching the further side of some extra deep slough, the man bedraggled with mud to his middle, the good steed shaking himself and looking about him with a perplexed air, which seemed to ask very plainly, "What next, I wonder!" and the carriage with its two hinder wheels still contrary to all reasonable expectation in due connection with their antecedent companions.

The road was assuredly, as we had been told, "unfinished." Almost all the streams were as yet unbridged; and as they were numerous, and turbid and swollen by the recent rain, the fording them was a difficult matter. We had to trust to the good horse "smelling" the stones at the bottom, as his master said. But it is needless to recount all our hair-breadth escapes. We *did* get through, and reached a comparatively good road four or five miles before arriving at Gubbio; and then our jovial Jehu treated himself to an unstinted amount of self-glorification.

"Did the old one at Fratta think that *he* could have done that? Not he! No one had done it in such weather; and no one else could do it! In fine dry weather? Ah! thank you! that was quite another thing! He was the lad to stick at nothing! *Per Bacco*, if a *Signor Forestiére* told him to drive through the Tiber, and paid him well, he would say, 'All right, Illustrissimo! Jump in! Here goes!'"

Nothing can be prettier in its own style than the country through which this new track has been pierced. It follows for the whole way the course of the mountain torrent Assino, which falls into the Tiber a few miles below Fratta. The hills are very richly wooded, almost entirely with oak; and during part of its course the valley narrows till it assumes the character of a rocky gorge. In the midst of the wildest and most (hitherto) inaccessible part of this difficult country is the little solitary convent of Campo Reggiano. It was several centuries old at the beginning of the thirteenth century, as we learn from notices of restorations then ordered by the Bishop of Gubbio,* on whom it depended. It is niched into a little, low, damp-looking meadow, which some shifting of the course of the stream in former ages has left available for the purpose. Now the monks have been turned out; and anything more desolate-looking than the place can hardly be conceived.

On a hill far back from the stream, among the thick woods, some three or four miles from the monastery, is the ancient castle of Danno. What a spot for a residence when no road whatever traversed this remote valley; when no wheeled carriage could have come within a dozen miles of it, and the only possible approach to it was by a difficult bridle track among the forests, and across the streams! The situation of such a home explains very intelligibly the old-world stories of ruffian and lawless nobles who carried off ladies or other stolen property to their castles in the Apennines. Little redress could be hoped for wrong done in the secrecy of such a lair!

About four or five miles before reaching Gubbio, as has been said, we came upon a tolerably good road, quitting the mountains and the narrow ravine of the Assino, and coming out into the peculiarly situated, mountain-enclosed basin in which Gubbio is placed.

A mile or two before reaching the city the road

* Mauri Sarti. De Episcopis Eugabinis, p. 131.

passes the well-head of the Assino, which rises in a singular manner from a pool in the midst of a green meadow in the bottom of the valley. The water wells forth in a very considerable stream, causing the river to commence its course at once with a volume of water deserving of that name. The phenomenon is by no means an unique one. But I do not remember to have heard in other similar cases what I was told here—viz., that no diminution of the water in the greatest heats of summer, or increase of it at the time of the melting of the snows on the mountains is to be observed in the case of the Assino.

# CHAPTER V.

POSITION OF GUBBIO—HOTEL THERE—ITALIAN INNKEEPING—AN ITALIAN RECEPTION—MONTE CALVO—PALAZZO PUBBLICO—FORMER POPULATION OF THE CITY—CURIOUS ANECDOTE—HOW THE DYNASTY OF MONTEFELTRO BECAME LORDS OF GUBBIO.

THE position of the city of Gubbio is a rather remarkable one. Lying along at the foot of the main chain of the Apennines there is an entirely mountain-surrounded basin, some ten or twelve miles long by about two in width. It is not the valley, nor part of the valley of any river; and one does not see why there should be this flat and completely enclosed tract in the midst of the mountains. In all probability it is the site of a long since dried lake. The whole shape and formation of the country are such as to suggest this idea; and the flatness and fertility of this little oasis in the midst of the mountains would seem to confirm the theory. The great mountains of the main chain of the Apennines shut in this basin to the north-east, and the smaller range of hills, among which we had been finding our way along the course of the Assino, complete the enclosure of it on the south-west, and at the two ends. The former of these enclosing boundaries is composed of a singularly bleak, barren, and rocky group of mountains; the latter of a region of wood-covered hills of more moderate elevation. The soil of the former district is mainly white in tone of colouring, the latter red.

The city of Gubbio is placed at the foot of the higher and sterner range of hills at about the middle of the length of the valley. Yet the phrase " at the foot of the hill," hardly succeeds in explaining the situation of the place. It would be more accurate to say, on the high instep of the foot of the hill. For the site of the town is raised considerably above the flat bottom of the valley, and occupies ground so far from level that many of the streets of the city are quite inaccessible to wheels.

As seen from the level of the valley below it, or from the wooded heights on the opposite side of the valley, Gubbio appears a very picturesque and handsome city; an advantage due partly to the position, which has been described and which hangs out, as it were, the whole town to view, in a succession of terraces; and partly from the singularly striking magnificence and prominence of the ancient municipal palace.

The steepness of its site has also the advantage of rendering it, at least after such weather as had preceded our arrival, a singularly clean town;—a circumstance which prepossessed us in favour of the accommodation we hoped to find at the one inn. Its uniqueness is perhaps the reason why it has been considered unnecessary to distinguish it by any name; at all events, it has none. But the stranger who visits Gubbio will have not the slightest difficulty in finding his way thither.

We drew up at the enormous doorway of an enormous house, a *palazzo* of course, which had been really such in its day by virtue of the rank of its inhabitants, as well as its own size and stateliness; situated in a silent little *piazza* in which the grass was growing thickly among the paving stones. Not a soul was to be seen. Our driver beat on the door which was wide open, with the huge old knocker, and the echoes rang through the great hall, and the little piazza; but that was the only result of his call. There was no sort of sign to indicate that the house was a place for the reception of travellers; and we inquired of the *vetturino* if he were sure that he had made no mistake.

"No! no! this was the place, sure enough! But then if the people were all asleep, or all dead since he was last in Gubbio, that was more than he could say." And thereupon followed another tremendous peal on the knocker. We begun to think badly of our chance of bed and supper in Gubbio. But at last a pretty smiling lass came tripping down the great staircase, and advanced with a bow of welcome to the door. Things looked better!

"Is it long since your lordships arrived?" said she, laughingly. "Pray come up! Why did you not come in? You might wear out the door, or at least your own arms, before you could make any one hear you! The house is so large, you see! And mother and I were in the kitchen ever so far away! This way, Signóri!"

And so she tripped up the stairs again, leaving the driver to take out the horse, and find his way to the stable, as best he might. We followed her up the grand old marble staircase, till we reached a very lofty "*piano nobile*," or first-floor; then passing through three or four large and wholly empty rooms, came to one that had apparently been, at some long since forgotten period, a grand drawing-room. Now there were two large square trestle beds in it, covered with counterpanes of coarse green serge.

We passed through this, and through a pair of once painted and gilded folding doors; and thus reached the "*sala da pranzo.*"

"There is another way through the kitchen," said the damsel, always smiling and showing two brilliant rows of even teeth, had it not been for which, her smiles would doubtless have been less frequent. For in this respect the *mores hominum* at Gubbio are singularly like those of London and Paris, and Timbuctoo.

"There is another way, through the kitchen; but mother is busy making *brigidini*,* and the kitchen is all *sotto-sopra;* so I thought it more "*convenevole*" (more proper and decent) to bring your lordships this way."

In answer to our inquiries about rooms, she said:

"Ah! yes! sleeping chambers! We have beautiful

* Brigidini are round, thin wafer-like cakes, made by baking between two irons, arranged forceps-wise. The plates which compress the dough, batter, or whatever it may be, between them, are about six inches in diameter; and are engraved with devices, which of course are reproduced on the cakes. Sometimes these are very handsome, and often of the fine work of the 16th century. *Brigidini* irons, with beautifully engraved arabesques, and other fancies, with coats of arms, and often with the date of their manufacture in the 16th century, are not unfrequently met with.

ones. I will show your illustrious excellencies some rooms, more *alla moda di questi tempi* " * than this part of the house, but they are a long way off."

So we followed her up more stairs, till we came to a sort of a vast garret under the huge naked rafters of the building, which was partly filled with hay and timber for firing and such like matters; and from this across a kind of long bridge of planks so placed as to form a steep inclined plane. What the nature of the space was which this bridge crossed I could not see; for there was very little light at all; and the abyss below was as dark as pitch, and might have been bottomless, for all the eye could ascertain to the contrary. A stranger way to a bedroom can hardly be imagined. However our conductress tripped on before us, apparently utterly unconscious that there was anything unusual in the arrangements of her household; and we followed nothing doubting. And the extraordinary bridge did, in truth, bring us to a region more " *alla moda di questi tempi.*" We seemed to enter through a thick wall a modernized part of the building; found an ordinary staircase of moderate dimensions, which we descended for awhile, and thus at length reached two clean and modern-looking rooms, with very tolerable beds in them.

And there our guide was about to leave us without more ado! But I was quite sure that I was incompetent to find my way back by the devious route we had traversed. I had no idea which door at the top of the modern staircase opened on the mysterious bridge. I assuredly could not steer my course aright by the bearings of haystacks and faggot-piles across

* More modern-fashioned.

the *chiaróscuro* of the huge garret. And I knew not how far I must descend the great stair, nor by what clue find my way through the maze of empty rooms to the kitchen and dining-room, in which all the life in the establishment seemed to be concentrated. So I demurred very decidedly against the contemplated abandonment, and signified to our pretty guide, who was the sole living being we had yet seen in the house, that where she went, thither I also would go!

So she took us back again to the eating-room; and there after a little attempt at making conversation about the weather, and if we had ever before been at Gubbio, ect., just as if we had been making a morning call, and had no needs to satisfy, or at all events as if she was in no wise concerned with the satisfying of them, she made another attempt to escape.

"But, Signorina! for the love of heaven, do not abandon us. This is the *sala da pranzo*, is it not?"

"*Sicuro!*\* Signori! see there is the table!" pointing to a great square one in the middle of the room, covered with a dirty white cloth.

"Yes! but there is nothing on the table to eat, and we are hungry!"

"Ah! you want to sup! I will call my mother!"

And with that she flitted out of the door opposite to that by which we had entered.

In a short time the mother made her appearance, a tall, pleasing-looking woman, who must in her day have been strikingly handsome. She, too, came in smiling and bowing welcomes; but at the first mention of eatables, her countenance fell.

\* To be sure!

## HOW TO GET SUPPER. 65

" What could we have for supper ? "

To say the truth, she feared there was nothing !

Everybody knows the stereotyped reply of the waiter in an English hotel to a similar question; how it at once promises everything that the imagination of a Lucullus could conceive, and by how rapid a process of elimination the prospect is reduced to the classical alternative of "beef-steak—mutton-chop." In the hostelries of out-of-the-way places in Italy, the process is generally exactly the reverse. Deeply impressed with notions of the unheard-of luxuries required by *forestieri,* and dismayed at their conscious inability to supply these unknown wants, the hosts will generally in pure desperation rush at once to the declaration that they have and can give you nothing. But a little further inquiry, if kindly and good-humouredly made, soon modifies the state of the case.

" A *minéstra di riso,* \* you can have to be sure; and a *lesso.*† Then for the *fritto,* one can find a few artichokes perhaps. Do you prefer a pigeon or *uccellini* ‡ for the *arrósto* ? "

All this our Gubbio hostess promised us, if we would give her a little time. To our suggestion that a few potatoes might be added to this magnificent bill of fare, she said that that was the most difficult of all; but that she would forthwith despatch messengers to scour the city, and if a potato could be found in Gubbio, we should have it.

In short, the blank announcement that nothing

---

\* Rice soup.  † A bit of beef boiled.

‡ Small birds, *i. e.* sparrows, thrushes, robins, chaffinches, or anything of the kind that can be caught.

F

eatable was to be had, was only intended to reduce gradually the inordinate expectations we were supposed to entertain down to the level of what turned out to be a repast quite sufficient to be very cordially welcomed by hungry travellers.

The next morning the rain had to our great delight ceased; and our first ramble through the city sufficed to assure me, that Gubbio has abundantly enough of interest of many kinds to make it well worth the traveller's while to overcome the obstacles to visiting it, arising from its out-of-the-way position.

The nature of its situation has been already in some degree described. The peculiarly stern-looking and barren mountains immediately behind it, and against the last steep slopes of which the city is built, are cleft exactly at the spot which it occupies by a singularly narrow and wild-looking ravine, through which runs a road to Scheggia, a post-town on the other or eastern side of the Apennines on the great road from Rome to Bologna. And by this road, which comes out from its passage *through* rather than across the Apennines, (so deep and cleft-like is the gorge along which it passes), was the best access to Gubbio before the tracing of the new road described in the last chapter. By this road also Gubbio was connected with Urbino, the capital of the Ducal family who were lords also of the former city. Monte Calvo* the mountain is called, and it well deserves the appellation; for I have rarely, in any part of the world, seen so large a mass so nearly approaching the condition of absolutely naked rock. The passage through the defile is one, which a small

* Bald.

number of resolute men might defend against an army.

The splendid princes of the House of Rovere had a residence at Gubbio, which must have vied with the magnificent and more celebrated palace at Urbino. But the traces left by the old free burghers of the time, when Gubbio was an independent community, before the princes of the House of Montefeltro had made themselves masters of the city, are even to the present day more plainly legible, and more indestructible than the impress of the later sovereigns. The most striking and most prominent building in Gubbio at this time is not the palace of its magnificent duke, but the town-hall of the old republicans of an earlier time.

The latter is indeed not only the most remarkable building in Gubbio, but is one of the most noteworthy in Italy; and has quite recently,—a few days only previous to my visit to Gubbio,—been declared by the Parliament a national monument, and its restoration and conservation at the public cost decreed. The townsfolk were greatly delighted at this determination, and were eagerly looking for the arrival of the architect to be sent by the Government; and hoping that the choice might fall on a gentleman who has shown himself so especially competent to undertake a work of this kind, by the very remarkably successful restoration of the Bargello at Florence, a nearly contemporary building.

The *Palazzo pubblico* of Gubbio is, however, a monument still more important and interesting in the history of architecture, than even the deservedly celebrated Florentine Bargello. For it is a more complete and homogeneous specimen of the epoch at which it was built. On the architrave above the principal doorway, is carved the following inscription in letters of the kind ordinarily, but not very reasonably called "Gothic:"—

"A . DNI . MCCCXXXII
CHOMENCIATA
QUESTA . OPERA.
E . QUANDO . FU . POSTA
QUESTA . PIETRA
MCCCXXXV . DEL . MESE
D' OTTOBRE.

"This work was commenced in 1332. And when this stone was placed here, it was October in the year 1335." And with the exception of a few degradations, and some altogether inconsiderable and most easily recognized additions and modifications, the fabric remains to the present day as the fourteenth century created it; whereas the Bargello or *Palazzo del Podesta* at Florence, is, as is well known, the production of several different generations.

At the date above given, in the first half of the fourteenth century, Gubbio was still, as it had been from a very high antiquity, an independent republic; and was at the culminating point of its prosperity. It fell towards the end of that century into the power of the lords of Urbino, of the House of Montefeltro. And although the dynasty it thus became subject to was in all probability by far the best on the whole of any of the numerous petty princes who governed Italy during those centuries, the city at once began, though slowly, to enter on the course of decadence, which it may be said with general correctness to have followed ever since.

A census of the population of the city taken on the 18th of April, in the year 1345, gives the following results :—

In the quarter of St. Martin, 1348 families.
In that of St. Guiliano, 1200 families.
In that of St Pietro, 1526 families.
In that of St. Andria, 1072 families.
Total, 5146 families.*

Allowing the moderate estimate of five individuals to each family, this would give a population of 25,730 souls. But it is to be observed, and the fact is a curious trait of the manners and ways of thinking of those times, that the possessors of real property only were taken into account in the above calculation. It is very remarkable also that this category should have included so large a portion of the population. But it is certain that the numbers of those who possessed nothing, and who were not thought worth counting even, must have amounted to many thousands. Further, the above numbers do not include the inmates of twenty-two convents of one or the other sex.

From another authority, cited also by Reposati, it appears that the population of Gubbio in the year 1400 was stated at 27,000; which would indicate a falling off from the previous numbers.

Already at an earlier period than this the flourish-

* Della Zecca di Gubbio; e Delle Geste dé Conti e Duchi di Urbino Opera del Prevosto Rinaldo Reposati. 2 Vols. 4to. Bologna. 1772. Vol. I. p. 45.

ing city had sent out colonies from the overplus of its population, and had founded the city of Pergola, and some other communities of less note. But its fall under the sceptre of a "tyrant," (using that term in the sense universally attributed to it in Italy in those centuries, to mean simply a single ruler), was caused in the midst of this prosperity by the same fault which has so often and in so many places wrought ruin in Italy;—the internecine feuds of the citizens.

A very curious and characteristic tradition, attached to a fabric still extant and visible in the city, gives a lively idea of the highly explosive condition of the social system, in which these pugnacious free citizens perpetually lived. The fabric in question is a stair, made to communicate with the "*Palazzo pubblico*," of which I have been speaking, from the lower part of the city. I have said that the town is built on the lowest slope of the mountain, just above the flat hill-circled basin that forms the fertile territory of the city. But this lowest slope is still so steep that the streets climb it in zigzags, in such sort, that in many instances the tops of the houses in one street are on a level, or almost so, with the foundations of those in the terrace next above them. The "*Palazzo pubblico*" stands in nearly the centre of the city, on a level *piazza* formed at the steepest part of the hill by supporting the outside portion of the space on a range of colossal arches springing from the level of the street next below it on the mountain side. It may easily be imagined how much such an arrangement adds to the imposing appearance of the building, which thus stands projected out, as it were, from the hill-side, and showing to the valley below it a façade of immense and almost unmatched altitude. But this position of the "*Palazzo pubblico*," the centre, mainspring, and heart of the republican political life, was attended by an important inconvenience. There were three directions only, by which it could be approached; up the street in which it stood; down the same street in the opposite direction; and thirdly, from the higher part of the town by a very steep street descending the hill nearly in face of the building. Thus by these three roads the public officers and citizens of the three wards, which lay in the three directions indicated, could approach the palace, and arrive at it simultaneously, so that no appearance of precedence should be claimed by or conceded to either of them.

But unfortunately the city consisted of *four* wards, as has been seen from the above statement of the population. And how were the representative men of the fourth ward,—that situated on the lower ground below the palace,—to come to that great centre of meeting on all the grand occasions, when the eyes of all the world of Gubbio were on them! To follow in the wake of one of the others, their fellow-citizens and equals, was not to be heard of! It was absolutely necessary, if they would avoid deadly animosity and constant warfare, that all the four wards should arrive at the burgher parliament hall so as to prevent the possibility of any appearance of precedence being enjoyed by either of them. And this could only be accomplished by finding some fourth road by which the fourth ward might approach the palace. The object was accordingly accomplished by constructing, at a vast expense, the stair which has been mentioned.

Not even this elaborate precaution, however, availed in the long run to keep the leading families in the city from deadly quarrel and hereditary feud. And towards the close of the fourteenth century, the state of things in the city became so intolerable from the consequence of these intramural wars, that a large party of the citizens became anxious to obtain peace even at the price of submitting themselves to a "tyrant." And the manner in which this was eventually brought about offers us another characteristic scene from the strange tragi-comedy of the mediæval republican life.

The year 1383 was one of disaster and trouble in Gubbio. To all the manifold evils of a state of civil war, which had for some time past been ruining the little republic, were added those of an extreme scarcity approaching to a famine. In those days, when want of physical as well as of moral communication with other parts of the world precluded the possibility of supplying the wants of one district from the superabundance of others, no mode of providing against the consequences of those years of scarcity, which a primitive and unscientific system of agriculture caused to be of frequent recurrence, was known, save the simple one of saving up the overplus of years of abundance, as a supply on which to fall back in the time of need, which was sure to come ere long. And if this supply, necessarily very limited in its amount, was exhausted before the return of plenty, all the horrors of famine were inevitable. A state of civil war in the city was not likely to be propitious to the agriculture of the surrounding district, which depended on and supported it. And the winter of 1383-4 was a terrible one in Gubbio.

On the 24th of March, 1384, a great meeting was held in the "*Palazzo pubblico*," to endeavour to devise some remedy for the evils which were apparently bringing the State to complete destruction. It was decided to send conciliatory letters to Francesco Gabrielli, the head of one of the great factions, which were ruining the city by their quarrels. But there was a large party in the city, who thought that no such palliative measures would be of any lasting avail; who cried out for "new blood;" and who were determined, rather than bear the ills they had, to fly to those others, which as yet they knew not of, inseparable from the domination of a foreign power.

Letters were prepared in accordance with the decision come to by the Council, addressed to Francesco Gabrielli; and they were left in the evening with the Gonfaloniere Niccolò di Sforzolini, " a man, of whom," says Reposati, the historian of Gubbio, "I cannot but think, that he was as simple and unversed in public affairs, as he was illustrious by birth;" that he might append to them the great seal of the Community, which was in his sole keeping. Meantime the adherents of the House of Montefeltro contrived to have other letters, inviting the Conte Antonio di Montefeltro to come and receive possession of the city, prepared, and in the dusk of the evening, as it would seem, so substituted these for the others addressed to Francesco Gabrielli as to cause the Gonfalonieri to affix the city seal to the former. With the earliest light of the next morning the conspirators were *en route* with the fraudulently obtained letters in their saddle-bags. But they had not to journey very far. For *it so chanced* that the Count Antonio happened to be at Cagli, just on the other side of the mountains. And it further happened most opportunely that the Count had with him at Cagli as many as two thousand foot-soldiers and four hundred horsemen, and what was yet more to the purpose, eight hundred loads of victuals. And with all this following, he made his appearance before the starving city, on the 31st of March, delaring to the men of Gubbio, exactly as another citizen king once upon a time told his subjects, that he was come, "not to be Lord of Gubbio, but Captain of the Eugubbians." \*

Even if the citizens could have denied their own letter, and resisted the two thousand bowmen, they could not resist the eight hundred loads of food. Cries of " Viva il Conte Antonio ! " rung through the city ; the fortress of St. Ubaldo was given up to the new comers; and whether as Kings of Gubbio, or Kings of the Gubbians, the Counts and Dukes of Urbino remained thenceforward rulers also of Gubbio, till both cities fell at last in the seventeenth century into the maw of the all-swallowing Church.

"Thus hunger," says Reposati,† "and civic discord, the denial of assistance implored by the citizens from the Court of Rome, and the dexterity of four

---

\* The adjective from Gubbio is *Eugubbian*, from the ancient Ikuvium or Eugubium.

† Vol. I. p. 109.

clever citizens attached to the Count Antonio, were the causes of the loss of liberty to Gubbio, and the notable increase of the states of the House of Montefeltro." *

* Mr. Dennistoun, in his admirable "History of the Dukes of Urbino," speaks of the Count Antonio having been "invited by the people of Gubbio;" and he mentions Reposati among the authorities consulted by him; but he wholly ignores the history of the trick by which the invitation was procured.

# CHAPTER VI.

THE RESIDENCE OF THE DUKES OF URBINO AT GUBBIO — THE DUKE'S CABINET—THE PALACE OF THE MUNICIPALITY — DESTROYED LOGGIA—MAURO SARTI'S DESCRIPTION OF THE PALAZZO PUBBLICO—COST OF THE BUILDING—PUBLIC LIBRARY —REMAINS OF A ROMAN THEATRE—THE "BOTTACCIONE"— AQUEDUCT—SOULAGE COLLECTION—" MOMO NICCHI"—STATUE BY MAESTRO GIORGIO—PICTURES AT GUBBIO—PICTURE BY DAMIANI—FRESCO BY NELLI—LOCAL HISTORIANS—ITALIAN SOCIETY.

It was about an hundred years after this acquisition of Gubbio by the Count Antonio, that the residence of the Dukes of Urbino in that their second capital was built.

"Sanzi describes it," says Mr. Dennistoun,* " as facing the south-east, and flanked by mountains on the north, overlooking fertile valleys, and smiling champaigns, and excelling the attractions of Urbino in charming prospects and pleasant pathways. Notwithstanding the general truth of this eulogy," continues Mr. Dennistoun, "nothing could be more inconsistent with beauty or convenience than its site, planted on a slope, with the Cathedral right in front, crowded round with poor buildings and accessible only by precipitous alleys. Its architecture is dis-

* "Memoirs of the Dukes of Urbino." Vol. I. p. 162.

puted between Francesco di Giorgio, and Baccio Pontelli; nor would it add much credit to either, its sole merit being minute decorations in hewn work and inlaid panelling. . . . The constant recurrence of the Garter among its ornamental devices is gratifying to the very rare English visitors of this Apennine town, but no traveller of taste and intelligence can be otherwise than shocked to find this once chosen sanctuary of Italian refinement and high-breeding, the residence in which Castiglione recounted his reception at the Tudor Court, and where Fregoso and Bembo were successively Bishops, degraded to vile uses and menaced by speedy ruin. It is now in the hands of a person who there manufactures wax candles and silk; but on my second visit in 1843 was closed up entirely and inaccessible."

It seems to me, that these disagreeable circumstances have unconsciously influenced the writer to under-estimate the merits of this remarkable specimen of the domestic architecture of the fifteenth century.

The position is a peculiar one, by no means without many advantages, which would be recognized as such at the present day, and others, which were thought to be so at the period when the palace was planned. It is planted not only on a slope, as Mr. Dennistoun says, but on so very steep a slope as to have very greatly increased the difficulties with which the architect had to contend, and the credit he deserves for having overcome them. The phrase "flanked by mountains," should rather have been *backed* by the mountain, which rises so immediately behind it, as to leave no foot of intermediate space. And in front the ground falls away so precipitously, that the way by which the "*Corte*," as the half-ruined palace is still called, can be most conveniently reached, is by entering the hall-door of a private residence in the street next below the terrace on which the palace stands, mounting the staircase of that house to the height of three storys, and then passing out from the garret floor of it by a little door opening on the hill-side in the immediate vicinity of the palace. And this strange approach has been found convenient by so many generations of the citizens, and has been for so long a period permitted to be used by the owners of the house in question, that the law holds that they have no longer the right to close their own hall door, or refuse the use of their staircase to the public.

It is true that the "*Corte*" of Gubbio could never have been approached save by paths almost deserving the epithet of precipitous; but it does not follow that they were "alleys," or that the palace was surrounded by poor buildings in its palmy day. There are indications on the other hand that the nearest buildings were houses of the better class.

The Cathedral is curiously close to the residence of the Sovereign, not "in front of it," as Mr Dennistoun says, in any other sense than as it is in front of the main entrance. The real front of the palace is that which looks out from the hill over the city. The main door of the palace is at the side; and it is indeed so close to the west front of the Cathedral that a flagstone-paved space of not more, I think, than about ten feet, is all that there is between the palace door and the steps leading to the portal of the Church. But this was deemed no disadvantage in days when it was really thought that "the nearer the

Church, the nearer to God!" was the true rule; and when an outward and material manifestation of closeness of union between the temporal and spiritual rulers was considered desirable and creditable by both of them.

Nor does the phrase "hewn-work," which Mr. Dennistoun says constitutes together with inlaid panelling the sole merit of the palace, at all do justice to the very exquisite arabesques, which decorate the stone-work of the window and door-frames and fire-places. All these are of *stone*, and not of marble. But the workmanship is of the finest and most delicate finish and admirable design.

The truth is that no modern architect would dream of erecting any building of pretension, save a fortification, on such a spot as that occupied by the palace. But the different needs, and different notions of what is desirable, prevailing in the fifteenth century and in our day, must not be forgotten. And even in the latter, as it seems to me, it is impossible not to be greatly impressed by the grandeur of the situation, with the city all immediately beneath it, and its magnificent out-look over a prospect of near valleys and more distant richly wooded hills beyond it, assuredly far superior in beauty to that wider but less rich prospect commanded by the palace at Urbino.

As to the "vile uses" to which this fine old building has been degraded, I am sorry to say, that the wax candle manufactory which Mr. Dennistoun seems to have found shut up in 1843 is now again in full operation; and the speedy ruin which he found menacing the palace is more menacing than ever.

For overtures were made to me by the proprietors for the sale of all the beautiful stone-work in the palace. And nothing save the difficulty and considerable cost of removal has prevented these exquisite specimens of the work of the fifteenth century from having passed ere now into the hands of dealers, who would find a ready sale for them in Paris or London, could they be transported thither for any moderate sum.

The intarsia work in wood, of the Duke Federigo's private cabinet, is in yet greater danger, in consequence of its greater transportability. Mr. Dennistoun quotes from the note-book of Mr. F. C. Brooke, of Ufford Place, Suffolk, the following account of this little cabinet, which he deems the most interesting feature of the palace:—

"The small cabinet has shared a better fate than that of the remainder of the apartments; and requires little else than cleaning up to restore it to its original state."

[I am sorry to say that, if such was the case at the date of Mr. Brooke's visit to Gubbio, the woodwork of this once exquisite little closet, must have suffered considerable injury since that time. Even yet, the work is by no means past restoration; and there are plenty of artists in *intarsia* at Florence competent to put the whole of it into perfectly good condition. But the cost of such repairs would be considerable.]

"The ceiling is divided into several scanty* compartments, of octangular form, and relieved with

---

* Of size however quite well-proportioned to that of the little room.

gold; while the wainscoted walls are inlaid with
*tarsia*, representing book-cases, or rather cupboards,
with their contents; amongst which are a ship, a
tambourine, military weapons, a cage with a parrot
in it, and, as if for the sake of variety only, a few
volumes of books, over one of which containing
music with the word ROSABELLA inscribed on its
pages, is suspended a crucifix. On the central case
opposite the window, and occupying, as it were, the
post of honour, is the Garter with its motto, HONI
SOIT Q. MAL I PENSE ; a device which has been sculptured on the exterior of the stone architrave of the
door of this apartment. It appears again in *tarsia*
in the recess of the window, where may also be seen
within circles, G. UBALDO DUX and FE. DUX. On the
frieze, and in a single line interrupted only by the
spaces occupied by the door and window, is the
following inscription in *tarsia :*—

"Aspicis æternos venerandæ matris alumnos
   Doctrina excelsos ingenioque viros.
 Vi nuda cervice cadant ante . . . .
   .   .   .   .   .   genu.
 Justitiam pietas vincit reverenda nec ullum
   Pœnitet ultrici succubuisse suæ."

"I might also have mentioned as amongst the
devices, the crane standing on one leg, and holding
with the foot of the other, which is raised, the stone
he is to drop as a signal of alarm for his companions.
Among other feigned contents of a book-case are an
hour-glass, guitar, and pair of compasses; in another
are seen a dagger, dried fruits in a small basket made
of thin wood, and a tankard; while in a third is represented an open book, surmounted with the name

of Guidobaldo, who probably made the selection inscribed on the two pages of the volume, comprising verses 457 to 491 of the 10th Æneid."

All the beautiful wood-work thus carefully and accurately described, may now be torn from the walls and carried off by any one willing to pay a moderate price for it. And it would doubtless long since have vanished were it not, that the proprietor has hitherto refused to sell any part of the spoils of the palace piecemeal. And the difficulty of moving the stone-work has as yet had the effect of keeping the wood-work in its place. One very beautiful stone door-case has been removed from the palace, and erected in the house of the owner in the lower town. But this also he is desirous of selling together with the rest.

I cannot concur with Mr. Dennistoun, as I have already intimated, in the censure he casts on the architect of the "Corte" at Gubbio; nor agree with him in thinking that the sole merit of the building consists in the details of its stone carvings and wood *intarsia*. But it must be admitted that its shattered remains make but a poor figure by the side of the sterner and grander handiwork of a previous century, as seen in the still unchanged *Palazzo pubblico*. The position of each of these buildings, as they have already been described, is appropriate and character-istic of their several purposes. The palace of the free people stands as nearly as may be in the centre of the city. The dwelling of the prince is am-bitiously placed on the highest ground, looking down on the subject-townsfolk and their residences. The latter building, dating from an epoch when artists were courtiers, is still rich in remnants of the splendour and elegance which surrounded a race of highly cultured and mostly well-intentioned princes. But the shattered fabric seems typical of a social system, which contained in itself the germs of inevitable decay, and under the operation of which the arts, as well as every other department of civilization, were doomed, despite all the fostering sunshine of magnificent patronage, to quickly advancing corruption, and the lethargy of effeteness.

The older building on the other hand, the architect of which, whoever he may have been,* was inspired by the sentiment of independence, and free self-government, and who laboured for the applause of his fellow-citizens and equals, stands now fit to endure as many ages as have already passed over it. The simple grandeur of its massive strength is durable as the social principle which it symbolizes. And even as the fabric, sharing the fate of that principle, has suffered abeyance of its functions and degradation to far viler uses than that wax-chandlery the presence of which so offended Mr. Dennistoun in the half-ruined palace of the extinct dynasty of princes, so it is still ready, vigorous and indestructible as ever to resume its old duties and significance, at the call of the resuscitated social idea, to which it owed its creation.

There are in fact two entirely separate buildings, which together constituted the old municipal palace. One stands at either end of the piazza, which has been mentioned as supported on the steep hill-side by a range of enormous arches. But though now

* It was probably built by Matteo di Giovanello, a native of Gubbio.

thus entirely separated, they were formerly united by an open *loygia*, running along the length of the terrace thus formed. The appearance of this range of arches as seen from the town below, and from the valley beyond, must have been grand in the extreme; and the place of meeting, and enjoyment thus afforded to the citizens, must have been one of the finest things of the kind ever seen, and unrivalled for the magnificence of its position and the view commanded from it over the city and the valley and the hills beyond. This *loggia*, moreover, served to unite the two *corps-de-logis*, of which the *Palazzo pubblico* consists, into one magnificent whole.

Unfortunately at the back of the piazza, on the slope of the hill, stands the large palace of the ancient family of the Marchesi Brancaleoni, with its great length of modernized frontage; so that the public *loggia* running along the front of the *piazza* came exactly between the wind (including the magnificent view) and the nobility of the Marchese Brancaleoni. And far more unfortunately still, the Marchese being a member of the town council, had sufficient influence to cause this superb old *loggia* to be pulled down, that his own palace might enjoy the view and the air!

Some gentlemen of the city to whom I spoke on the subject, endeavoured to excuse the Marchese, and the city (for truly both almost equally need excusing) by saying that the demolished *loggia* was not a building of the same period as the rest of the *Palazzo pubblico*; and that the junction of the two edifices at either extremity of the *piazza* by means of it, was no part of the original architect's design. It is difficult, however, to give much faith to the latter part of this statement. It may very well be, that the *loggia* was not executed till long after the completion of the two buildings, between which it formed a communication. In a very great number of instances in Italy—as indeed elsewhere also, but more especially in Italy—several generations were suffered to elapse between the first conception and the ultimate completion of architectural designs, the prosecution of which depended on the funds and the will of popular bodies, and which were destined to gratify the taste and the ambition not of an individual, who would never enjoy them if they were not completed within his life-time; but of a corporate body, which lived through the whole prolonged time of their slow progress to perfection. But there is a manifest fitness and appropriateness in such a building as this *loggia*, the place so unmistakably invited it, and the creation of such a place for the recreation and use of the citizens is so consonant with the almost invariable practice of the mediæval Italian municipal communities, that the assertion that no such edifice entered into the conception of the original architect seems to me to need more than simply negative proof. In any case, I think that no one can stand on the site of the demolished *loggia* without most strongly feeling that its destruction is very much to be regretted.

Of the two buildings thus disunited, that which stands on the right-hand of a person, looking from the terrace of the *piazza* over the valley, is the principal and the more remarkable.

The learned Camaldolese monk, Mauro Sarti, in

his history of the Bishops of Gubbio,* speaks as follows, of this very note-worthy building:—

"The public palace of the Eugubians is a vast edifice, which plainly proves what the money power of Gubbio must have been in those days. The whole of it is constructed of cut stone, with a stability and perfection of skill that rivals those great works of the ancients, the remains of which still fill us with admiration. Throughout the building there are neither fastenings nor beams, nor any even the least quantity of any material liable to fire. The whole roof rests on an arch of immense thickness; and the entire mass of the building is held together by its own natural forces. And I judge that the object of such a method of construction was to avoid all danger of fire, arising either from accident or from the perfidy of men; a danger which in those days was of very frequent occurrence by reason of the ever-recurring turbulences of the armed citizens."

Reposati tells us that he finds, from accounts still extant, that the entire cost of the building was 16,336 *liri*, 2 *soldi*, and 1 *denaro*. And he calculates the quantity of metal contained in each *lira* to be worth at the time of his writing (1772) rather more than one Roman *scudo* and one-third of a *scudo*, or nearly seven francs. This would give, as the cost of the palace in silver at the close of the last century a sum of 114,352 francs, equal to rather more than £4,500 of our money. But it is very clear that five times that sum would not suffice to raise such a

* Mauri Sarti Monachi et Cancellarj Camaldulensis de Episcopis Eugubinis. 1 vol. 4to. Pesauri. p. 188.

building at Gubbio at the present day. And it is evident that the proportion of value between labour and silver must have differed to a very much greater degree than that which Reposati assigns to the diminution in the value of silver.

The appearance of the old edifice, as it stands at the present day empty, save for the residence of a "*custode*" in one corner, high up in the neighbourhood of the bell tower, is just what the reader might imagine from the above description of its construction—the very symbol and most perfect expression of stern, hard, solemn durability. Stonehenge itself conveys to the mind hardly a more vivid impression of indestructibility. The two vast and very lofty halls—of which, one above the other, nearly the entirety of the ground-floor and the first-floor consist,—are empty, as has been said, and present their naked stone walls to the eye, unmitigated in their sternness by furniture, or upholstery, or ornamentation of any sort. For the various offices which formerly had their seat there have been removed to a large convent, from which the monks have been recently ejected, in the lower part of the city at the foot of the hill. Among other things of less interest the celebrated bronze Eugubian tables—which have been minutely described and engraved so often, that it is needless to speak further of them here—have been removed hence to the new seat of the municipality. And many of the purposes to which the huge space of the old fabric was destined have ceased to exist under the regimen of a radically changed social system.

"There are also," Reposati tells us,* "in this palace, magazines for the conservation of grain for several years, under the authority of the board for corn-supply, by means of which not only the poor of the city and its territory, but travellers also are provided with bread, which even in the years of greatest scarcity never fails them. There are also magazines for the oil-supply, where the oil for the need of the city and the territory is kept in vases of the best kind; and there is always a store sufficient for several years. There are, besides, places destined to the fish-market, where the sellers of it are obliged to bring their fish and sell it there. Finally, there is a furnace for the baking of vases of clay, and other conveniences necessary for such an edifice."

All is gone now. But the colossal walls, and floors and arches remain, and will remain for many a generation to testify, as the old Camaldolese monk says, what was the money power of Gubbio in those days.

One cannot help wondering whether the orthodox ecclesiastic ever paused to ask himself why and how it came to pass that the "money power" of the little city "in those days" was so very remarkably different from what it was, after it had had the advantage of a few centuries of despotic and priestly government.

In one of the walls of the upper hall there is a large cistern, handsomely decorated with carvings in stone; and in the middle of the floor a still more unusual decoration for an upstairs chamber.

"*Fons est,*" says an old writer cited by Riposati,† "*in medio superioris aulæ, quo per admirabilem*

* Vol. II., p. 411.   † Vol. II., p. 411.

*Aquæductum altius conscendunt cristallinæ ac murmurantes undæ."*

The stair by which this upper hall is reached from the lower one is at one end of the latter and is open, being constructed in a very similar manner to the well-known stair in the courtyard of the Bargello at Florence; only that in that instance it is exterior instead of interior. Outside this upper hall, on the side looking over the valley, there is a very beautiful small *loggia*, from which a great part of the territory of the little republic could be seen. A bell-tower of no great height completes the edifice. But although the entire altitude of the building is but slightly increased by this addition, it is stated on the good authority of the well-known writer, Scipio Maffei, that the entire height of it is equal to that of the Campanile of St. Mark's at Venice. Of course, by this is to be understood the height of wall on the side looking towards the valley, which, as will readily be comprehended from what has been said before, is increased by all the height of the vast substructure which supports the *piazza* on which the palace is built. It will be understood also, that the building as seen from below, and from the valley, and from the hills on the further side of the valley, gains the full advantage of this additional height, and makes a proportionably striking and imposing appearance.

The men of Gubbio may well be pleased that the nation has determined to take on itself the restoration and future care of this unmatched memorial of the palmy days of old; and it will be an interesting question to decide to what purpose the renovated fabric shall be devoted.

The other building at the opposite side of the *piazza* now contains in it a very tolerable public library, the gift to the city of Alessandro Sperelli, a former Bishop of Gubbio, who died about the middle of the seventeenth century, and left some small funds for the increase of the collection. I found on the shelves rather a remarkable collection of the local historians of this and the adjoining districts of Italy, and of rare biography specially connected with the same provinces.

The upper part of this building has suffered the same degradation to which the recently-restored *Palazzo del Podista* at Florence was subjected,—that of being turned into the city prison; and it has materially suffered from the ill usage. The architectural construction of it is very peculiar,—the vaults which support the different floors and the roof springing from and resting on a central column. And it would seem that the additional floors which were introduced for the construction of prison cells, and the number of partition walls necessitated by them, overweighted the supports calculated to bear only the burthen which the original architect placed on them. The result has been that the vaults in the several floors have manifested very serious symptoms of giving way; and the architect to be sent to Gubbio by the Government will not arrive there an hour too soon.

There are in the valley below the city, about a mile from the walls, the remains of a very considerable Roman theatre, which suffice to indicate the importance of this locality under the Empire; as the work has been judged by competent authorities to have been begun and completed within the Augustine period. It would seem from engravings and descriptions by writers of the last century that the remains were then far more considerable than they are now. But after having been for many years the prey of any one who chose to carry off the stones, till nearly all that remained above the surface of the soil had been removed, the renewed interest in every memorial of Italy's past has recently moved the local antiquaries to take the remains under their protection. Excavations have been commenced; and it seems probable that sufficient portions of the original building have been concealed beneath and protected by the soil, to make the recovery of them well worth while.

To me however the traces and memorials of the times, when that civilization, of which our own is the immediate successor and heir, grew up and flourished and died, are even more interesting than the remains of a social system immeasurably more distant from our own. And I turned from the anxious speculations of the gentlemen who are hoping to discover enough of the foundations of the Eugubian Roman theatre to enable them to prove that it was exactly like all the other Roman theatres in its arrangements, to look with 'much livelier interest on a work executed by the free mediæval burghers of Gubbio, for the more effectual prosecution of the various industries, especially that of cloth-weaving and dyeing, which produced the "money power" that so much astonished the monk of a subsequent age.

The monument in question is known as the *Bottaccione*, and is simply an immense cistern intended to obviate the scarcity of water, which was often experienced during the summer months. But it is the grandiose and noble manner in which they set themselves to accomplish this object, which strikes us with admiration and curosity. "They determined," says Reposati,* "to supply by art the deficiency of nature. How, then, did they proceed?" he continues. "On a foundation of rock of extreme hardness they built from one Apennine to another—from Monte Calvo that is, to Monte Ingino—a lofty wall of such extraordinary thickness, that it seems mere hyperbole to tell the measurement of it. It is almost impossible to believe that it is an hundred and fourteen Roman palms † thick; and of such stability, being admirably wrought throughout with stone hewed from the living rock, that despite the lapse of many ages, and despite the action of the waters, which ordinarily make some breach in the strongest moles (especially when they fall with rapidity, as is the case in the present instance), neither time nor torrents have been able to make the slightest impression on it. This reservoir of water forms a deep and ample lake, 450 Roman palms ‡ long, 300 wide, and 105 deep. The wall which has been described has an aperture, closed by a massive door of iron, furnished with a smaller opening in it; and constructed in such a manner that either one or the other may be opened from a distance without danger. So that in summer or any season of drought the small door may be opened, from which a stream of water issues sufficient to form a river running for many days, and capable of turning eleven corn-mills, as many oil-

* Vol. II., p. 423.    † About 83 English feet.
‡ The Roman palm is equal to 8¾ inches.

mills, supplying several tan-yards, and furnishing water for all general purposes. And since this lake from time to time becomes clogged with sand and mud,* which the water brings down with it from the mountains, the aforesaid ancient men of Gubbio took thought and made the above-mentioned larger aperture, so that the reservoir might be cleaned out without cost or difficulty, by opening wide the large iron door, and allowing the waters to rush out and sweep with them the sand and mud brought down from the mountain."

The historian goes on to relate however, that on some occasions, this operation had caused very great mischief in the city, and even in the country below, with the loss of several lives. "In order, therefore," he concludes, "that everybody may have the means and opportunity to avoid such dangers, some days before the opening, notice is given to the citizens by sound of trumpet."

The Eugubians were not content however with this supply of water for industrial purposes. They determined to bring into the city the waters of a living spring that rises in Monte Calvo; and for this purpose constructed a covered channel two miles in length, "not of lead," says Reposati, "nor of brick, nor pipes of baked earth, but of living rock hewn out by the chisel." This channel, which is large enough for a man to walk upright in throughout its entire length, is supported for the greater part of its course by an enormous wall, and when the inequalities in the flank of the mountain require it,

* Reposati says "with *bitumen;* but he probably means merely slime.

by vast arches; "so that," says Reposati, "it astounds one to hear tell of it."

It was the water from this channel that supplied the fountain in the upper room of the *Palazzo pubblico*.

In the course of my rambles about this interesting little city I fell in with a curious indication of the former wealth of this district of the Peninsula in all those various branches of the artistic industry, mainly of the *rénaissance* period, which have of late years engaged so much of the attention of the art-loving world. All, who have ever taken an interest in such matters, have at least heard of, if they have never seen, the celebrated "Collection Soulage," which formed so prominent a feature of the great exhibition at Manchester. It would seem that by far the greater part of that extraordinary assemblage of articles was the result of gleanings from the rich harvest of past centuries in this district.

It was while that bright-eyed "maid of the inn," of whom I have spoken, was ministering to us in the half-and-half capacity of courteous hostess and active waiting-maid at supper, that she remarked, in total disconnection with anything that had gone before, that "Momo Nicchi was very old now!"

This was said so evidently in the full conviction that no human being could be ignorant as to who or what Momo Nicchi was, that I hesitated to convict myself of such a degree of greenness as would be involved in the confession, that I was doubting whether Momo Nicchi were her own grandfather or the popular nickname for the tower of the Palazzo, or any similar Gubbian antiquity. On second thoughts the "now" at the conclusion of her speech seemed to point to an antiquity, which had been appreciably less within her own experience. But I was cautious, and only answered—

"*Altro che vecchio!*"\*

"Yes! he rarely comes down here now! he used always to come when any *forestieri* arrived."

This somewhat narrowed the field of conjecture, and encouraged me to hazard the reply that—

"If necessary, we could go to him."

"I could send for him to come here," said she; "but really I doubt whether he could get up the hill again, poor old Momo!"

"Oh! do not ask it of him by any means. It is easier for us to go up the hill than for him to come down."

"Yes! and I will send little Sunta to show you his house. I dare say he will go round with you, if he can walk at all; but I do not think he has got anything!"

"Poor fellow!" I said at a hazard.

"There is nothing to be found! Why, what would you have? The country has been regularly cleared out!"

This was more puzzling than ever! But the result of a considerable amount of further beating about the bush, was the gradual discovery that old Momo Nicchi was a sort of cicerone and antiquity dealer, and broker;—that our pretty hostess had deemed it quite a matter of course, that our business at Gubbio was to purchase remnants of the artistic wealth of the city's palmy days, that apparently being the only object that ever within her experience brought

\* "Other than old;" meaning simply "Old indeed!"

strangers to Gubbio;—and finally, that it was the invariable course of all persons bound on such a quest to address themselves to Signor Girolamo Nicchi, manufacturer of rosolio by profession, but cicerone, antiquarian, and dealer in art by taste and preference.

So we determined to begin the morrow by a visit to this ancient worthy. Our arrival at his house seemed to give him great satisfaction, poor old man. He had been anxious to come down to the inn, which is situated quite at the foot of the hill, when he had heard of our arrival, but had feared that he would not be able to get back again. He too told us that he was very old, and had "got nothing, except this bit of Venice glass," he said, producing a curiously-shaped and daintily-ornamented vase, badly cracked, "which I unfortunately cracked in bringing it home." "Bah! I am old and cracked myself now!"

I bought his bit of glass for the few pauls he asked for it, and thus effected probably his last transaction with the old dealer, through whose hands had passed, as I afterwards learned from him, the greater part of the Soulage collection. The old man insisted on "going round with us," as the girl at the inn had said. As a cicerone his company was far more an impediment than an assistance, poor old fellow! But it was impossible to refuse him; and his talk of the good old times when magnificent pieces of Majolica and Venice glass, and ancient furniture, and chiseled and chased arms, and sculptured wood and ivory were to be found in every house, and to be bought for anything offered for them, was amusing enough.

Of course the abundance of these gleanings was

due to, and is evidence of the luxury, wealth, splendour, and refinement which prevailed in this part of Italy under the Dukes of Urbino of the two successive dynasties of Montefeltro and Della Rovere; and to the sudden extinction of all this, when the dukedom fell to the Church, aided by the remoteness of the district from the ordinary track of travellers.

Of course the name of Gubbio is familiar to all admirers of Majolica, as having been one of the principal seats of the manufacture, and the native country of the most celebrated master of the art, "Maestro Giorgio." But in all the city, from which such large quantities of this remarkable ware have gone forth to all the museums of Europe, I could see but one specimen of it remaining. That one however is a very remarkable one, if it be indeed genuine. It is a life-size sitting figure of a saint in the church of the Dominicans, which the Gubbio folk declare to be a work of Maestro Giorgio, and to be radiant with the famous iridescent varnish, for which his finest works are celebrated. But it seems almost incredible, that if it be so, the statue should have been, as that in question has been, painted and gilded, so that as now seen, it might just as well be of wood, or any other material, as of the celebrated *terra-cotta* of Maestro Giorgio.

In the different churches, and in a few of the palaces of Gubbio, there are a considerable number of pictures of much interest to the instructed student of art, mainly as showing that there existed in the fourteenth and fifteenth centuries a school of art in this secluded district, undeniably its own, and separated by decided characteristics from the great Umbrian school, of which Perugia is recognized as the head quarters. The study of these ancient works is really valuable to a thoughtful artist or critical historian; and the fact that this little mountain-fenced community generated and maintained a native school of its own, furnishes curious and interesting testimony to the isolation, which sundered cities separated by a few miles more entirely, than half the circumference of the globe avails to do in our own day. But there are not many among these ancient pictures which will really give any pleasure to the generality of even intelligent visitors. And it is the less necessary to point them out severally to the reader, as this has recently been done in the most modern editions of "the red book." It may be mentioned however, that the late expulsion of the monks and nuns from their convents throughout Umbria, has, since the date of the most recent notices in the guide-book, caused the gathering together of a considerable number of pictures, mainly of the native school, in a couple of rooms at the convent now occupied by the municipality. One especially, by Damiani, will attract the notice and admiration even of the unlearned, both as a very vigorously painted picture, and as containing a singularly interesting collection of portraits of the Gabrielli family, whose tyrannous usurpations and feuds caused the city infinite trouble in the days before it submitted as has been above related, to the dynasty of Montefeltro.

There is a fresco also by Ottaviano Nelli, in the church now belonging to the *Confraternitià* of the *Misericordia*, which may really delight any lover of the beautiful, by the truly remarkable purity and grace of the conception, the wonderful delicacy of the execution, and the rare degree of its preservation. I believe that this beautiful work has been, or will shortly be reproduced in chromo-lithography, by the excellently useful Arundel Society.

The best local works to be consulted for the history of Gubbio are, "*L'Esemplare della Gloria, ovvero i Fasti sacri, politici, e militari della Città di Gubbio,*" By Bonaventura Tondi. 1 Vol. 4to. Venezia.

"Mauro Sarti; De Episcopis Eugubinis, Prœcedit de Civitate et Ecclesia Eugubina dissertatio. 1 Vol. 4to. Pisauri."

The preliminary dissertation is the most valuable part of this work.

"Della Zecca di Gubbio, e delle Gesta de' Duchi d'Urbino. 2 Vols. 4to. Bologna. By Rinaldo Reposati."

This last is the best book on the subject, and may indeed be deemed sufficient by itself for the needs of any one, save a collector of this species of literature. It is a somewhat scarce book; that is to say, it is rarely to be met with in the ordinary book-market; but it is to be found at the price of a couple of pounds, or so, by those who will make inquiry for it in the proper quarters.

Our stay at Gubbio was one of a few days only. I should have much liked to make it longer; and would counsel any one who has time on his hands to do so. It is an attractive little city in many respects; and one or two letters of introduction would at once secure for a stranger the agreeable and instructive society of several men extremely competent to assist him in seeing and appreciating their country, whatever special direction his inquiries may take.

Italians, it may be observed, will be found, especially in those districts here treated of, far more ready to associate on pleasant terms with Englishmen than was the case a few years ago. They are, as we all know, an eminently sociable race, proverbially courteous to strangers, and I may say almost always particularly ready and inclined to show themselves so to Englishmen. And it is not meant that any change has taken place in this respect in the people. But under the old *régime* it was often a dangerous and imprudent thing to associate with foreigners, Englishmen especially, who were but too likely to say all sorts of things, which it was not safe for a subject of the priestly government even to listen to. Besides that, the mere fact of being marked as prone to associate with heretics and liberals (for very few Englishmen, indeed, are otherwise, relatively to the rule of the Pope-King), was sufficient to render a man unpleasantly noted by the ever-vigilant and suspicious authorities. All this, thank God! is changed now; and an Italian has no more reason to shun the free interchange of thought and opinion on any subject under the sun, than an Englishman. The prudent restraint, which an Englishman must still continue to put on his tongue when he quits the shores of our own island, may now be freely removed as soon as he finds himself on the sunny side of the Alps. And the change, which this new freedom of the tongue is operating with wonderful rapidity in the social and moral characteristics of the Italians, is one of the most suggestive, as it is one of the most valuable results of the new order of things in the Peninsula.

## CHAPTER VII.

ROUTE FROM GUBBIO TO PERUGIA—LIMITS OF THE ANCIENT PICENUM—NO GUIDE TO BE HAD—VALINGEGNO—FRATTIC- CIOLA, A ROBBER TOWN—APPROACH TO PERUGIA—POLITICAL CHANGES—PERUGIA DESERTED BY TRAVELLERS, AND WHY— AN ITALIAN JURYMAN—THE FORTRESS AFTER THE EXPULSION OF THE PAPAL GOVERNMENT — ITS DEMOLITION — FORMER PRISONER — THE SWISS IN THE BENEDICTINE CONVENT— POLITICAL FEELING—OLD CARBONARO—CURIOUS ANECDOTE SHOWING THE ISOLATION OF THE PAPAL PROVINCES FROM ONE ANOTHER.

IN leaving Gubbio difficulties arose before us of the same nature with those which we had encountered in approaching it. We wished to go thence into the district bounded by the Apennines to the south of Gubbio; by the coast of the Adriatic from Ancona southwards to the Tronto and the frontier of the old kingdom of Naples; and by a line drawn from east to west from Ancona to Gubbio. And the first point, for which we would have made, would have been Camerino, the ancient *Camerio*.

The district so enclosed would correspond with considerable accuracy to the Picenum of the ancient geographers, called under Augustus, the fifth region of Italy; and at a later date known as " Picenum Suburbicarium," in contradistinction to the district lying along the coast immediately to the north of it, and extending as far in that direction as Rimini and the Rubicon, comprehending Gallia, Senonia, and a part of Umbria, forming the sixth region of Italy under Augustus, and afterwards called " Picenum Annonarium."

But want of roads renders it impossible to travel by wheeled conveyance in anything approaching to a direct line from Gubbio to Camerino. And I could not meet with any encouragement in my proposals to get across the country on foot, with a horse, mule, or ass, to carry our baggage. Nobody could be found who would undertake to act as guide in such an unheard-of expedition. And the general disinclination to the adventure was probably increased materially by the firm persuasion that the persons proposing it must be, if not altogether crazy, yet sufficiently eccentric to render it imprudent to have any part in their plans. Who could say whether a mad English "*milordo*" might not be engaged in strict accordance with the well-known habits of his kind, in a wager for an hundred millions sterling, that he would conduct an Italian citizen to the summit of Monte Catria and there prove that the English constitution could endure famine and frost longer than the Italian. Nothing more likely! At all events it was clear that there was something "*sotto*,"* it was not "*liscio*."† And in short, nobody could be found who would embark in so mad a scheme.

The way people who are *not* mad go from Gubbio to Camerino, is by Perugia, Foligno, &c. But as my object was to explore a region little known to English-

---

\* Underneath. † Clear.

men in general, and for the most part new to me, I had been anxious to avoid the necessity of falling into the old beaten tracks. I knew Perugia, and all the many objects of interest in its neighbourhood well. But then my companion did not; and he was anxious to see it as well as Assisi, which would lie in our road from Perugia to Foligno. So that the upshot was that I was obliged to fall into the old ruts for a few days and a short space. But as this portion of my route in no wise deserves to be classed among the less known parts of Italy, I intend in the following pages to pass over it very quickly.

The route from Gubbio to Perugia, though not an uninteresting one, is less so than that new road across the hills from Fratta. For the first few miles it covers the fertile low-lying basin, which spreads itself out beneath Gubbio; then mounts by a long well-managed ascent, the wooded hills on the other side of it, and for about half the distance to Perugia continues, mostly on high ground, to traverse a country of well wooded hills and valleys. Two or three castles in ruins, which from the style of building, must date from some century previous to the fifteenth, and which must, when their sites were first selected, have been surrounded on all sides by many miles of all but pathless forests, are past during this first half of the journey. One very picturesque building, hardly to be called a ruin, but apparently not inhabited, called Valingegno, stands a few hundred yards from the road, on the left hand of one going towards Perugia, at the head of a very beautiful ravine, thickly clothed with oak-wood. The ground on which it stands, and over which the road passes—

for the castle is rather below than above the latter—
is sufficiently high to command a very extensive view
over a wide region of billowy hills and valleys, all
more or less covered with oak-wood, and stretching
away towards the south-east, till the horizon is shut
in by the high Apennines, dividing Umbria from the
ancient Picenum.

The latter part of the route is less pretty. The
hills become more bleak, and the country less rich
in wood and water. At about the highest and
bleakest part of the pass, just before the road begins
the long descent, which following the course of the
little mountain torrents, the Grande and the Primo—
both singular misnomers, one would think—brings
the traveller at last into the valley of the Tiber, a
large village is seen on the left, some three or four
miles from the road, in as miserably barren, cold,
and naked a position, as it is well possible to conceive. It is called Fratticciola, and is marked in the
Austrian Ordnance map (the only good one which
has ever yet been made of the Papal territories) as
being 2,934 feet above the level of the sea. It must
be visible from a great distance over a wide tract of
country; and the view from it must command a
similarly wide extent, and many a mile of more
roads than one. And this circumstance, together
with the impossibility that anybody should approach
the village without being seen by the inhabitants a
long time before their arrival, are probably the most
valuable features that any residence could possess in
the eyes of the inhabitants of Fratticciola.

"There," said our driver, pointing to the place
with his whip as soon as ever the road brought us

within sight of it, "There is Fratticciola! All the inhabitants are robbers! *All* of them!"

On the road, as far as we could see it before us, there was not a human being to be seen; and I remarked to the driver, that Fratticciola did not seem to have thought it worth while to send out any of her sons to stop our humble equipage.

"Ah! things are not as they used to be;" he said in reply. "The *carabinieri* keep a pretty sharp look out nowadays. They are well watched up there; and they know it. But for all that I had much rather not pass along here by night."

As the road comes down to the valley of the Tiber, the country it crosses grows richer and greener. But this part of the course of the river did not seem to me to be marked by such exuberant fertility as had struck me in the higher part of its course near Città di Castello. The stream is crossed by an ancient hog-backed bridge, called Ponte Felcino; and immediately afterwards the ascent of the hill on which Perugia stands is commenced. The city has been seen by the traveller, superbly crowning its lofty and long-backed hill, for some time past; and now that he is at the bottom of the hill, it is difficult to believe that his journey is not all but over. It seems, as he looks up to the long lines of walls on the brow of the hill immediately above him, as if half a mile was the utmost of the distance that separated him from them. But the road winds and winds, heading by turns towards almost every point of the compass, and affording him a variety of quite different views over the low grounds he is leaving behind him, till it seems as if an unsuccessful attempt had been made to enter the city on three or four different sides, and that the persevering road was still trying for better luck in another direction.

After those three or four great cities of Italy, the annals of which form pre-eminently important chapters of the history of European civilization, there is perhaps no more interesting city in the Peninsula than Perugia. The story of its art, of its arms, of its political vicissitudes and struggles have all been such as to make the study of them worthy of a larger share of the world's attention, than can be generally accorded to the history of a single city. The importance and interest which attaches to it in all these respects has been fully recognized by a great number of native writers; and few, if any one of the secondary cities of Italy, has received more abundant illustration of every phase of its past social existence. It has always received a large share of the attention of English travellers in Italy; and its artistic history is pretty well known to those among us, whose tastes and culture lead their inquiries in that direction. Its social and political story is less well-known; and it would not be difficult to write a volume on this subject, as it connects itself with the extant and visible monuments of the city, which should be new and interesting to English readers. But it does not enter into my present scope to make any attempt in this direction, partly for the reasons I have already assigned, and partly because it would require nothing less than a volume to do anything like justice to the subject.

My present visit was not my first, by many, to

the old Etruscan city; and that which possessed most of the interest of novelty for me was to observe how far I could detect symptoms in the social aspect of the place of the great political change that has recently been accomplished there.

With respect to that sort of movement, which falls most readily under the observation of a traveller, —the movement of travelling that is to say,—Perugia has been a sufferer rather than a gainer in these latter days. Two or three circumstances have conspired to produce this result. Because an inoffensive family of American travellers narrowly escaped being murdered by the Pope's troops in the principal hotel of the city, while they witnessed the murder of the landlord at his own door, and were forced to be the spectators of other horrors, which were wellnigh if not quite fatal to one lady of the party, it is certainly not rational to anticipate the recurrence of any such events. But such things make a deep impression on that large portion of the public mind, which does not take the trouble to examine the foundation of its impressions. Perugia has got a bad name among such people, since the date of that terrible day. Then two or three instances of travellers having been stopped in other portions of that route to Rome have aided in turning the stream of visitors to the Eternal City into another channel. But perhaps the railroad from Florence to Sienna, by which that road to Rome is made so much shorter and easier, has been the most actively operating cause of the desertion of the Perugia route. The fact at all events is that one of the two great hotels, which used to compete with each other here, is shut up; and the other is very different from what it used to be.

We got beds there with difficulty; and in answer to inquiries for food, were told that there was absolutely nothing in the house.

"What! when the house is so full, that you could hardly find us rooms?"

"Yes! full; but we have not a traveller in it. None come; and we are glad to let our rooms as we can. They are almost all inhabited by officers of the garrison, who do not eat here."

Nevertheless, in the general aspect of the town, there was certainly an improvement; though not marked as yet by outward and material signs in the same degree as in some of the cities of Tuscany, where the load of oppression, which has been shaken off, was less severe, and where the energy and recuperative force of the people were less broken and destroyed. Still, as I say, signs of the change might be detected. There was more noise in the streets; there was the sound of human voices. There was talking; and newspapers were being read in the cafés. One little word, that I chanced to hear, fell strangely on the ear with a pleasant, constitutional, English-like ring in it, that seemed full of the promise of a bright future. I was inquiring for a gentleman, with whom I had some acquaintance, and was told that I should hardly be likely to see him before the evening, because he was serving on the jury in the Assize Court! I did however meet him in the course of the day; for, as he told me, he had been challenged by one of the parties, and set aside accordingly.

My last previous visit to Perugia had been shortly after the final recovery of it from the Papal Government; and the destruction of the enormous fortress raised by Paul the Third for the more effectual repression of the citizens was then just being commenced. Few buildings have ever been laden with a heavier amount of long accumulated popular hatred than this; and few have more richly merited it. The Perugians were for many ages—nay, it may pretty well be said that they never ceased to be—a hard nut for the grinding teeth of Papal tyranny to crack. This huge Bastille was, at the time of its erection, a symbol of the final destruction of liberty in Perugia, as well as a provision against all possibility of future resistance; and it has served during the long dreary course of priestly tyranny as one of those hopeless prisons over the door of which might well be inscribed the celebrated epigraph of the Dantescan hell.

When I had last been in Perugia the entire building was open to the curiosity and free examination of the public. There was no crowd when I wandered over the labyrinth of its stairs and passages, guard-rooms, barracks, casemates, and prisons of every sort and size. I had the foul place then all to myself, with the exception of a few workmen, who were beginning to take the roof off one of the upper buildings; for the public of Perugia had already satiated their curiosity. There were probably few men, women, or children in Perugia, who had not, in the first days after the dreaded and detested prison-house was thrown open to them, wandered at will over its bastions and through its dungeons, with such feelings and interchange of talk, as may readily be imagined. But when I came there all was deserted and still. I saw the large dungeons, accessible only by a circular opening in the pavement of the less dreadful dungeons above them; I saw the fearful cells, constructed in the thickness of the colossal masonry, in such devilish sort, that the wretches, who had dared to question the deeds of Christ's Vicar on earth, once introduced into the cavity through appertures barely sufficient to admit a crawling figure, could neither stand nor sit in them. I paced the lofty battlements, which commanded such a panoramic view as can hardly be matched over the beautiful country and the many cities within its circuit, all priest-trampled and poisoned; and I marked the narrow light-holes in some of the less dreadful prisons, through which a miserable tantalizing strip of far-distant sun-lit horizon was dimly visible by the immured victim, who knew too well, that he should never, never return to the light of day.

When I returned on the occasion I am speaking of, the good work of demolition had made considerable progress. There were willing workmen labouring with mattock and crowbar, to sever the huge masses of masonry which had been dislodged from their places, into fragments of a size capable of being carted away. An inscription had been placed on the wall of the *piazza* fronting the former main entrance to the fortress, which struck me as ironically satirical in its simplicity. It merely stated that the magistrates of Perugia had removed the fortress raised for the oppression of the citizens " for the improvement of the prospect from the Piazza!"

There were a number of people, on the occasion of my second visit, gloating over the progressing destruction of the detested walls, as crowbar and pickaxe did their work. I saw one remarkable looking old man, with long a flowing white beard, sitting on a fallen fragment of wall in the sunshine, and never taking his eyes from the workmen who were tumbling down the great masses of concrete, as fast as their excessive hardness would permit of their being detached. The gentleman I was with noticed the direction of my look, and said :—

"That old man comes here at break of day, and remains till the workmen knock off at night. He was many years a prisoner in the fortress, and was liberated at the fall of the Papal Government."

I felt that his presence there was fully accounted for, and that I could guess without any difficulty "of what was the old man thinking?" as he watched the demolition of his prison-house.

I might fill the remainder of this volume with the stories to be met with at every turn in Perugia, of the horrors of that dreadful day and night when the Vicar of Christ wreaked his vengeance on this unhappy city. But much has already been told the English reader of all this, and I need the pages for other purposes. One circumstance which fell under my observation, I will mention, because it strikingly indicates the utter lawlessness and wantonness of the violences committed by the Holy Father's soldiers.

The celebrated and wealthy Benedictine Monastery of St. Peter, unlike all the other convents in the city, sided with the people in that terrible day, at least so far as to endeavour to save any lives they could by admitting fugitives into the monastery. The Swiss, in consequence, broke into the convent, and did a vast quantity of mischief there. Now, in the church of this monastery is the celebrated choir, all lined and fitted up with carved walnut-wood, after designs by Raphael, the whole of which has been admirably engraved, on fifty or sixty sheets, purchasable at the convent. I possessed a copy of the work, and my companion was now desirous of purchasing one. But when, on our demand, a copy was brought into the sacristy, a higher price was asked for it than I had formerly paid; and in reply to our objections on this head, it was answered that the increased charge was made, because the work was now very scarce in consequence of the Swiss having wantonly destroyed a great number of copies, when they broke into the monastery.

The conversation on political subjects, which I was able to hear in Perugia, all agreed in representing that part of the country as still suffering from the effects of political disturbance, but nevertheless as well affected towards the present Government, perfectly understanding that such a change as Italy has passed through cannot be accomplished without the disturbance of many interests, and the production of partial distress, and still persuaded that the day, which saw the change from priestly misrule to a system of constitutional government, was the birthday of a new era of prosperity and happiness for Italy. The most remarkable testimony to the prevalence of these views was afforded by a conversation I had with an aged *carbonaro* chieftain, whose long

## OLD CARBONARO.

life of conspiracy and resistance to the Papal despotism had seen at various times during the present century many a hope of better days dawn in Italy only to be quenched in blood and disaster. This patriarch of rebellion, while avowing that the *carbonaro* association still existed, spread over every country of continental Europe, that the discipline and means of co-operation were kept up in undiminished efficiency,—all the signs and watchwords of the Order having been changed, he assured me, subsequently to the Orsini attempt;—nevertheless declared, that the present Government of Italy had nothing to fear from the republican principles of the adepts; that the great majority of them were of opinion, that the essential characteristic of a " republic," as opposed to an absolute government, was self-government; that this was quite as attainable under a constitutional monarchy, as under any other form of rule; and that they had no preference whatever for a chief magistrate, bearing the title of "President," over one of which the head was styled " King."

One of the great advantages which will be most immediately realized from the formation of the various extinguished Italian governments into one homogeneous nation, will be the increased communication of one district with another. The isolation of the various provinces from each other—even of those which were immediate neighbours, and were subjected to the same despotism—was greater than it is easy for a nineteenth century Englishman to credit. And I cannot forbear mentioning the following curious instance of this in a department of social life, where it would seem the least to have been expected.

There exists a work on the ancient and mediæval Antiquities of Picenum, by the Abbate Colucci, in thirty-one volumes, folio, printed at Fermo in that province, at various dates during the last quarter of the last century. It is a very complete and erudite book, and the great recognized store-house of all that the past has left us on the subject. It is very difficult to meet with a complete copy, certain volumes being of extreme rarity. But scattered volumes are common enough. And I have no doubt that the work is well known, both in London and Paris. But it is not known in Bologna ! And when I say this, I mean that it is not known to those who might most be expected to be acquainted with it. I could hardly believe my ears, when the librarian of the public library of Bologna, and several other gentlemen, whose tastes and occupations were such as should have made them conversant with such matters, all agreed in declaring that they had never heard of the book in question ! At the distance of a day's journey, just on the other side of the Apennines, it would seem to every bookish man, as impossible as it did to me, that Colucci's Picenian Antiquities should be unknown in any part of Italy. And the people there are probably just as uninformed respecting the local literature of Umbria. The Apennine chain running between the two provinces, had acted for centuries as a barrier more effectually shutting out all intercommunication of interests, ideas, and intelligence, than the semi-circuit of the terraqueous globe to more fortunately circumstanced nations.

## CHAPTER VIII.

DRIVE TO ASSISI—ST. FRANCIS—THE GREAT CONVENT—THE CHURCH SERVICES—SERMON BY ONE OF THE FRIARS—SCENE IN THE CHURCH—BELL OF SANTA LUCIA—THE GREAT REFECTORY—THE KITCHEN—THE NO LIBRARY—THE AMBULATORIES—EXCURSION TO LE CARCERI—MOUNTAIN SUBASIO—CONVENT AT THE CARCERI—THE SUPERIOR—LEGENDS.

A PLEASANT morning drive brought us from Perugia to Assisi, by the well-known and well-beaten Roman road. As this celebrated little city lies on the hillside, only about two miles on the left-hand of the great road which pursues its way Romewards, along the valley formed by the mountain torrents Topino and Chiascio, hurrying to join the Tiber at the foot of the hill of Perugia, it is almost as well known as if it formed one of the necessary stopping-places on the route. For who would not go so far out of his way to visit the head-quarters and special home of early Christian art? Surely not the one man in an hundred, who really understands and cares either for the sentiment of the *trecentisti*, or for what may be called the genealogy of artistic history! And still more certainly not any one of the ninety and nine, who in obedience to "*la mode*" have substituted for raptures on "the Correggiosity of Correggio" an intense gusto for the Giottesqueness of Giotto! So every body visits Assisi; and the *vetturino* horses take the turn, which leaves the great road to mount the short steep hill that leads to it, without any hint from the rein.

But there is much that is worth seeing and thinking over in Assisi, besides the extraordinary wealth of thirteenth-century art still extant on its walls. For myself I humbly confess, that the materialistic tendencies of my mind are such as to force me to find more pleasure in looking at a landscape by Constable, Calcott or Cowper, than in the contemplation of any representation of a miracle by St. Francis ever painted. But this misfortune does not prevent me from seeing in the buildings and on the walls of Assisi, a vividly suggestive gloss and commentary on some of the most interesting chapters of the history of our civilization.

The entire city of Assisi, as it exists at the present day, and has existed for four or five centuries, may be fairly considered as one vast monument to the memory of St. Francis. Some few other instances might be pointed out in Europe, of localities similarly filled with the abiding presence of some individual man, by and for whose remembrance they exist, and hold their place in the recognition of the world. But nowhere else is this the case to so extraordinary a degree as at Assisi. Had the cloth-dealer, who is said to have lived in the darksome little house still pointed out to the curious as the birthplace of the Saint, (and who probably did really live on the site of it; but the existing building, ancient and solidly built as it looks, cannot be a dwelling of the twelfth century); had that obscure citizen *not* had born to him a son characterized by great qualities and defects as exceptional as those which caused the Saint to leave so indelible an impress on the history of the human race, Assisi would have been as unnoticed and unnoticeable a townlet as might be. Everything there is due to that cloth-merchant's son. Even the very remarkable and specially characterized beauty of the place, as it now is, would not have existed. For it depends mainly on the architectural features, which would have been wanting to the landscape, had no motive arisen for gathering the best artists in every kind that the thirteenth century could furnish to do honour to the memory of Francis the Saint.

It is six hundred and thirty-six years since Saint Francis died there, his macerated and extenuated body covered by a cloak, thrown over it by the hand of charity. And still the momentum of the forces he set in motion has not entirely expended itself. The large community of monks who inhabit the monastery attached to the church, or rather group of churches, under which the Saint lies buried, have so far "reformed" the rule he left them, as to get rid of the obligation of absolute poverty. They are not mendicants, these black-robed "*Minori Conventuali*," as they call themselves; and insomuch are less faithful disciples of their master than the brown-frocked professors and practisers of absolute beggary. But none work harder, as one of the brethern assured me not without a certain degree of bitterness. Twenty-eight full choral services in a week was, he begged me to believe, no joke. Certainly I never entered the "middle * church," as it is called, without finding some sort of service or function in progress there. On the occasion of this last visit a sermon was being preached. It was the festival of the Annunciation, and the preacher was eager in turning to characteristic account the sacred history of the day.

The tidings announced to the Blessed Virgin must have seemed wholly incredible and impossible to her intellect. Yet she implicitly believed them. This was her merit. "Faith, my brethren, etc. etc. etc." "My sisters," he should have said; for the congregation consisted almost entirely of women. The monk spared neither voice nor gesture; and frequently paused to wipe the perspiration from his face. But he only reiterated the same thing, almost in the same words again and again. Had his subject been, as those selected by Italian preachers often are, of a nature calculated to address itself to the imagination, the place in which he was preaching was admirably adapted to assist in producing such a result.

The roof-arches of this middle church are low and cavernous; and the imperfect light, which to eyes newly come from the outer daylight seemed almost darkness, was yet sufficient after one had been in it for awhile, to enable the eye to penetrate the recesses of the lateral chapels, and here and there distinguish

---

* The position, architecture, and art-decoration of this very remarkable pile of building, consisting of an upper church, a second church lower on the steep hill-side beneath it, and a third, which is in fact merely a crypt containing the tomb of the Saint, below that, have been so often and so sufficiently described that I abstain from saying anything on the subject.

## THE MIDDLE CHURCH AT ASSISI. 119

the outline of some of the figures painted on the walls. At the upper and further end of the church beyond the preacher and the little congregation gathered around the pulpit in the middle of the nave, the gilded grating of very elegant iron-work which encloses the altar and the small choir behind it, was rendered very visible by its gilding. And gradually as the eye became accustomed to the obscurity, the figures of monks behind the grating, listening or affecting to listen to the sermon, could be discovered. It was nearly mid-day when the preacher concluded his discourse; and a musical service, the third which had taken place that day, was immediataly commenced — so immediately, that the choir started off in full swing, before the preacher had time to descend the steps of the pulpit.

The wonders of the middle church, almost every inch of the vaults and walls of which is painted by the greatest artists of the thirteenth century, had to be examined by my companion, as best he could, while this service was in progress. But the upper church, almost equally rich in fresco, and with far higher claims to architectural beauty, was wholly empty and silent. There was the scaffolding in the nave, which had been erected to enable a painter to copy one of the frescoes of Giotto; but he was absent from his work, and we had the vast church entirely to ourselves. There hung from the lofty vault immediately behind the high altar, the rope of the bell of Santa Lucia, much celebrated among the rural populations of the surrounding districts. On a certain day in August, according to the popular creed, unlimited "indulgence" is to be obtained by whoever can and will ring this bell by taking the rope in his teeth, and so pulling it, without any other aid. I pulled and rung the bell; but entitled myself to no indulgence, as I did the feat with my hands; and so assured myself sufficiently of the soundness and strength of the jaws of the Abruzzi peasants, who, I was told, form the great majority of those who ring Santa Lucia's bell on the appointed day. They come, I was assured, in considerable numbers from their distant province for the express purpose of thus entitling themselves to the indulgence attached to the adventure.

We visited every part of the immense convent; and I confess that to me, the observation of the domestic details of the life of these disciples of the man, who refused the luxury of a bed to die on, was certainly not the least interesting part of what Assisi has to show. The "great refectory," a noble hall, some two hundred feet or more in length, which was formerly, in the palmy days of the Order, used constantly, and was not too large for the inmates of the establishment, is now put in requisition only on occasion of a few grand festivals in the year, notably on the 4th of October, the day especially dedicated in the calendar to the memory of the Saint, when even still in these degenerate times, a very large gathering of Franciscans of all the various branches of the Order is assembled in Assisi, and all are feasted in the great refectory of the convent. This fine hall had been recently used as a dormitory for a regiment of soldiers; and the straw which had served them for bedding still lay in long lines down either side of the immense chamber.

## THE CONVENT.

We looked into kitchens, where a posse of lay brothers were busy in preparing at colossal cauldrons and stewpans the feast-day meal, which was about to be served in the "small refectory" as soon as the service in the church was concluded. We walked through the airy corridors, on which the long lines of cells opened, and saw the handsome rooms of the *forestieria* for the reception of honoured guests. We inquired for the library; but could obtain no satisfactory reply on this head; which reminded us that we were not visiting a Benedictine Convent, and that the Sons of St. Francis have always been very much of the opinion of the old gentleman in the play, who "never knew no good come of book-larning." The ambulatories are such as probably no other convent that ever existed could match; long galleries supported on rows of arches running along the side of the hill, and commanding in different directions the most delicious views over the valley, the hills of Perugia in one direction and the distant mountain-range behind Spoleto in the other. The imagination, as one paces these quiet, ample, and most lovely arcades, can hardly avoid falling into the gross error of fancying in the words of the song, that

"Sure if there's peace to be found in the world,
The heart that is weary might hope for it here."

But the outside world has had abundantly sufficient revelations of the interior of cloister life, to be well aware, that a community of monks, shut up in forced and constant association with each other and with no one else, is perhaps the very last place in which to look for an immunity from those faults and follies by which men make life unpleasant to each other.

The sights of Assisi are all registered in the guide-books, and need not therefore be mentioned here. But there is one little excursion beyond its walls, which is worth making; but which somehow or other does not form part of the regular tourist's programme, and is therefore generally neglected. It is to a spot called the "*Carceri,*" celebrated in Franciscan history as that to which the Saint was wont to retire for the purpose of solitary meditation, prayer, and penance. Behind Assisi rises in an immense mass one of the advanced bulwarks of the Apennine chain, called Subasio. The latest observations fix its altitude at twelve hundred and eight metres; and it is on several accounts interesting to a geologist as well as to a mere admirer of the landscape effects produced by the varieties of geological arrangement. Subasio rises from the great Umbrian valley wholly isolated from the neighbouring mountains, both materially and by the nature of its formation. A region of more recent geological formation surrounds it on all sides, from which it rises like an island from the sea. It turns its rounded back towards the main chain of the Apennines, and its more broken and precipitous front to the great valley through which the Roman road pursues its way to Foligno and Spoleto.

On the nearly precipitous face of this mountain, at a distance of about three miles and a half from Assisi, is the "*Santuario delle Carceri.*"

The walk thither—or ride if the traveller please, but wheels are out of the question—is a very pleasing one, commanding during its whole length a noble terrace-view of the beautiful vale of Umbria, and the varied outlines of the mountains, which enclose it to the south and south-west. A little stream has eaten away a deep ravine in the rugged front of the mountain, and has deposited soil enough on its sides to favour the growth of a small grove of ilex and other trees, which forms a veritable oasis amid the bleak and stern nakedness of the vast slope of the mountain. This is the site of the little priory of Le Carceri; for, as a matter of course, a place sanctified by such reminiscences, could not be left in other hands than those of the little band of the disciples of the Saint; and as a matter of course also, a spot so inviting and yet so isolated could not but be selected as the site for a convent. But the community established at the *Carceri* is a very small and a very poor one. The Franciscans who guard this favourite haunt of their founder, have not reformed away the poverty of his institution. They are mendicants; and are not more than seven or eight in number.

The monastery in which this miniature community dwells is really a curiosity. An overhanging ledge of rock, harder and offering greater opposition to the action of the weather, than the stratum immediately below it, forms a sort of grotto into which the buildings of the monastery have been niched; while three or four caverns hollowed out of the rock at different altitudes by the action of the little stream at some period, when its waters were much more abundant and more violent than they are at present, serve for as many little chapels, each more intensely holy than the other, and each sanctified by some special anecdote of the Saint's presence. A tiny paved court, in front of the main grotto, surrounded by a humble range of little cells, now vacant (for the community is not numerous enough to occupy them), and a picturesque old covered gateway, approached by an ivy-grown bridge across the ravine, completes the "*clausura*," and supplies the absolutely essential means of excluding the outside world, or at least the female half of it, from the sacred precincts. At one part of the enclosure of the little court, it should be observed, at a place where a precipitous fall of the hill-side makes more complete enclosure superfluous, the continuity of the "*clausura*" is maintained only by a low parapet wall on the brink of the precipice, thus admitting air and sunshine into the court, and affording the inmates a view over the lovely valley. In the middle of this court was a picturesque well, with its little antique copper bucket, full of the beautifully cool and clear water of the spring below hanging over it.

The Superior of the establishment received us at the gate, and introduced us into the little court; where we found the whole of the community basking in the sun, some grouped around the well, and some lolling on the parapet wall, watching the Spoleto mountains change from blue to purple, and then to orange colour, with summits crimson-tipped, as the declining sun poured its slanting beams on them.

There are two great categories of monks, those who grow thin, and those who grow fat upon monastic discipline, corresponding with considerable accuracy of analogy with the two pilgrims, the one of whom crippled himself by walking with peas hard as stones in his shoes, while the other complied with, but modified the penance by boiling his peas. The Father Superior of the "*Carceri*" belonged to the latter category; and might have been selected for his dignity by weight, so palpably did he excel the members of his flock in rotundity of person and face. He had great round eyes, always opened to their utmost extent, which seemed capable of no expression save that of wonder. Whether his features had acquired this expression from the frequency with which he was called on to recount the marvels of his convent to visitors, and the propriety of appearing to feel the marvellousness of his own tale, I cannot say. But at all events his bearing was admirably well adapted to his office; and there was something really and truly marvellous in hearing and seeing a sane man stand up face to face with you and make the statements he did with the *naïf* air of undoubting belief and profound wonderment, that characterized his manner. If he did not implicitly believe all he asserted, he did his part most uncommonly well.

There was of course a crucifix, or a picture of the Virgin, in each little rock-hollowed chapel; and they all were in the habit of talking. There was a very grimy-looking and severe-visaged Virgin, who had waked brother Serafino by a box on the ear, and asked him what he meant by going to sleep when he came into her chapel to meditate! There was the crucifix, which had belonged to St. Francis, and which he had used in his devotions at this place. After his death, it had been carried to Rome, and set on an altar magnificently decked with precious stones and gold. But *che!* the very first night, as soon as ever it was left alone, it returned to its old place in the poor little chapel at the *Carceri!* "All kinds of splendid ornaments," said our friend, "were then offered to this convent to deck this poor altar, which *He* (with a jerk of his thumb towards the crucifix) so manifestly preferred. But they were declined; for it was judged," said the Father Superior, "that if He had wished to dwell among riches, He would have stayed at Rome when he was taken there."

Then of course there was no stint of local legends of the Saint himself: the abyss among the rocks by the side of the chapel door, " down which he used to pitch the devils," said the Superior, suiting the action to the word, "when they came to interrupt him at his devotions; the ilex tree still standing by the oratory window, on which the birds used to come and make the responses as regularly as possible, when the Saint offered up a litany; "the tree would long since have been carried away, bit by bit, by the devout," said the friar, "were it not that, as you see, it stands on the side of the ravine in a spot difficult to get at." Then there was of course the spot where the Saint had worn away the hard stone with his knees, and the coffin-shaped hollow in the rock where he slept, when nature exhausted by fasting and long vigils could endure no more.

But the wonders our guide had to tell were not all belonging to that far distant past, the haze around which seems in some sort to soften and mitigate the monstrous incredibility of such assertions. There were some, in the telling of which, the "*quorum vars magna fui*" was dwelt on with infinite *gusto* and a proud humility, which was a perfect study. There was the Cardinal (I forget his name, but it is recorded there on a marble tablet), who came from Rome so ill, that it was with the utmost difficulty that he could be brought to the *Carceri* on a mule, and his imbecile and diseased body be introduced into the little chapel down the narrow awkward rocky stair and through the low entrance.

"I thought we should never have got his Eminence to the foot of the altar, he was so unwieldy, and so utterly unable to help himself. But I saw him walk down to Assisi the same afternoon, a hale and active man!"

This was said with the most perfect appearance of believing simply and implicitly in the truth of the facts as he stated them. I found it difficult, as I stood before him, and looked at his face as he spoke, to suppose that he was consciously speaking falsely. I presume the story to have been made out of a little imagination, a little humbug, a good deal of acted exaggeration on the part of the Cardinal, and a certain amount of *growth* in the mind of the friar who chronicled it.

I recommend any one who has two or three hours to spare, and who is not afraid of a steep and rough three miles' walk, to make the little excursion to the *Carceri*. Those who care nothing for such studies of humanity as may be found there may still be sufficiently recompensed for their toil by the queer picturesqueness of the strange little convent, by the unexpected beauty of the oasis of verdure around the spot, bright with an extraordinary wealth of wild flowers,—primroses, violets, and crocuses, thriving beneath the shade of the ilex trees; and above all, if they will so time their visit as to enjoy the returning down-hill walk when the setting sun is gilding the panorama of mountain sides to the south-west, by the extreme beauty of the view commanded from the terrace-path along the steep front of Subiaso.

## CHAPTER IX.

FROM ASSISI TO FOLIGNO—BASIN OF ASSISI—SPELLO—FOLIGNO—MAKING BARGAINS AT INNS—FOLIGNO TO CAMERINO—BELFIORE — SCOPOLI — COLFIORITO — SERRAVALLE — DISTRICT OF CAMERINO—SITUATION OF THE CITY — THEATRICAL CICERONE—WANDERINGS IN SEARCH OF A RARE BOOK — RAVAGES OF EARTHQUAKE AT CAMERINO—PALACE OF THE VARANI—WEALTH OF THE CITY UNDER THEIR RULE — DECADENCE UNDER THE PAPAL GOVERNMENT—HISTORY OF THE VARANI — DENNISTOUN'S MEMOIRS OF THE DUKES OF URBINO—PASSAGES FROM THE HISTORY OF THE VARANI — FRATRICIDE, AND EXTERMINATION OF THE FAMILY—ESCAPE AND ADVENTURES OF GIULIO CESARE VARANI—A GOOD AUNT—THE CHIAVELLI FAMILY AT FABRIANO—SECOND ESCAPE OF GIULIO—FINALLY MURDERED BY CESARE BORGIA — RELIGIOUS EXPERIENCES OF CAMILLA VARANI — BEAUTY OF THE CAMERINO WOMEN — QUOTATION FROM A POEM OF THE FIFTEENTH CENTURY ON THIS SUBJECT—LEGEND OF ST. ANSINUS — HISTORY OF CAMERINO BY CAMMILLO LILLI.

NOTHING can be pleasanter than an afternoon—or, if it be somewhat later in the year, evening—drive from Assisi to Foligno; at the foot of Subiaso, for the greater part of the way, as far as the little city of Spello, which is built on a projecting spur of the huge mass; and, after that, for four or five miles across the valley of the Topino. This wide, flat and very fertile basin, separated from the valley of the

Tiber below Perugia by a long but not lofty spur of the hills, which the Italian geographers call the Anti-Apennine range, and enclosed to the south-west by a higher Anti-Apennine range, which unites itself to the main chain to the south of Spoleto, and to the north-east by the outlying buttresses of the great backbone of Italy, is visible almost in its entirety from Assisi, and is called in the different parts of it by the various names of the Valley of the Chiascio, the Topino, the Teverone, or the Maroggia, as its waters are drained into the Tiber by means of one or the other of these streams. But such appellations are apt to give an erroneous idea of the nature and formation of the country. These various "valleys" are but parts of one extensive basin; and there can be little doubt in the mind of a person looking down on this flat expanse from any one of the heights which command it, that the wide extent of rich alluvial soil spread out before them was once the bed of a vast lake. And such a description of the district is far more conducive than that generally adopted to the conception of a true notion of its features and appearance.

An hour of light should be reserved in making this little afternoon's journey, for the purpose of seeing the very fine frescoes by Pinturicchio in the Baglioni chapel of the church of Santa Maria Maggiore, which has been made known to the English public by the admirable chromo-lithographs of the Arundel Society. There are a considerable number of other good frescoes by the masters of the Umbrian school in the churches of the little, ill-built, dark, steep and tortuous streeted city of Spello. A real art-student must set up his tent there for a while. But for any other, an hour devoted to the examination of these very remarkable and, in their way, beautiful works of Pinturicchio will suffice.

Foligno is a great travellers' station, being the converging point of two roads across the Apennines —that by the celebrated Furlo, the old Flaminian Way, to Fano, and that by Tolentino to Ancona—as well as a much used station on the great road from Perugia to Rome. The city has not much to interest the traveller at present, though its past has a history of some importance. But its situation on the well-known great road takes it out of the scope of this volume; and having been brought thither solely by the necessities of the road, which would only take me whither I desired to go by this round-about way, I on this occasion used the place only as a shelter, from 7 P.M. on one evening, to 5 A.M. the next morning. For this purpose Foligno is not badly adapted; as the inn, *La Posta*, is a very fair one. But I mention this for the sake of introducing a little piece of advice to travellers, which my own experience dictates, in opposition to that often repeated in the guide-books. It is again and again written in those classical pages, with reference to various hostelries, "Make your bargain!" My own long experience of Italian travelling would lead me to say, "Never do anything of the kind!" It indisposes the people to you; it is contrary to the habits of the country; it will much diminish your comfort; and in nowise profit your purse. Neither imagine that any economy will be achieved (except in the cases of the great cities, where accommodation of different degrees of luxury is provided at recognized and avowedly different scales of charges), by limiting your demands to anything less than the best the house can give you in point of rooms and fare. Tell the host good-naturedly and cheerfully to do the best\* he can for you in both respects. Say nothing about prices. But when the bill is brought, if it is an extortionate one, just cut it down to a fair charge, taking care of course that the sum you fix is *rather* more than less than the absolutely strict rate. If this be done good-humouredly and quietly, and with evident knowledge of what the charges ought to be, the traveller will find that it will always be acceded to with a good grace, and that the operation will not be attended by the disagreeables inseparable from the work of making a bargain for your entertainment on entering the house. The striking-off of this "*tara*" on the bill presented for payment ought not to be done in anywise as if the objector considered the innkeeper a rogue for overcharging, which the latter in his inmost conscience does not at all consider himself on any such grounds, but as simply a matter of course, as a merchant considers defalcations under the heading of "tare and tret."

Immediately on quitting Foligno, the road to Ancona begins to climb the Apennine, leaving the ancient Flaminian Way on the right to follow the course of the Topino. The country through which the road passes is not a beautiful one, but is by no means void of interest.

\* Of course it is hardly necessary to say that it is not meant to include in this "best" foreign wines or any other such extra articles as are usually supplied only on special demand.

Shortly after starting on this upward course the traveller looks down on the delicious little village of Belfiore, nestling in its green ravine, where a mountain stream forces its way out from the hill-country into the plain. But a few miles more of climbing brings him to Scopoli; and the two names denote accurately enough the change in the nature of the region through which he is passing. The changeful Apennine is seen hereabouts in its sterner mood and more naked appearance. But at the top of the pass, nevertheless, the wayfarer falls in with Colfiorito, which also is a fairly-deserved appellation. For the flat table-land, which the road crosses, is moistened into rich verdure by one of those little mountain lakes which are of frequent occurrence in the Apennine, and is in the early spring enamelled in colours of every hue by a singularly abundant growth of wild flowers.

Then by a long descent excellently well engineered, the road comes down to Serravalle, and here again the name perfectly well describes the locality. Serravalle is a name often met with in this land of mountains and mountain passes, and the places so called are always found in similar positions; at points where the " valley is closed" by converging hill-sides, and where often it is yet more completely shut by a fortress intended to defend the passage. This is the case in the instance in question; where the remains of a large castle and adjoining fortified walls serve now only to beautify the landscape by their picturesque ruins, but must in the olden time have effectually closed the valley against any hostile passenger. The old road rose from the village of Serravalle, creeping humbly beneath the castle wall up a stony, narrow, and almost precipitous track, the remaining traces of which disclose plainly enough that, when that castle was built and that road planned, impediment to free locomotion was a very much more important consideration than facilitation of it. The new road indicates in an equally striking manner how completely this order of ideas has been reversed. For it pursues the easy slope of its descent right through a gap in the buildings of the old fortress, which have been thrown down to admit the triumphant course of modern commerce and intercommunication.

Two or three miles beyond Serravalle, the way to Camerino branches off to the left from the high road to Ancona; which falls a mile or so further into the valley of the Chienti, and follows it to the Adriatic. About four or five miles from this fork in the road, the traveller reaches the mountain capital of the ancient nation of the Camerti, of the mediæval duchy, and of the modern delegation of Camerino.

The ancient geographers do not furnish us with the means of determining exactly the limits of the country inhabited by that proud and high-spirited little nation, which in the fifth century of Rome was admitted to alliance with the Empire City, "*æquo fædere;*" and whose thousand citizens contributed so much to the Roman victory over the Cimbri by Marius. Nor is it even quite clear what were the exact bounds of the mediæval duchy, which belonged to the Varano family from A.D. 1260 to 1534. But the limits of the territory are marked so strikingly by Nature, that it is probable that they have been very nearly the same under every successive phase of history. From the vast knotty mass of the Monte Sibilla, where the Apennine rises to the height of 7184 Parisian feet, to the south of the territory in question, a lofty range, forming an Anti-Apennine chain, as the Italian geographers call it, branches off towards the north in a direction almost parallel with the main range. And between these two, the ancient Camerti, the mediæval subjects of the Varani, and the inhabitants of the Papal delegation of Camerino, were enclosed, and to a considerable degree shut out from communication with their neighbours, especially during the second of the above periods of their history. The district thus enclosed however must by no means be supposed to be a valley or basin; but is a congeries of lower hills, traversed by two main valleys, that of the Chienti, and that of the Potenza. And Camerium or Camerino, the capital, is built on an isolated hill, rising to two thousand and twenty-six feet above the level of the sea, and situated between the two wide valleys of the Chienti and the Potenza above named. It is a very fine and commanding position; and from it the little capital can survey nearly the whole of the territory belonging to it.

For him who has patience enough to persist in being dragged up the hill in his carriage, the approach to Camerino is a very long and tedious affair. There are the inviting and picturesque old gateways of the city tantalizingly close above your head; and the patient road goes winding and zigzagging about, showing you now one part of the city wall and now another, till it seems as if the gateway would never be absolutely reached. All this I noted not in going up, but subsequently on my way down. For I could not muster patience sufficient for continuing in the carriage during the ascent. A foot-path, very steep, but proportionably short, brought me to a different gate of the city from that by which the carriage entered, full three quarters of an hour before its arrival. There was no chance of failing to be rejoined by it and by my companion at the inn door, for Camerino boasts but one *hospitium;* but that though a modest is a very tolerably comfortable one.

Here again, as at Gubbio, the motive of our coming was taken by our hostess as a matter of course; and the preconceptions thus formed are evidence of the ordinary experience of the locality. At Camerino it was supposed that we were travelling to obtain subscriptions to some literary undertaking. And the hostess, impressed with this idea, proposed at once to send for the ticket-taker of the Camerino theatre, as the most proper person to assist us in our supposed object, inasmuch as it was his professional business to know everybody in the city, their addresses and who and what they were. And, although unable to avail myself of his assistance exactly in the manner proposed, I at once accepted the ticket-taker's services. For the only person to whom I had a letter of introduction in the city was absent from it; and it is absolutely necessary, in a city in which one is perfectly a stranger, to have somebody in the capacity of "guide, philosopher, and friend," of whom one may ask questions; and often obtain information of a kind that might hardly be expected from the character of the informant.

For example, it struck me as a curious trait in the

social manners and ways of the place, and a queer indication of the sort of terms on which all classes of the citizens of these remote little cities must live with each other, to get the answer I obtained from the theatrical official I have mentioned, on one of the subjects on which I consulted him, scarcely imagining that I should get any available hint from him on such a matter. There is, the reader must be told, a "History of Camerino" by one Camillo Lilli, which is a very rare book, and of which I was anxious to obtain a copy.

Did my "guide, philosopher, and friend" know, by any chance, I asked, whether there were anybody in the city likely to be the possessor of old books, and to be induced to part with any of them, should they be such as I was in search of?

What class of books was my Excellency looking for?

"*Stória pátria;*" municipal history, especially of Camerino.

"Ah! yes!" replied the ticket-taker at once; "the best book on the History of Camerino is Lilli. But it is very rare! Let me see!"

And then he went on to tell me of an old *avvocato*, who to his certain knowledge had possessed the book, and who would not have dreamed of parting with it. But he had died eight years ago; and his property had all gone to a nephew, who must have the volumes still, and might probably sell them, as he was a different sort of man from his uncle. So we went forthwith to one of the best houses in the town, and were very courteously received by the pretty young wife of the fortunate possessor of a

copy of Lilli's "Camerino," who unfortunately was
absent at a villa some four miles from the city. Of
course the lady knew nothing about the object of our
quest; but we were most welcome to go into the
library and search for ourselves. Whether her husband would part with any of his books or not, she
could not say; but knew that he would not object to
sell some pictures. That was quite a matter of
course. I do not believe that any Italian man exists
above the rank of an agricultural labourer who has
not pictures that he wishes to sell. But I explained
as well as I could to the pretty little chattering
woman that it did not come to the same thing to me
whether I bought books or paintings. She went on
depreciating the books and extolling the pictures,
while we looked over the old *avvocato's* library; and
succeeded, sure enough, in finding the two quarto
volumes of the work we were in search of, as well as
sundry other rarities of the same kind. As to the
probability of her husband's parting with them, however, the little lady would hazard no opinion; but
volunteered to despatch a messenger to bring him
home, if we would return in the evening. I fancy
she still hoped that we might be induced to do a
stroke of picture dealing. The upshot of the matter
was, that her husband returned; but alas! absolutely
declined to part with any of his book-treasures.
Pictures he could sell, as many as we pleased, but not
a volume of "*pátria stória.*"

Nevertheless the resources of my theatrical friend
were not at an end. He remembered to have seen
the book in the house of a certain Conte; and without the least hesitation led us off to knock at this

nobleman's palace-door, and open negotiations for the sale of the desired volumes. Here again we were received with perfect courtesy, and our overtures listened to without the smallest manifestation of surprise or offence. But they were equally unsuccessful; this gentleman also proposed to sell us pictures, if we were bent on buying of him; but absolutely declined parting with the History of Camerino. Two or three other tentatives, equally strange according to our code of manners and ideas, were made with no better success; and I eventually had to leave Camerino without the history of the town by Camillo Lilli; but was subsequently more fortunate in another neighbouring city.

At Camerino we found ourselves again on the track of earthquake. This little city, on its lofty, isolated hill, was visited by a series of severe shocks in the September of the last year of the last century. It seems to have been especially fatal to the ecclesiastical buildings of the city. The ancient cathedral was totally destroyed; and the epoch at which the calamity occurred is sufficient assurance that the new church which was raised to replace it has neither architectural merit nor interest of any kind. Another large and handsome church in the lower part of the city was also entirely destroyed, with the exception of the west front; the highly ornamented doors and windows of which are interesting specimens of the ecclesiastical architecture of the thirteenth century in this part of Italy, indicating a decidedly distinct and earlier style than that prevailing at the same period in Tuscany. This fine church has remained in ruins till, a year or two ago, the reconstruction, which is still in progress, was commenced. The vast superiority of the style and taste of the work in progress, to that which prevailed when the cathedral was rebuilt at the beginning of the century, is a gratifying proof that the great improvement in such matters, which has been attained in the great centres of European civilization has penetrated also into this remote district.

It is strange that the convulsion which sufficed to throw down these two churches should have left uninjured the immense palace of the Varani, the mediæval lords of Camerino and its duchy. This vast building, the back part of which rests on and forms part of the walls of the city, is but a few steps from the cathedral, on somewhat higher ground, and must have been, one would have thought, far less able to stand the effect of a shock than the church. Resting on the city wall, which encircles the top of the hill, and in this part of its course closely skirts its almost precipitous edge, the wall of the palace as seen from without the town is of very great height, and makes a picturesque and imposing appearance; but does not suggest the idea of great strength nor stability. Neither the front of the palace within the city, nor the interior of it, occupied as they have been for three hundred years by a variety of offices and institutions connected with the Papal Government, have retained much that is worthy of notice; with the exception of fragments of the ancient architecture scattered here and there among the degradations and restorations—(the terms are well nigh equivalent)—of later times. There is enough to indicate, that the petty despots of this obscure little mountain territory, who made for themselves this home so disproportioned to the extent and dignity of their dominions, found the means to expend wealth and employ art on the decoration of it, to an extent that would now exceed the resources of the owners of many a more valuable lordship.

The most obvious explanation of such a phenomenon, which at first sight presents itself, would be the supposition that these tyrants drained to their own uses the whole wealth of their dominions, that their greatness and splendour was the accurate measure of the misery and poverty of their subjects. And yet the aspect of Camerino, as it stands at the present day, seems to supply a decisive contradiction to any such theory. The city is full of the traces of past wealth and "money power," as the monkish historian of Gubbio phrased it. And these traces all belong to the anti-papal epoch. There are *facades* of a considerable number of private dwellings, which now but serve to conceal interiors the abode of poverty and decadence, but which must have been the homes of opulent and lordly citizens in the days when the Varani ruled in Camerino. And small scattered fragments of architectural ornamentation to be seen every here and there built into the walls of mean modern constructions, seem to declare very unmistakably that Papal "order" and tranquillity have been more fatal to the place than the stormy tyranny of its old native lords. One would imagine that nothing could be worse, more ruinous, more fatal morally and economically to all prosperity, than the kind of social condition that discloses itself to us in reading the local details of the history of these little principalities. It is impossible to deny that the Papal Government brought with it comparative legality, repose, and quiet. It is difficult to deny that it is better that those halls of that huge palace, which the Varani stained with the blood of their domestic murders, should be occupied by the peaceful members of the Papal University, even though there be seventeen professors to one hundred and twenty students. Yet the fact is patent and unmistakable, that this order, this *régime* of legality and tranquillity, brought with it some element more fatally poisonous to human society than all the turbulence, lawlessness, and violence of the social system which preceded it. And such facts are worthy of all the attention of economists, historians, and politicians.

These Varani were perhaps among the worst, as the Montefeltro and Della Rovere dynasties of Urbino were among the best of the petty sovereigns who divided central and Eastern Italy among them during the Middle Ages. And curiously enough, while almost all the males of the family were either worthless imbeciles, or atrocious monsters, several of the ladies of the house have been celebrated in history for their virtues, acquirements, and beauty. The history of their domination at Camerino would be well worth writing, not on such a scale as Mr. Dennistoun has devoted to that of the Dukes of Urbino, but yet with sufficient detail to give the reader a vivid picture of the sort of life and social system which existed from the twelfth to the sixteenth century in these more remote and less known districts of Italy. Such a volume would assuredly lack none of the elements of interest, which strangeness of incident, and the play of undisciplined passions could impart to it. It would moreover be for the most part new to English readers, having to be drawn from sources that are wholly so. For the imperfect notices supplied by the popular works in the hands of readers in general,—as for example "Sismondi's History of the Italian Republics,"—are full of error. This much-read book is a charming, but it cannot be called a conscientious work. Mr. Dennistoun, whose "Memoirs of the Dukes of Urbino," *is* an eminently conscientious work, in the casual notice which his subject has led him to give of the Varani, has pointed out a number of Sismondi's very gross mistakes in this part of his book, as the present writer has had occasion to do with regard to other subjects. But Mr. Dennistoun himself has not, I think, understood aright some parts of the Camerino history, on which he touches, probably for lack of having consulted that best authority on the subject, my unsuccessful search for which I have above related. The work of Lilli does not appear in the copious catalogue of authors used by him for his "Memoirs;" and I note the absence of several other writers who might have been consulted with advantage.

A passage in this history of the Varani, to which Mr. Dennistoun alludes cursorily,—his own subject not requiring him to do more,—but in speaking of which, he has misunderstood the motives of the citizens of Camerino in the part they played in the matter, may furnish a specimen of the sort of incidents to be met with in their annals.

Ridolfo Varani, tired at length with a life of

continued turmoil, comes to an agreement with Guido Antonio of Montefeltro; and by solemn instrument bearing date the 3rd of August, 1414, the two potentates "*fecerunt finem de represaliis omnibus, robbariis, arrestationabus, violentiis, extorsionibus, injuriis,*" etc.* And having thus satisfactorily arranged his affairs, and, more satisfactorily still, having in the following year been confirmed in his sovereignty by the authority of "Antonius Archiepiscopus Ragusinus, Bertrandus Episcopus S. Flori, et *Johannes Strokes V. I. D. Anglicus,*" who were, it appears "*Nuntii et Commissarii per Sacrum generale Constantiense Concilium sufficienter deputati,*"† he shortly after died and left his small dominions divided by a deed ‡ dated 1430, into four parts between his four sons; the two eldest Gentile-Pandulfo and Bernardo by his first wife Elizabetta Malatesta; and his two younger sons Giovanni and Pier-Gentile by his second wife Costanza Smeducci. An arrangement more sure to lead to a series of family tragedies could hardly have been contrived. And the result which might have been expected was not long in coming to pass.

Under Pope Eugenius IV., who was elected in 1431, a certain Giovanni Vitelleschi became Governor for the Holy See in the March of Ancona. "He was," says Lilli, § "a seditious man, born in

---

*. Lilli, Hist. Cam. Vol. II., p. 142.

† Lilli, *Ibid.*, p. 145. He says nothing further respecting this John Strokes which can at all enlighten us as to who he was.

‡ Ughelli, Italia Sacra. Tom. I., p. 607.

§ *Ibid*, p. 170.

Corneto, an infamous* place in Tuscany, who being of turbulent and greedy mind, set at nought no less divine than human laws." This dangerous man conceived the idea of extirpating the whole family of the Varani, and then usurping their dominions. And with this view, being aided by the perfidious counsels and suggestions of a certain Arcangelo di Fiordimonte, a courtier and hanger-on of the Varani, whose object was the establishment of freedom (*i. e.* self-government as a republic) at Camerino, he carefully and skilfully fomented a feeling of jealousy and suspicion in the mind of Gentile Pandulfo and Bernardo against their half-brothers Giovanni and Pier-Gentile. From this to a resolution to compass the murder of them was a very easily made step. It was plotted that Vitelleschi should come to San Severino, a little city and fortress a few miles to the eastward of Camerino, and should invite all the four brothers to meet him there, as he wished to have some conversation with them on business. It was arranged that the two eldest should excuse themselves; and that Giovanni and Pier should be detained and murdered in the castle. But the design was all put off to another time in a hurry, on the sudden passage through the country of the Emperor Sigismund on his way to Rome. It is curious to observe how the coming of the Emperor, like that of a schoolmaster

* Why the Umbrian historian should call the little Maremman town of Corneto "*térra infame*," I cannot guess. It is a curious instance of the prejudices and hatreds which divided town from town, and province from province in Italy for so many hundred years; the feeling which led Dante to brand Pisa as "*vituperio delle gente.*"

L

among a lot of mischievous boys, causes all these
abominations to be suddenly laid aside as long as he
is within sight or hearing, to be resumed as soon as
ever his back is turned.

It was August, in the year 1433, before the
accomplices could put their design in execution.
In that month Vitelleschi came to San Severino, and
invited the four brothers, as had been agreed.
Giovanni, probably suspecting foul play, absolutely
refused to quit Camerino. The two elder brothers
pretended to be laid up with the gout, but sent their
sons with their excuses to Vitelleschi. With these
his nephews went Pier-Gentile. The young men
returned in the evening to Camerino. But Pier-
Gentile returned no more. He was seized at San
Severino, and conveyed to Recanati, a city at that
time wholly in the confidence of Vitelleschi, and was
there beheaded outside the wall of the city on a spot
which retained the name of Varano in memory of
the deed for many generations afterwards.

When the two young men returned to Camerino,
they found their other uncle Giovanni in a chamber
of the palace with his two half-brothers Gentile Pan-
dulph and Bernardo, engaged in a dispute arising
from the reproaches cast by the two latter on
Giovanni for the mischief he had done to the family
interest by his refusal to meet the Papal Governor.
From words the disputants soon came to blows; and
as Giovanni, being in the minority, turned to quit
the room, he was cut down by the young men at a
sign from their father Bernardo.

This double fratricide however seems to have
shocked public feeling throughout the little Duchy

in an unusual manner. And in the July of the following year Bernardo, who had gone to quiet some sedition at Tolentino, was put to death there by the citizens as he was in perfect security taking an evening stroll round the walls.

The news of this fact at once stimulated the people of Camerino to do as much for the last of the four brothers, Gentile Pandulfo; and an opportunity was soon found. One Festa morning the whole of the survivors of the family, Pandulfo and his nephews and their children all went to attend mass at the church of the Dominicans. The bloodstained tyrant seems not to have conceived the slightest suspicion that he was in any danger from the hands of his subjects; and yet it would appear that the whole city was engaged in a conspiracy to rid themselves of him and his for ever.

Mr. Dennistoun is evidently mistaken in thinking that the men of Camerino were only anxious to avenge the death of Giovanni, whom they loved. For the infant children of Giovanni and Pier-Gentile were with difficulty saved from the popular rage. The object evidently was to extirpate the race entirely, and restore Camerino to that condition of "liberty" which the citizens of all the municipalities were always longing for, and always misusing as soon as they attained it.

Pandulfo and five of his nephews, and some of the children of the latter were slaughtered in the church; the infants being put to death by knocking their brains out against the walls of the building. Two others of the family, who on the first signs of tumult had shut themselves up in the palace were hunted out and slain, and the palace sacked.

The race of the Varani was thus extirpated, *with the exception of* two infants, the one Rodolfo, a little more than a year old, the son of Pier-Gentile, who had been beheaded at Recanati; the other, Giulio, aged only five months, the son of Giovanni, murdered in his brother's chamber in the palace. The people of Camerino eagerly sought for these infants, that they might be put to death, and the race of their tyrants be thus utterly extirpated. Both were however got out of the city in safety; and both lived to become successively lords of Camerino, and the progenitors of two new branches of the old family.

The story of the escape and subsequent fortunes of Giulio, the son of Giovanni, who was five months old at the time of the great slaughter in the church of the Dominicans, is full of romantic incident.

His widowed aunt Tora Trinci, on the first outbreak of the disturbance snatched the infant, swaddled as it was into a compact bundle, after the fashion still prevalent in Italy, and rushing off with it from the palace, delivered it to a trustworthy man of the name of Pascuccio Geminiano, with directions to smuggle it out of the city as best he might. This he succeeded in doing, carrying it through the guarded gateway in a bundle of hay on his shoulder. Tora had in the meantime herself escaped from the city, and making her way across the mountains to the northward of Camerino, awaited the arrival of her friend Pascuccio in the solitude of the ruins of the ancient city of Attidia, a spot still marked a mile or two to the south of the little city of Fabriano by the name Attigio. There this good Aunt Tora received the little bundle in the shape of an Egyptian mummy-case of a cat, which contained the future lord of Camerino, from the hands of her confidant; and hurried with it to Fabriano, then an independent little lordship, under the rule of the Chiavelli family, where Tora's sister Guglielma, was the wife of the reigning lord, Battista.

But Giulio Varano's cradle adventures were not yet ended. He had been under the roof of his new protectors hardly a year, when the fortune which appears always to have been overhanging these despots of miniature dominions overtook the Chiavelli. Probably the men of Fabriano were stimulated to revolt, by the exemple of their neighbours of Camerino. The fate of the two princely families was also singularly similar both in the manner in which it overtook them, and in the details of the catastrophe. It was in the church of St. Venanzio that the citizens of Fabriano, in the May of 1435, made a sudden onslaught on the family of their tyrant and slew him, his two brothers, and five of his children. In this case also, two infants, the youngest children of the murdered prince, were saved by the Sacristan, and were subsequently smuggled away in safety to Piedmont, "where," says Lilli, * "their posterity still inhabit Pinerolo to this day."

One does not see why this event should necessarily have endangered the life of the infant Giulio, who was only a guest at the court of Fabriano. But he was great danger; and the historian seems to consider it quite a matter of course, that he should have been so;

* Lilli, Hist. Cam. Vol. II., p. 177.

as if the insurgent citizens would have been anxious to put to death any member of the class of " tyrants," and strike a blow in favour of their neighbours of Camerino, when their hands were at the work on their own account.

Giulio was however a second time saved by the energy and vigilance of his Aunt Tora. She managed to hide him, at the first outbreak of the tumult, in a nunnery; and he was subsequently carried out of the city, hidden in a bundle of cloth, by Niccolò Giunta, who had been sent express to Fabriano from Pesaro by Galeazzo Malatesta, the lord of that city, at the urgent request of Tora. The getting out of the city however was a difficult matter. The guards at the gate wanted to stop Niccolò and examine his big bundle, "but giving the spur to his horse he dashed on at full gallop to San Donato, a castle three miles distant from Fabriano, where he was met by a band of 300 lances, sent by Malatesta for the purpose." \* They escorted Giulio and his deliverer to Sassoferrato, a neighbouring city, where the child "remained seven years, and was then sent to be educated by Blancina, a daughter of Tora, and the wife of Giorgio Antonio Manfredi." †

Here is already incident and adventure enough for one life; but there was much more in store for Giulio Cesare Varani. He lived a stormy and troubled life, till it might have been said of him, as of Hardyknute in the old ballad :—

> "Some seventy years he might have seen,
> And scarce seven years of rest !"

And he was doomed at last to a violent death,

\* Lilli, Hist. Cam. Vol. II., p. 177. † *Ibid.*

having been strangled in the castle of Pergola, on the night of Sunday the 9th of October, by a *brávo* in the pay of the infamous Cesar Borgia, in the sixty-eighth year of his age. As soon as ever the deed was done, the murderer rode off in all haste to La Cattolica, where the three sons of the old duke were kept in prison by Borgia, and put them all to death in the same manner.

The city had been taken, and the duke and his children made prisoners by fraud a few months previously. Here is a Roman diarist's account of the manner in which the news of Cesar Borgia's success was received by his father, the Pope, in Rome. The original latin is quoted by Lilli*:—

" On Saturday the 23rd of July, two hours before sunset, news was brought to the Pope that the Duke of Valentino had gained possession of Camerino by a capitulation. Therefore, many bombs were let off from the castle of St. Angelo. In the evening there was a great illumination, and rockets were let off, and a great festival was made in the Piazza of St. Peter. On the Sunday evening the great bell of the Chapter was rung; and with great triumph, still bigger fires were made than the previous evening. The victory was in this wise. A truce having been made with the Lord of Camerino by the Duke of Valentino, the latter rushed into the city when the Lord of Camerino least supposed himself to be in danger of being attacked."

The imperturbable diarist as usual permits no word of comment to escape him; but surely that dry

* Lilli, Hist. Cam. Vol. II., p. 260.

"*Victoria fuit hujusmodi,*" was not written without a feeling of irony.

Abundance of highly curious and interesting matter of quite a different kind, is to be found in the records of the Varani. For instance Camilla the daughter of Giulio Cesare, a lady of eminent sanctity, has left us an extremely curious account of her religious experiences. After having minutely and really graphically described the fierce struggle which had continued for some time in her soul on the question, whether she should give up the world and take the veil, or no; and, when this was at length decided in the affirmative, having dilated at large on the intimate nature of her communion with the Second Person of the Trinity, with copious illustrative quotations from the Song of Solomon, she writes thus:—

"Being one day in prayer, and having clearly felt that He was in my soul, He said, when He chose to leave me; 'If you wish to see me, look at me.' And it was as when a person leaves another, and turns his back to him, and goes his way. So exactly He did to my soul. When I began to see Him, He was distant from me more than six paces off in a room, at the end of which is a small door, like the door of a chamber."

[Here Lilli,* from whose extracts from the lady's MS. my quotations are borrowed, interrupts his citation to remark: "This was the great hall of the ancient palace, built by Venanzo Varani, at the end of which there is to the present day a communication with other rooms by that little door."]

"I continued to see Him," Camilla proceeds,

* Vol. II., p. 233.

"until He bent His head by reason of His tallness, and passed in at that door. And I saw neither Him, nor the hall, nor the doors any more. He was robed to the ground; and the dress was bordered at its extremity with a border, having letters of gold on it, a full finger large, which I could not read, because they were too far off from me; and He walked away quickly, and did not stop. He was girded very tightly at the girdle with a band of massive gold, two fingers wide. He was taller than all other the tallest men. Falling from His shoulders, His hair appeared all golden, and reaching almost to His girdle. The hair was rather wavy, but I could not see all the top of His head, so as to perceive whether He wore a crown, or diadem, or garland of flowers and roses. This He did not choose me to see. I suppose that He wore on His head something so beautiful, that I was not worthy to see it. But those blond tresses falling in such abundance over those large and well-proportioned shoulders, set off by that exquisitely white garment, declared well enough that it was something marvellous."

*This* was the "religious experience" of a young girl, for whose energies of intellect and feeling no fitting outlet was furnished by the social system in which she lived, four hundred years ago!

From these specimens it may be seen that the story of the rulers of this little highland dukedom and their people is not deficient in romantic passages and interest of many kinds. I do not remember a more picturesque incident in the pages of Italian history, than that of the noble fifteenth century dame, waiting in the solitude of the oak-embowered ruins of the ancient Roman city, with anxiety proportioned to the importance of the life she was trying to preserve,—an importance to all concerned as great as the preservation of any other royal or imperial line to the country whose fortunes were bound up with it,—and there receiving the precious bundle of wailing swaddled humanity from the devoted servant of the house.

One of the first things that struck my companion and myself at Camerino,—though I have left the mention of it to the last,—was the beauty of the women. The type is quite a different one from that of either Tuscany or Rome; having a nearer relationship however to that of the former country. The features are generally small and delicate, eyes full of vivacity and intelligence, faces generally pointed at the chin, brilliant teeth, figures remarkably good, lithe, round, elastic, with well formed and well attached extremities. Having noticed this first for myself, I found afterwards a confirmatory notice of the beauty of the Camerino women four hundred years ago. One Ludovico Lazzarelli, a poet of the neighbouring city of San Severino, in a poem composed about the middle of the fifteeenth century on the life and legends of Ansinus, the patron saint of [Camerino, writes thus of the festival held in the city in his honour :—

> "Octo dies totum venalia quæque per urbem,
> Tunc impune patent; advena turba venit.
> Vestibus ornatæ nuptæ pariterque puellæ,
> Incedunt, multo fervet honore via.
> Tuncque Varanæas flagrans potes advena Nymphas,
> Mirari, atque illas esse referre Deas."

It may be that the poet intended his compliment

## SAINT ANSINUS.

to be applied only to the ladies of the reigning family. But I should rather imagine from the context, and from the habit, common in the Italian writers of that period, of applying an adjective formed from the name of the lord to all his followers and subjects, that the " Varanean Nymphs," whom the enamoured stranger would take to be Goddesses, were in general those wives and maidens of Camerino, who walked dressed in all their best through the fair.

Those who are fond of the legends which give the psycological *signalement* of the darkest ages, may find a curious collection of them in connection with this Saint Ansinus, who was Bishop of Camerino about the middle of the ninth century. But his fame was by no means confined to his own part of Italy, for Lilli * cites the following verses, copied from an inscription existing in his time in a chapel of the Chiesa degli Eremitani at Naples:—

> " Ansinus Sanctus capitis fugat iste dolorem ;
> Quilibet hoc fidei lumine tutus erit.
> Huc properant populi, concurrunt undique gentes,
> Nam Divo Ansino tollitur omne malum.
> Ansini precibus, si quis se subdet, habebit
> Protinus immensum, quod peragebat, opus.
> Gloria summa Deo, laus Sanctis, gratia cunctis,
> Defunctis requies, Ecclesiæque decor."

Besides the work of Lilli, and the great collection by Colluci already mentioned, the curious may consult for Camerino and its territory, " Francesco Dino, De antiquitatibus Umbrorum, Thuscorumque sede ac imperio, dequi Camerino et Camertibus a Sylla excisis. Venetiis. 1704."

* Vol. I., p. 131.

But the one indispensable book on this region of Italy, is the stumpy little quarto of Camillo Lilli, printed in two parts at Macerata, in 1652. Should the collector meet with a copy wanting the sheets from page 218 to 225, and from 256 to the end of the first part, and wanting likewise the engravings of portraits, seals, medals, &c., which should be inserted in the text, and the blank spaces left for which will be observed, he will not too summarily reject it; for all the copies extant are thus defective, in consequence of these pages having been destroyed as soon as printed, because of certain offence contained in them against a powerful family of the city.

## CHAPTER X.

ROUTE FROM CAMERINO—CASTLE OF VARANO—ORIGIN OF THE FAMILY—TOLENTINO—MEDIÆVAL POLITICS—REMARKABLE REPORT TO ALEXANDER THE SIXTH—THE ACCORAMBONI FAMILY—A SENTENCE ON TREASON—ST. NICHOLAS—CASTELLO DI RANCIA—GREAT BATTLE IN 1815.

A VERY pleasant drive of four or five miles brings the traveller back from Camerino into the great road which he left for the purpose of climbing the hills on which the old city is, according to ancient fashion, built. Soon after descending from the city gate the first and steepest part of the isolated hill, the steepness of which was the merit that attracted the first builders there, who shall say how many tens of centuries ago, the road dips into the valley of the little mountain torrent called the Scortachiari, which it follows till that stream falls into the Chienti, at the spot where the little road also falls into the great one. For the last mile or two of its course, this valley is picturesque to a very high degree. It is narrow; the bed of the stream is rocky, and the very steep sides of the hills between which it finds its devious way are abundantly clothed with oak.

On a singularly commanding hill-top, which stands out isolated from the hills behind it, at the mouth of this narrow and beautiful defile, where the Scortachiari falls into the Chienti, stands the castle of Varano.

Whether this ancient fortress gave its name to the family who were so long sovereigns here, or received it from them, is perhaps doubtful. Lilli and the local antiquaries would assert that the latter is unquestionably the case, and would utterly scout the notion that the reverse could be true. For they claim a Norman origin for the family, and relationship with our Earls of Surrey, of the race of that William who accompanied William the Conqueror, and who executed an extant deed of gift " pro salute D. mei Willielmi Regis, qui me in Angliam adduxit, et pro salute D. meæ Matildis Reginæ matris, Uxoris meæ, et pro salute D. mei Willielmi Regis filiæ suæ, post ejus adventum in Anglicam terram hanc cartam feci, et qui me comitem Surregiæ fecit."

When and how any branch of this family came into Italy however, the historian avows himself unable to say. But he thinks that a relationship and connection between the Varani of Camerino and the English family in question is rendered probable by the fact, that Gentile Varani, who in the last half of the thirteenth century became tyrant of Camerino, " was captain-general of the forces to Edward the Fifth of England," (as the Italian historian has it, evidently meaning the monarch whom, counting from the Conquest we term Edward the First.) This captain-generalship, however, must, I suspect, be reduced to the fact that Gentile had at one time under his orders a band of English mercenaries, who were furnished by him to Pope Alexander the Fourth. This

## VARANO CASTLE.

Gentile was the first Varani, says Lilli, who called himself "*di Varano*," thus affecting a territorial designation. And if so, the probability is, that the Varani who built the castle I have been speaking of, gave it their name. But the case is a rare one; the territory having almost invariably in similar instances given its name to its possessor.

The stronghold in question must have been a very important place, which could evidently have been suffered to remain in no hands save those of the sovereign lords of the district. A very little improvement of the locality by the hand of man, has rendered the rock on which the castle stands altogether isolated on all sides, and accessible only by a drawbridge. The position commanding, as it does, not only the valley of the Chienti, which formed the main avenue of access to this mountain-circled district from the east, but also the smaller and more easily defended pass of the Scortachiari, which led directly to the capital, was one which it evidently behoved the possessors of the country to fortify to the utmost of their power. And the natural advantages of the spot were turned by them to the best account. The castle is still worth a visit, as it yet retains most of the arrangements of the old feudal mode of life but little changed. There is the great keep, the enormous hall, the dungeons, and the lady's bower, much as they were when the Varani lords were plotting fratricides, and the Varani ladies were passing their days in erudite study or ascetic devotion.

Of course there are the usual stories and traditions at Camerino of a subterranean communication from the city to the castle. But I could not learn that the assertion rested on any verification of the fact by examination. There were not wanting occasions in the history of the family when such a passage might have been a most welcome means of safety to more than one of its members. But we hear nothing of recourse ever having been had to the facilities afforded by it.

As the family of the Varani are now merely an object of curiosity to the historical student, so their castle has no longer any purpose to serve in the world save that of an interesting and beautiful object in the landscape. And this function it discharges very satisfactorily. It is a building of imposing size; and the lofty masses of its grey stone almost windowless walls, rearing themselves on their cliff amid and above the surrounding oak woods, are as attractive to the eye of a scenery-loving traveller as they were once forbidding to that of an invading enemy.

After falling into the valley of the Chienti, the way becomes less picturesque. This part of the river however runs among high mountains through a pass sufficiently narrow, and with a course so winding, as to present various points available for fortification; and three or four ancient castles accordingly are passed, now on one and now on the other side of the river, which give interest to the scenery. At the point where the Chienti or rather the valley through which it runs, finally opens out into a broader basin, and the shallow bed of the river becomes a world too wide for its scanty stream, except at times of floods, stands the city of Tolentino; the fourteenth century inhabitants of which would have been greatly astonished, could they have foreseen that the principal European reputation of their city in the time to come would arise from its having been a scene of, and giving its name to a treaty by which the Papal Government ceded to a lay conqueror a part of its dominions, and thus established a precedent fatal to the "*non possumus*," by which the still harder pressed successors of that unfortunate 6th Pius would one day vainly seek to protect the last shreds of their temporal power. For it was the great boast of Tolentino that it had never been subject to any other sovereign than the Holy See.

Various writers, either natives of rival and jealous neighbouring cities, or animated by dynastic tendencies and anti-liberal sympathies, have endeavoured to show that Tolentino was at some period of the thirteenth and fourteenth centuries subject to the dominion of the ancient family of the Accoramboni. And the disputations and arguments of the local historians, who have debated this point, illustrate in a very curious and instructive manner the relationship, which commonly subsisted in those centuries between the Holy See and the cities of all this part of Italy,—the views, which led the citizens to prefer the supremacy of Rome,—and the sort of way in which most of them fell under the tyranny of some powerful noble.

When Cesare Borgia by force, by treason, and multiplied assassinations, as we have seen, obtained possession of Camerino professedly for his father the Pope, but in reality for the purpose of forming with his father's connivance a Duchy for himself, the citizens of Camerino for a moment took part against their old tyrants. But as soon as they found that they were to be governed as despotically as ever by a dynasty of Borgias instead of a dynasty of Varanis, they turned about and attempted by a new revolution to throw off the new yoke. Alexander the Sixth, the infamous Borgia Pope, was surprised at this sudden change in their politics and wishes, and desired an agent in whom he could confide to report to him upon the subject. In that report we find the following curious passage:—

"These men,—(the citizens of Camerino)—have an immutable desire, which always tends to liberty. All the men of Camerino, who have property, or family connections, or spirit, or talent, all I say without exception wish this same thing. I include in this statement both the partizans of the Varani and those of the Borgia. In a word they have no other desire in the world; they think only of this. And in their political changes they labour only towards this immutable object. All their revolutions therefore, as well those made in favour of your Holiness, as those made in an opposite direction, tend in reality to this desired and longed for end. They disturb the Government and revolutionize the city for the sake of acquiring a retinue and state, enjoying for awhile freedom from control, becoming *Signori*, eating their meals with accompaniment of fifers and trumpeters, and dividing among themselves the revenues, as they have done on other occasions."

Now although it is natural to expect, that a person consulted on this subject by the Pope should speak contemptuously of the state of liberty desired by the rebellious city, there can be little doubt, that the reporter characterized in this remarkable passage the political views of the popular leaders with very considerable justice. It was the same thing all over Italy, in these little communities as in the great and powerful cities, the history of which is better known. The "liberty" so ardently desired, was the liberty of sharing in the grandeurs and profits of the ruling tyrant. Even in Florence, that "most republican of republics," it was the same thing, with the only difference that wealth and prosperity had made the number of those, who were determined so to share, much larger not only absolutely but relatively to the entirety of the population.

Recent historians, and none more than Sismondi, the writer from whom the nineteenth century has mainly taken its ideas of mediæval Italian history, have been sadly led astray by the constant use of this word "*libertà*" by the politicians and historians of the old Italian municipalities. "Tyranny" was the possession of the revenues and powers of the state by one individual,—"*il governo di uno solo,*" as the old writers phrase it again and again;—"liberty" was the sharing of these among a larger or smaller number of the peers, or those who claimed to be peers, of that one. No difference in the administration of the government, in any political or economical ideas, or in the condition of the governed, was contemplated in the exchange of the one for the other form of government. And the desire so frequently met with in these communities to place themselves under the supremacy of the Church, arose solely from the expectation that practically the Church would leave the profits and sweets of power to the leading citizens.

"They never made any difference," says Lilli, speaking of the citizens of Camerino,* "between being free and being subject to the Apostolic See."

And in after times, when all were alike reduced to the quiet dead level of subjection to the regular Papal Government, in those dull dead seventeenth and eighteenth centuries, when no Italian dared to employ tongue or pen on any public matter of present interest, and the few men, who could not find sufficient occupation for their minds in the drowsy routine of the stagnant life around them, were driven to exercise themselves in academical antiquarianism, it is curious to observe the anxiety of writers, who had no more conception of the meaning of civil liberty than a Chinese, to maintain that their city had ever been free from tyranny, and subject only to the Church. The meaning in the minds of these writers, who all belong, it must be remembered, to the families of the old municipal nobility, in as much as no others were men of any education at all, was this. "Our forefathers, great-great-grandfathers, and uncles, whose names are preserved in genealogical trees, whose portraits hang on the walls of decaying, tumble-down palaces, and of whose greatness and standing in their native city each man is as proud, and as jealous of those of his neighbours, as the utter absence of any thing else to be proud of can make him; these our forefathers were as good as any other in their city. No one of their fellows lorded it over them. That wretched, poverty-stricken, snuff-begrimed little, old Marchese B. or C. whom I meet at our evening gossip in the apothecary's shop, is as proud as Lucifer

* Part II., p. 2.

because his maternal grandfather's grandmother was an Accoramboni. What then? The Accoramboni were never Lords in Tolentino. It is false to assert it. We were always free under the Church. The Tolentinans would never endure tyranny. The Camerino men submitted to it; but we were made of different stuff down here!"

This is the meaning of the constantly recurring anxiety of these local historians to prove that their city was either never subject to, or quickly freed itself from the "*governo di uno solo.*" And the facts adduced by Don Carlo Santini, who dedicates his book to a Cardinal in a strain of the most fulsome adulation, to prove that Tolentino was never subject save to the Church, which have suggested the above observations, show curiously how gradually the tyranny of some one great citizen over his fellows was established, and by what sort of means it was mostly at last achieved.

It is asserted, as has been said, by many writers that the family of Accoramboni were Lords of Tolentino. To this Santini * replies by relating an event, which proves, as he argues, that such was not the case, and adduces documents, which he has discovered in the archives of the city, in proof of the accuracy of his story.

He admits that towards the middle of the fourteenth century the power of the Accoramboni family had "increased beyond measure." † So that Berardo, or Bernardo, and Francesco, "studied to gain the

* Saggio di Memorie della Città di Tolentino. Raccolte ed illustrate da Don Carlo Santini. 1. Vol. 4to. Macerata. 1789.
† *Ibid*, p. 226.

favour and adherence of many of their fellow citizens, and succeeded in drawing to their alliance the Boni family, and others of the richest nobles." They also succeeded in persuading the priest of Santa Maria to share in their designs. And then on the 31st of July, in the year 1342, "being instigated," as is said in the legal proceedings, " by a diabolical spirit, they conspired together to take possession of our country; so that a great quantity of people, with arms in their hands, on foot and on horseback, went through the streets, crying out, ' Long live the sons of the Lord Accoramboni!' in such sort that they placed the city in a position of rebellion against the Holy See."

At this time a certain Friar, John Rivora, was Governor of the March of Ancona for the Church. And Frà Giovanni, despite his frock and his shaven crown, seems to have been quite equal to the emergency. For immediately on hearing the news of what was going on at Tolentino, he got together a number of horsemen, and riding hard to the scene of action, succeeded in putting down the disturbance and bringing the authors of it to their trial before the " *Vicarius super spiritualibus,*" sitting at Macerata. And the sentences which were then pronounced against them, have been printed at length by Don Santini, in his Appendix. Inasmuch as being " sons of iniquity," (and a great many other hard names) they had endeavoured to subject the city of Tolentino "in pravam tirapniam," to a wicked tyranny —(which, the document goes on to recite, they would have succeeded in doing, had it not been for the Virgin Mary and Frà Giovanni the Rector,) they are condemned first to a fine of ten thousand golden florins to the Apostolic exchequer. Secondly, to confiscation of everything belonging to them. Thirdly, they are excommunicated with the greater excommunication, and branded with perpetual infamy. Fourthly, they are deprived of whatever offices or benefices they or any of them may hold of the Church; they are declared incapable of ever acquiring others for the future; and the benefit of any spiritual indulgences, privileges, or immunities which they have ever or might ever gain, is taken from them, and the same made null and of no effect. Fifthly, they are declared incapable of making a will, (which under the circumstances above provided for, would seem to be of little consequence,) and of ever inheriting any thing. Sixthly, no man shall be obliged to plead to any judicial complaint of theirs; but they shall be obliged to answer all accusations against them, and shall not be permitted to have any advocate or defenders. And finally, if ever they shall be found in any place within our power, (by which it appears that the culprits had slipped through Frà Giovanni's hands, despite his promptness and energy;) they shall be kept in perpetual prison, "on the bread of pain and the water of sorrow, and so finish the residue of their lives, weeping for their misdeeds."

In truth the "*Vicarius super spiritualibus*" seems to have felt the luxury of condemning so keenly, that he could hardly make up his mind to hold his hand, when he was at it.

It may be conceded that Signore Santini has conclusively shown that the Accoramboni did not upon that occasion succeed in establishing themselves as

Lords of Tolentino, and that they were not in that position in the middle of the fourteenth century. He admits however that they had become beyond measure powerful; and his narrative shows the easy way in which such "tirapnia" was often established in the cities.

A few miles before reaching Tolentino the road passes the villa in which Pius the Sixth was lodged at the time of the signature of the celebrated treaty. There is an inscription commemorative of the event on the front of the building, in which the writer exclaims on the *happiness of the dwelling that kissed the feet of the Pontiff*, in a tone of exultation which seems to accord but ill with the sentiments of any thing save happiness, which poor Pius the Sixth must have felt at placing his feet on that threshold.

The old Gothic gateway by which Tolentino is entered is picturesque, and there is still something of Italian mediæval character about the group of public buildings in the Piazza. But there is little else of interest at Tolentino, which cannot be in this respect compared with its more out-of-the-way and old-world neighbour, Camerino.

St. Nicholas of Tolentino, who lived, and worked miracles, and died here, has achieved a very high reputation among the peasantry of his own district, and some degree of fame throughout Catholic Christendom. And of course the local historians have a great deal to say about his life and wonderful deeds. Of these, that which is most celebrated among the people of the district is a periodical miracle, which the saint was in the habit of performing occasionally for three centuries. It seems that in the year 1345,

## ST. NICHOLAS OF TOLENTINO.

a certain monk attempted to steal the arms of the Saint, having for this purpose cut them from his body. He was however miraculously stopped in his flight, and rendered unable to move in the cloister of the church, where the body was preserved; so that in the morning he was detected, the arms were recovered, and restored to the body. But, wonderful to relate, the dry arms on being brought back to the body from which they had been sacrilegiously cut, began to bleed. And more wonderful still, this prodigy has again from time to time taken place. It is recorded to have happened once in the fourteenth century; once in the fifteenth; seven times in the sixteenth, and sixteen times in the seventeenth century; the last occasion being in the year 1700. The varied frequency of the miracle in the different centuries, is not altogether unsuggestive of observation. Since the year 1700, Saint Nicholas of Tolentino, setting an example of discretion in this matter which might be advantageously imitated by certain other saints, has contented himself with his laurels won, and has made no further sign.

A drive of about fourteen miles brings the traveller from Tolentino to Macerata. But the latter city, like Camerino, lies three or four miles to the left-hand of the great road to Ancona, which continues to follow the valley of the Chienti.

A short distance before leaving it, the attention of the traveller will be attracted by a large and imposing looking castellated building on the right-hand of the road called "Il Castello della Rancia." It has long since been abandoned, and from its position in the midst of the low ground of the wide basin of the

Chienti, could never have been a military position of much importance. It now serves to mark the site of the great battle between Murat and his Neapolitans with the Austrians under Bianchi, in May 1815. When night fell on the day's work, two thousand men lay dead and dying on that fertile plain, now once again green with the thick growing wheat-crops. There are battle-fields, many of them, on the earth, which, when nature has dropped her veil of beauty and renovation over the scene, men may tread with exultation and admiration for the heroism which there made stand for the right. But few, alas! of Italy's battle-fields have, unless in these last days, been such. The very names of the generals in this great slaughter in the Chienti are enough to show what Italy's interests in the matter were. There were Austrians under an Italian on one side, and Italians under a Frenchman on the other! And it is difficult to say what termination to the fight could have been least injurious to Italy;—unless indeed it could have ended after the fashion of the notorious battle of the Kilkenny cats. Probably, as far as it may be allowed to us to judge from our imperfect estimate of the value of subsequent events, the issue that was best for Italy was that which happened. Had Austria not triumphed then, she might not have been forced to other battle-fields, which ended in a different result.

How far dare we hope that these valleys have been enriched with human blood for the last time?

## CHAPTER XI.

MACERATA — ITS POINTS OF SIMILITUDE AND CONTRAST TO CAMERINO—ORIGIN OF MACERATA—ITS MEDIÆVAL HISTORY—PROSPERITY—TERRACES AROUND THE WALLS—VIEWS FROM THEM—DIVISIONS AND HATREDS BETWEEN CITY AND CITY—LITERARY QUARRELS—REMARKABLE ONE BETWEEN MACERATA AND CAMERINO—ORIGIN AND PROGRESS OF THE DISPUTE—REAL BITTERNESS OF FEELING ATTENDING SUCH DISPUTATIONS—MACERATA AND RECANATI—ORIGIN OF RECINA—WORK OF FRA BRANDIMARTE — ABSENTEEISM AT MACERATA — BRICK PALACES — BRAMANTE'S CHURCH OF LA MADONNA DELLE VERGINI — ENORMOUS BALL COURT — PROBABLE FUTURE DESTINY OF MACERATA.

THE situation of Macerata resembles in many respects that of Camerino; yet the points of contrast between the two cities and the landscape around them are quite as numerous, and are all the more striking from the general similarity in their position. Like Camerino, Macerata occupies the summit of an isolated hill, rising in the midst of a district of lower hills, intersected by large water-courses. As at Camerino the views from the terraces around its walls are charming and varied; and they themselves, with the gates, and towers and cupolas of the city within them, group into a variety of pleasing landscapes, as seen from the lowlands on the sides of the neighbouring hills. But with these general features of resemblance the similarity ends. The country around Macerata is softer, richer, more garden-like than that in the midst of which its rival city is situated. The lofty barrier of stern and naked mountain tops, which shut in the horizon on all sides at Camerino, are not to be seen at Macerata. All the slopes and hill-sides around the latter are gentler, less rugged, and less steep than those which make up the more romantic scenery around Camerino. Then the general aspect of the two towns is curiously different. The past has left its impress on the ancient capital of the Varani, in a visible and unmistakable manner, which is not the case at Macerata. And it is curious that the social aspect of the two cities seems to correspond accurately with this difference in their material features. Macerata is, for a Papal town, a busy, active, lively, thriving place. At Camerino, all is sleepy quietude, stillness, and stagnation. Grass may be found in the streets at Camerino. At Macerata there seems to be sufficient movement to keep such growth down. Echoes to passing footsteps may be heard from the grey and grim old stone fronts of silent palaces in the capital of the mediæval feudal Duchy. But there is bustle and traffic in the shop-lined streets of the residence-town of the Papal Delegation.

Camerino is in point of fact the elder of the two cities by many centuries—by so many that the number of them cannot be counted. For it was a city and a capital when Rome was young; and none can say for how long before that epoch; while Macerata arose from and after the destruction of the ancient city of Recina by Alaric in the fifth century, according to some opinions, or by Teia, the last King of the Goths in the sixth century, according to others. But this difference in age can produce no sensible effect save on the imagination. For assuredly the old-world character of Camerino arises from features implanted in it long subsequently to the foundation of Macerata in the fifth or sixth century. The marked difference therefore in the aspect of the two cities in this respect must be attributed to some other circumstances of difference in their histories. And here we are led again to a consideration of the different social results produced on the communities of the Middle Ages by the government of the Church, and that of the old "tyrant" families, who ruled in most of them. Macerata seems at no period to have been subjected to any family of native lords. Always Guelph in its tendencies and politics, it remained faithful to the Popes, as long as it could do so without bringing itself into trouble. During the contest between the Church and the Empire indeed Macerata would seem to have been a veritable Vicar of Bray in its politics, if not in its affections. These seem to have been always with the Popes. But the first show of force on the part of the Imperialists always sufficed to induce the Maceratese to bring their keys in humblest fashion to the feet of the Imperial representative, and shout for long life to whatever Cæsar happened to wear the Imperial purple on his shoulders.

It might seem that a consistent course of such worldly wisdóm should have secured a condition of wealth and prosperity to the prudent city. And the fact is that at the present day it possesses far more of these than Camerino. But it is remarkable that the signs of mediæval magnificence which are so striking in the latter city are not to be seen in the former. And as a corollary fact, Macerata possesses a far less interesting and eventful history than Camerino, with its lineage of ferócious lords and saintly ladies. Perhaps the reader who has the story of the two towns before him, will be led to remember the axiom, which declares, that the happiest communities are those which leave the least for history to tell. There can be no doubt that at the present day the old Papal city is a more thriving and prosperous place than the ancient capital of the Varani. But this is in all probability due simply to the greater fertility of the surrounding district, the somewhat softer climate, and more accessible position.

Perhaps the most pleasing external feature of Macerata, and that most calculated to strike a stranger, is the magnificent terrace-road which runs round the base of the walls on their outer side for a considerable portion of their circuit. The walls themselves, though of brick instead of stone, are so overgrown by a variety of wild plants as to be objects of exceeding beauty, and invaluable studies of colouring to a landscape painter. Then the view over the surrounding country is as varied as it is charming. Throughout all this district the most remarkable peculiarity of the scenery consists in the extraordinary number of towns,—cities, very many of them,—which crown almost every pre-eminent hill-top, and of which some half a score may be seen from the walls' of each one of their neighbours. At least this number may be counted from different parts of the terrace-drive around the walls of Macerata, several of them ancient cities of renown, with each its independent history of its own; and all testifying to the exuberant richness of the country, and assisting in the composition of a landscape of extreme interest and beauty.

No rulers of mankind in any age or part of the world, have better understood or more consistently practised the maxim "*Divide et impera,*" than those who have successively held power in Italy. And the result has been, that during all ages of its history, till this last one, when a long experience of the suffering entailed by division seems at length to have inspired the Italians with an overruling passion for unity, no nation on the face of the earth has ever been so "divided against itself" as Italy. In the old days, as all the world knows, internecine wars between city and city, often between village and village, were unceasing. No people ever were such "good haters,"—to use the Johnsonian phrase,—as the Italians. It was an implicitly received part of every man's creed, that all the inhabitants of the opposite side of the river,—of the townlet on the mountain above his own, or that in the valley below it,—of the rival city on the opposite hill, whose walls were visible from his own, were absolutely and necessarily odious and contemptible, and "our natural enemies." And when the less rude and more law-abiding ages came, when it was no longer possible for neighbouring cities to wage active war with each other, the old hatreds, vigorous and inveterate as ever, often took a more amusing and less harmful mode of showing themselves. When blood could no longer be shed, ink might be used as a means of deadly hostility. And the quantity of it, that has been shed in such quarrels in Italy is astounding.

Some patriot, most probably a member of some Academy, with an extraordinary name, himself bearing also an academic nick-name, as for instance, "Corydon" of the "Inflammable Shepherds," or "*Il Stolido*" (for such uncomplimentary soubriquets were sometimes adopted) of the "Unutterable ones," writes a quarto, of perhaps some twenty pages only, to prove that the rival city over the way there, on the opposite slope of the valley, was not, as its inhabitants vainly boast, a Roman colony, and that its Bishop was in the fourth century subject *in spiritualibus* to our bishop. Instantly some champion on the other side fulminates a reply; and some other patriot of the attacked community comes out with a treatise, questioning whether the miracles attributed to Saint Somebody, the "protector" of the hated city, were not in fact performed by quite a different namesake of his? And quarrels of this sort, kept up for years by men who had nothing else on earth to do in the utter stagnation of provincial Italian society in the seventeenth and eighteenth centuries, were carried on with a degree of bitterness and real hostility, which it would seem impossible that such differences could engender.

A contest of this kind arose in 1777 between Macerata and Camerino, which raged for several years, and has left a literature which gives an amusing notion of these learned tournaments. In the year named, Pius the Sixth promoted to the Cardinalate a certain Guglielmo de' Pallotta, who happened to be born in Macerata, but who was, by inscription of his family in the lists of the Camertine nobility, a citizen of Camerino. Thereupon a Camerino poet composes a cantata to be sung by four voices in the theatre at Camerino, with the following title :—" Religion Comforted ;" a "Dramatic composition to be sung in the theatre at Camerino, to celebrate the exaltation to the purple of the most Eminent and most Reverend Prince Cardinal Guglielmo Pallotta, Patrician and Joint-protector* of the said city."

Now in this poem, the river Chienti addressing Religion tells her that he comes from the "*Camerti lidi,*" for the express purpose of offering her

"*Un raro spirito egregio,*
"*Ch' oggi s' adorna di purpureo fregio ;*"

a gift, the river-god goes on to remark, which "invidious *Elvia*" begrudges ;

"*Quell' Elvia stessa, che ne' di vetusti*
"*Della Camerte donna*
"*Baciar lo scettro, e il sacro fren dovea ;*

"that same Elvia, who in ancient days was obliged to kiss the sceptre and the sacred curb of the Camertine lady."

Now Recina, from the ruins of which Macerata arose, was called Elia, or Elvia Recina, from the Emperor Elius Pertinax; and therefore Elvia meant Macerata. And bitterly was the insult in the above quotation felt and resented at Macerata ;—especially as a long note on the offensive passage explained its

* "Comprotettore." He could not be Protettore, seeing that Saint Arsinus already held that dignity. This term "Comprotettore" was an invention constantly used for purposes of adulation.

meaning by maintaining that once on a time the Bishop of Macerata had been subject to the spiritual supremacy of him of Camerino.

All Macerata was up in arms—or at least in pen and ink—to repel this insult. The most galling of these replies seems to have been one by an "*eruditissimo Cavaliere Antonio Lazzarini*," which ran through three editions, and called forth a host of counter-attacks from the champions of Camerino. The title of one of these, for example, is "*Il Cavalier Maceratese frustrato dal Bidello del Università di Camerino.*"—The Cavalier of Macerata whipped by the Beadle of the University of Camerino. The contents of some of these publications seems to have been such as to have made it necessary or at least decorous to veil their real origin under title-pages, with such dates as—"In Calcutta. xv Decembre. MDCCLXXII. per Meer Jaffier, Stampatore della Compania Inglese di Bengala." Another is dated "Cosmopoli."

Of course, as might be expected, the original point in dispute became enlarged, as the battle raged and fresh champions entered the lists, to a vast number of other matters connected with the history and antiquities of either city. Macerata being unable to pretend to any higher antiquity, prided itself much on being the heir and representative of the ancient Recina. And it was the unkindest cut of all, when one of the Camerino champions wrote as follows:—
"The men of Macerata, eight centuries after Recina was destroyed and levelled with the ground, and when it was impossible to indicate with certainty the site on which it stood, dreamed in their Pythagorean

delirium that they arose from the ruins of that city." And another maintained that it was "by no means so certain, as the Macerata people would have it believed, that Recina was situated in their territory at all!"

This was very hard to bear; and called forth a flood of erudition on the subject of the whereabouts of the Roman city, which proved abundantly, if nothing else, that any attempt to indicate its precise locality is but conjectural. This however only rendered the contest fiercer and more interesting. And it was carried on with an amount of real hostile feeling that seems scarcely credible, till towards the end of the century, when events and interests of more real importance began to occupy men's minds.

The genuine bitterness of animosity generated by this controversy, which I have mentioned as a sample of many similar literary tournaments, and as a curious illlustration of the mode in which the educated society of these provincial cities strove to find some relief from the leaden dullness and stagnation of their lives, is curiously shown by a MS. note in the handwriting of that Cavaliere Lazzarini abovementioned, written on a title-page of a treatise "*Dell' Antica Città di Recina, Dissertazione di Domenico Troili Macerata*, 1790," in my possession. Under the name of the author, the Macerata partizan adds "Ex-Jesuit, who in order to defend and maintain the malignant impostures vomited forth by his colleague the Ex-Jesuit Zaccaria, in the controversy between Macerata and Camerino, which arose in 1777, has chosen to trample on the laws of integrity, of truth, and of sound criticism, and of citizenship, ignorantly obscuring the memorials of Recina, and of Macerata his native country, with his conglomeration of lies, sophisms, and paradoxes, rather than leave his friend exposed to the blame of the learned."

*Tantæne animis* academicis *iræ!*

As regards the reality of the descent of Macerata, it is to be observed that another neighbouring city a few miles to the northward, Recanati, claims the same heritage. And another erudite Jesuite—the Padre Diego Calcagni, in his very rare folio volume of "*Memorie Istoriche della Città di Recanati,*" printed at Messina in the year 1711, brings a great many authorities to support the claims of that city; among whom however one impartial writer, Raphael of Volterra, declares that the inhabitants of the destroyed city built Recanati *and* Macerata.

The name of Recanati seems to furnish strong evidence in favour of its claim to be the veritable heir and descendant of Recina; the name of which, however, is, though all the above-mentioned authors so write it, more correctly written " Ricina ;" and was in all probability derived, not as the older writers are inclined to believe, from a king Cinus, "who reigned in these parts four centuries after the deluge," but from a temple to Venus Erycina.

For those who may take any interest in the question at issue, a work, written at a period when something more of the principles of historical investigation had begun to be understood, and entitled "*Plinio Seniore illustrato nella descrizione del Picino,*" by Fr. Antonio Brandimarte, printed in 1 vol. 4to, at Rome, in 1815, will be more to the purpose. And I am afraid that they will there find cause to believe that Macerata can claim no antiquity higher than that of the twelfth century.*

A few walks through the streets of Macerata sufficed to show that there also, as in so many other similar places, absenteeism, and the tendency of society to gather itself together, as far as each individual's means permit, into masses in the great capitals, is rife among the class of local nobility, which had once the reputation of forming one of the best provincial social circles in Italy. We observed a great number of palaces of much architectural pretension, and many of them of such vast size, as to make it a matter of wondering speculation what purposes of accommodation or splendour such immense masses of building, containing evidently suites of magnificent apartments, capable of receiving guests by the thousand, could have served. But almost all, if not every one of these were shut up, the owners absent, inhabiting, probably, a furnished lodging in Rome, Florence, or, mayhap, Paris!

These handsome buildings are all of brick, and evidently of a later period than the more dilapidated, but not so entirely deserted, stone-built palaces, which still give a character to the streets of Camerino. The brick used is of a very fine quality, very white, and ground to a fine surface for those parts of the building which meet the eye. It struck me however that the effect was far poorer than that of our deep-red coloured brick in buildings of the seventeenth century.

* "Plinio illustrato," p. 83.

About a mile out of the city there is a celebrated church dedicated to "La Madonna delle Vergini," built by Bramante. It is therefore very fine; and everybody with any pretension to taste must admire it very much. My own private opinion is, that it would be difficult to imagine a more repulsively cold, nude, and characterless building; a Greek cross with a white cupola in the middle, all pilasters, plaster, whitewash, gilded altars, and windows *alla* Little Zion tabernacle. The Madonna who lives there is a wholesale miracle-worker; and innumerable little pictures, daubed in colours, of the wonders she has done, are hung up as votive tablets. The inhabitants of the district seem to have an inveterate habit of tumbling, always head foremost, out of fruit-trees. And the Madonna always saves them from getting anything worse than a good bruising. But she never keeps them from tumbling; or if she does, she gets no thanks for it.

No stranger will be likely to leave Macerata without having his attention called to the amphitheatre which has been built there just outside the city-wall for the accommodation of the players at the favourite game of *Pallone*.* Should he fail, which is almost impossible, to observe the huge, hideous building himself, his attention will infallibly be called to it by any Maceratese with whom he may come in contact. And his wonder as to the purpose for which such an edifice could have been raised, in the case of his discovering it for himself, will not be greater than his astonishment when he has been informed of the

* "Pallone" means a great ball; as does the analagously-formed word "balloon."

object of it. It is an enormous building of white brick, consisting of a vast semicircular range of "*loggie*," or boxes, each with its private room behind it, an equally vast range of open brick benches, tier above tier, and a colossal wall forming the chord of the arc, and thus enclosing a wide open space.

Other cities of Italy are fond of the popular game of "*Pallone:*" and many of them have some appointed place, with more or less of preparation and convenience for the sport, an open space level and free from herbage being all that is absolutely needed for the purpose. But one would suppose to look at the temple here provided for the game, that the one great object of life at Macerata was to play, or see others play, at *Pallone*. The population of the city is somewhat less than eleven thousand; but the accommodation here provided for spectators is capable of receiving a very much larger number, and that with a degree of luxury as regards the boxes, which no other theatre in Italy, or I suppose in Europe, can boast; for every box in the huge circle has its own withdrawing-room behind it! And it is very evident that real practical ball-play, and the looking on at it, has been the sole object of the builders, and no vain notion of raising an edifice that should be in itself beautiful or ornamental to the city. No illusion has been permitted on this point. The mere vastness of the building, ugly as it is in its material and all its details, would have produced a fine effect in the architect's spite, if the form had been either a perfect half-circle, or a perfect ellipse. But it is neither. It is a half oval, with the two ends cut short off;—a very deformity of figure. I ventured to observe to the gentleman who conducted me thither, and who in truth seemed, I thought, by no means proud of this manifestation of his city's energy, that the building could hardly have been raised as a speculation. Oh dear, no! The prices of entrance, on the rare occasions when it was opened, did not nearly pay the expense of keeping it in repair! And indeed it was visible enough that as little as possible was expended on this score. And the grass was growing thickly in the area. Its vast size however was not useless, he said. For occasionally strolling performers of some sort, rope-dancers, jugglers, or others such would come to Macerata, and hire the amphitheatre for their performances; and then all the people from the country round would come in, and fill the benches. If so, I should think that a visit to Macerata must assure prosperity and plenty to any such troop of wandering Bohemians for a twelvemonth!

If interesting in no other point of view, it must be admitted that the Macerata ball-court is a very curious monument of provincial pride and ambition.

Macerata is at present a thriving town;—doubtless, if Ancona be excluded, the most so of any within the district still known as "Piceno." But I should be inclined to fear that the future has only a destiny of decadence in store for it. Railways *will* draw the centres of population to their sides. And no railway can ever visit Macerata. Nor is it sufficiently near to either of the great valleys which run, that of the Potenza to the north of it, and that of the Chienti to the south, for it to struggle down the slope from its hill-top, and reach out a long arm, as it were—as so many other towns have done—to put itself in communication with the life-stream which henceforward will only flow in iron arteries.

## CHAPTER XII.

ROUTE FROM MACERATA TO FERMO—MONTOLMO—PAUSULÆ—DIF-
FICULTY OF ASSIGNING LOCALITIES TO THE NAMES OF DESTROYED
CITIES—ANCIENT PICENIAN CITIES BUILT IN THE PLAIN—ST.
GIUSTO—CURIOUS TREATY BETWEEN A NUMBER OF PICENIAN
CITIES—MONTE GRANARO—ST. ELPIDIO—LETE MORTA—TURN-
PIKES *v*. NON-TURNPIKES—DIFFICULTY OF DISTINGUISHING
THESE HILL-TOWNS FROM EACH OTHER—LONG ASCENT TO FERMO
—THE STREETS OF THE CITY—THE APPEARANCE OF IT FROM
WITHOUT THE WALLS—DALMATIA VISIBLE FROM FERMO—SITUA-
TION OF THE CATHEDRAL.

FROM Macerata the plan of our journey took us southwards to the archiepiscopal city of Fermo, a distance of some six and twenty miles.

It is extremely difficult to state the distances in this part of Italy with any precision; for no two persons of whom information on the subject may be asked, agree in their replies; and rarely do any of them profess to answer your questions with any accuracy;—always with the exception of your driver, whose arithmetic however generally fails to support the positive nature of his assertions; the half-way house in a stage of thirty miles, for instance, being often found to stand at a distance of twelve miles from one and thirteen miles from the other terminus of the journey.

The journey to Fermo is an interesting, although not a particularly beautiful one. It is interesting from the number of interesting objects which stud the landscape in every direction. The vast number of towns of more or less pretension and importance which, all of them built on conspicuous hill-tops, form a succession of landmarks, constantly changing in their bearing in regard to the traveller and each other, has already been mentioned as a peculiarity strikingly characterizing this district. And the strangely winding road to Fermo keeps the traveller's attention on the alert by constantly exhibiting to him a variety of these in such different aspects that it becomes a puzzling and amusing task to learn to recognize each, as during the progress of the journey it becomes an old acquaintance.

After descending the hill from Macerata into the valley of the Chienti, the road to Fermo follows it for a while along the great Flaminian way, then crosses, by an immensely long wooden bridge a quantity of water, about as large when we saw it as that which flows through the Paddington Canal, but which perversely chooses to change its bed every year or so. After that the road forthwith commences to climb the hills, among and over which it has thenceforth to make its way to Fermo, with no further assistance from any valley or river-course to help it. Thence it arises that this little journey brings so large a number of the neighbouring towns under the stranger's observation.

Immediately on starting, and before leaving the

valley of the Chienti, the traveller passes beneath the finely situated town of Montolmo, with which he has already become acquainted as one of the most prominent objects of the landscape seen from the walls of Macerata. It crowns the crest of a lofty hill on the southern side of the valley of the Chienti, across which it is seen from Macerata, so that the road by which we were travelling, passing first below it along the valley to the north of it, and then, after turning southwards over the neighbouring hills to the eastward of it, took us nearly round the hill on which it stands. The valley of the little river Cremone, which falls into the Chienti a little below the spot where the road crosses and leaves the latter, isolates the hill of Montolmo on its southern side, and makes the position rather a strong one.

The principal interest attaching to this picturesquely situated little town arises from the long disputed question, whether it occupies or no the site of the ancient Pausulæ;—for such, and not Pausula, as it is written in the Austrian Ordnance map—is the correct reading of the word. A large array of learned names, including, among several others less known on the northern side of the Alps, those of Cellario, Muratori, and D'Anville, may be cited in favour of the affirmative. But others have supposed that the site of the ancient Pausulæ was in the valley of the Chienti, on the north side of the river, at a spot now marked by a little hamlet called St. Claudio, about half-way between Macerata and the place where the road crosses the river. "Traces of *bassi rilievi*, of coins, of bronzes, of gems, all of them relics, which indicate that a rich city there lies buried," have been found, says Brandimarte,* in the fields around St. Claudio. Camillo Lilli declares that in his time the vestiges of an ancient city, traces of walls, pavements, encrusted marbles, inscriptions and other such-like things were found in this spot; and it would seem certain that this plain of St. Claudio was in truth the site of a destroyed Roman city. But it does not follow that that city was Pausulæ. For there are so many ancient cities known to have existed in this district, to which it is now extremely difficult to assign a position with any certainty, that it may well have been that Pausulæ occupied the site of the present town of Montolmo, according to the opinion of almost all the older writers; and that some other,—Plenina, perhaps, another ancient city to which it is difficult to assign a local habitation, stood where St. Claudio now stands. Brandimarte remarks, in favour of the theory, which would make the latter the true locality of Pausulæ, that in such case that city was situated in a plain, " as were pretty well all the cities of the ancient Picenum ;"—a curious indication of the difference in the state of the country, and the different objects of the inhabitants in the centuries inmediately preceding and those immediately following the irruption of the barbarians. It is curious moreover that the practice of the ancient inhabitants of this district should have been exactly the reverse in this respect of the habits of the Etruscans, who beyond all doubt almost invariably placed their cities on the hill-tops. It is clear that Pausulæ was not destroyed in the year 465 ; and further that it had at that time re-

* Op. cit., p 75.

ceived Christianity, and was a Bishop's See ; for
Claudio, Bishop of Pausulæ, subscribed the acts of
the Roman Council held under the pontificate of Pope
Ilario (Hilary) in that year.*

Lanzi, the well-known historian of Italian art, who
was a native of Montolmo, wrote a dissertation on
Patisulæ, which was printed at Florence in the year
1792. Colucci has also treated of the subject at
length in the fifteenth volume of his *Antichità
Picene*.

After leaving the river, the road ascends almost
continually for several miles, till it reaches St. Giusto,
a little walled town perched on a naked hill-top, which
must be swept by every blast from the "unquiet"
Adriatic. The road passes close beneath the fine old
walls of the little town, but does not enter it. *I* did
however, having reached the top of the hill long
before the carriage; and was surprised at finding,
even in this remote and inaccessible little fortress-
town, handsome stone-built palaces, which must at
one time have been inhabited by the families of resi-
dent nobles. Truly home was home in the olden
time. The owners of the soil were hardly less
"*adscripti glebæ*" than the cultivators of it; and
each territorial "Dominus" preferred to live where
he was best known and valued at the highest estimate. There must have been men, even within the
last couple of centuries, who thought it better to rule
in St. Giusto than serve in Rome.

But to look back a few centuries further, to the
time when the still solid walls of these little highland

---

* Brandimarte. Op. cit., p. 76.

towns were built, it is curious to reflect, that even these were independent communities, self-governed, and making war and peace, and signing treaties with each other as well as their betters. There is a very curious document extant in the archives of several of the cities of this part of Italy, which has been printed by several of the local historians,* and which gives a vivid idea of the "comminuted fracture" which the social system of these countries had been exposed to, and of the great progress towards resolving society into its primitive elements which the darkest centuries had achieved.

The document in question bears date 1202 or 1203, (for historians give it differently), and is a treaty of peace between a great number of these independent States of the dimensions of parishes. The towns of Fermo, Torre di Palma, Poggio St. Giuliano, Morro Valle (which may be seen on the other side of the Chienti valley from St. Giusto), Monte Lupone, Monte Santo, Monte Granaro (also in sight from the same point, and passed by the road a few miles further on), St. Giusto, Osimo, and Jesi made war against Ancona, St. Elpidio (also in sight from St. Giusto), Civitanuova (also in sight), Montolmo (also within sight), Recanati, Castel-Fidardo, Camerino, Monte Fano, Sinigaglia, and Pesaro. And by the instrument in question they all "*juramus et promictimus omnem finem et perpetuam pacem inter nos de omnibus offensis, et rapinis, maltoltis, furtis, in-*

* By Saraceni in his "Memoirs of Ancona;" by Amiani in his "History of Fano;" by Martorelli in his "History of Osimo;" by Baldassinio in his "Memoirs of Jesi;" by Marangoni in his "History of Civitanova."—*See* Brandimarte. Op. Cit., p. 117.

*cendiis, homicidiis, vulnerationibus, captionibus, quæ sunt vel fuerunt invicem commissa."* It is curious to observe, as may be seen at once by a glance at the map, that this war was by no means one of district against district. St. Giusto is in league with the comparatively distant towns of Osimo and Jesi, and at war with St. Elpidio and Montolmo, one on each side of her, and into either of which she could almost, as the phrase is, throw a biscuit. It is puzzling to imagine what the principle could have been, and of what sort the motives, on which such friendships and hostilities were formed. It would seem as if feelings much akin to what we should now call individual pique between man and man, must have led to such enmities. And it is terrible to think what the state of things must have been, when three or four towns, on as many neighbouring hills, separated only by small mountain streams from each other, were all busily exerting their utmost energy to commit "offences, rapines, *maltolta* (which I suppose means the same thing),* burnings, homicides, vulnerations, and captions" on one another!

The road continues after leaving St. Giusto, and passing beneath the walls of Monte Granaro, a still smaller and more inaccessibly rock-perched town than St. Giusto, to wind over a region of rather bleak hills, bringing into view at every crest some one or more newly-discovered town on its eminence. St. Elpidio, also the site, as all the antiquaries agree,

* *Maltolta, Tolta mala, Malatolta, Mantota, Malatosta, Malatoxa; Malum vel indebitum tributum; pecunia a subditis injuste et vi et male ablata sub specie telonei aut vectigalis.*—Ducange. Gloss.

of an ancient Roman city, though some believe it to represent Cluentum, and some Novana, remains in sight during a considerable part of the journey, and is also a landmark visible far out in the Adriatic.

Then the road commences a long descent, which, ending in a very steep, and not very well managed zigzag, dips down into the valley of a little stream, with the strange and melancholy name of the Dead Lethe, *Lete Morta*. This Dead Lethe seemed dead and sluggish enough to do justice to its name, when we reached it. But the fragments of a broken bridge were there to testify that Lethe could upon occasions be roused to life, and sufficiently dangerous in its liveliness. It seemed to have been long since the bridge was broken; and there were some small signs of a feeble attempt to construct a new one having been commenced. But as matters were, there was the Lethean stream before us, black and sullen looking enough; and there was no alternative, if we would reach the further bank, to dipping at least our steeds and chariot-wheels in its flood. In we went; and had barely reached the middle when we began to fear that the dread qualities of the stream had produced their well-known effect on the animals, who were now standing up to their girths in its dark waters. For they came to a dreamy, puzzled standstill, and appeared totally oblivious of the necessity of making an effort to reach the stable and food awaiting them at Fermo. They insisted on taking a long drink, too, of the torpefying water, and there we sat in the midst of dull Lethe, beginning to think that we should be obliged to try the effect of its water on our own persons. Our driver meanwhile was preparing to try the effect of a sudden shock, sometimes known to be efficacious, on the nervous systems of his cattle. Abandoning his first attempts to urge them forwards, he remained quite quiet for a while; and then noiselessly rising to his feet and raising his heavy whip high in the air, he suddenly brought down a tremendous lash across the loins of both his nags. Not even "Lethe's dull wave" could neutralize the effect of such vigorous treatment. With a plunge the two stout horses started to their collars, and after a rather tough struggle dragged us up the opposite bank. We had at starting that morning remonstrated against the necessity of having two powerful horses put to a light open carriage laden with only two passengers and two small portmanteaus. We had been assured that we should find them needed. And now our triumphant charioteer, turning on his seat, as we gained the top of the steep and soft bank, asked us where we should have been if we had had but one horse to pull us out of the Lethe!

I was reading somewhere the other day, some magazine or newspaper article contrasting our turnpike system with that continental administration of the roads, which knows no such barriers; and putting the matter in a point of view wholly favourable to the latter. And I could not help remembering our Lethean adventure, as I read; and thinking that the utmost amount of turnpike money ever paid over six and twenty miles of road would have made but a small portion of the expense caused by the necessity of hiring a second horse for that distance, owing to the non-repair of a bridge. And all continental travellers on any save the greatest of the great roads, can bear witness to the frequent recurrence of the same combination of circumstances.

When we emerged from the ravine of the river, there was Fermo on the top of a very high hill in front to the left of us.

" There is Fermo ! "

" No ! that is only a different view of St. Elpidio ! "

" Not a bit of it ! St. Elpidio must be more behind us. There it is ! "

" No ! no ! that is St. Giusto ! You may know it by that long bit of unbroken grey wall, which the sun is now shining full on; and by the neighbourhood of Monte Granaro close to it."

" Where is St. Elpidio, then ? "

" Hidden behind that hill close on the left, with Monturano on the top of it."

" That must be Fermo, then, in front. Besides, we have not seen all day any town with so remarkably shaped and angular a mass, rising sharp and well defined over all the rest of the buildings. That topmost square-looking mass of building must be a fort, and an extraordinarily fine position for one too ! "

" I suppose that it must be Fermo ! But we have been dodging about so all the morning among a morris-dance of towns, all situated much alike, and all changing their aspects so entirely as you see them from one side or another, that there is no remembering their relative positions, or feeling sure which is which."

This is a specimen of the talk, which had occurred between me and my companion again and again that morning with reference to the bearings of the numerous hill-towns and villages around us. A reference to the driver however, who at the commencement of the hill had dismounted, and hitching his rein to the rail of his box had left his horses to their own discretion, while he loitered behind to gossip with a woman standing at the door of a roadside cottage, and who had now returned to his duties, set the question at rest; and assured us that the town on the high hill before us,—the highest of all the towns we had seen in the course of that morning's journey,—was indeed the city of Fermo; and that the remarkable building which crowned the square-looking rocky lump which formed the apex of the hill, was, not a castle, but the Cathedral.

We had had sufficient experience, it might be thought, since the commencement of the present journey, of the ascents to these Umbrian and Picenian mountain towns, to have learned to moderate our expectations in regard to the amount of time and labour required to reach them, after arriving at the bases of the hills on which they stand. But all previous experiences of interminability were exceeded by the interminableness of the ascent to Fermo. The altitude is really considerable, —1116 Parisian feet above the level of the sea, which must be very nearly the same thing as the level of that dead Lethe stream, from which we had to climb to the city. But again and again the road seemed to approach the place, only to start off anew for a fresh huge circuit in a totally different direction. Up to the last we were quite at a loss to conjecture on which side of the city we should finally effect an entrance; and when at length we were absolutely within an hundred paces of one of the gates of the town, our driver turned away from it to follow a road running at the foot of the wall till he reached a different gate on another side of the hill. Our subsequent knowledge of the city abundantly satisfied us of the judiciousness of this course. For we very soon found that the streets of Fermo are not such as to be traversed by wheeled vehicles unnecesarily,—many of them being so steep as to make wheel traffic wholly out of the question.

The circuitous nature of the ascent had at all events brought with it the advantage of showing us the position and aspect of the city from almost every quarter of the compass. And it must be admitted to be a very fine one. Not above three miles from the coast—less probably in a direct line,—it looks over an immense sweep of the Adriatic, and itself serves as a landmark far away out towards the opposite coast of Dalmatia. An old writer in counting up the number of dioceses, part of which may be seen from the top of the hill of Fermo, reckons two in Dalmatia! And I have no doubt that on a propitious day the outline of the Dalmatian mountains may be descried from this vantage ground. For myself I must admit that I could not see them, for the same reason which accounted satisfactorily for the invisibility of the "Spanish Fleet." But then the weather during our stay at Fermo was not clear.

The landward view is a very fine one, comprehending, as may be understood from what has already been said, an extraordinary number of towns and townlets on the tops of the surrounding but somewhat lower hills. The appearance of the city itself from the outside is particularly picturesque, partly from the imposing masses, and varied weather-stained tints of the venerable old stone walls, and partly from the very remarkable position of the Cathedral, raised on its precipitous sided rock clear above all the other buildings of the town.

## CHAPTER XIII.

IMPRESSIONS OF FERMO—THE PICTURESQUE *v.* THE PROSPEROUS—DETERIORATED ASPECT OF THE COUNTRY—WEALTH OF THE CHURCH AT FERMO—ITS PROPORTION TO THAT OF THE COUNTRY IN GENERAL—INN AT FERMO—A BRIGAND HOST AND HOSTESS—CLEAN SHEETS AND GARLIC—ARCHITECTURAL FEATURES OF THE CITY—THE CATHEDRAL, AND THE "GIRONE."—FORMER MILITARY IMPORTANCE OF THE SPOT— TYRANTS IN FERMO—DESTRUCTION OF THE CASTLE—TUBA DA IMOLA—THE EUFFREDUCCI FAMILY—OLIVEROTTO EUFFREDUCCI —HIS STORY, AS MORALIZED BY MACCHIAVELLI—LUDOVICO EUFFREDUCCI—HIS DEATH SCENE—PAPAL RULE IN FERMO— THE THREE MARTYRS OF FERMO—A STORY OF PAPAL JUSTICE.

THE first impression on entering the city of Fermo is one of surprised disappointment. The expectations produced by the imposing, finely-situated and picturesque exterior, have been too favourable. The grand outside of the place is found to have been imposing in more senses than one; and the stranger is reminded for the ten thousandth time that picturesqueness and prosperous civilization do not go hand in hand.

The questions, why they do not? and whether the fact that they do not arise from the fault of the prosperous civilization, or from that of the searcher for the picturesque, would lead to the discussion of a curious and important chapter of æsthetics, far too large and wide-branching to be entered on here. The interior of Fermo so far keeps the promise of its exterior as to be by no means wanting in the elements of the picturesque; but it is not a pleasing city to the eyes of those who have other and less "æsthetic" requirements.

Already in passing through the district around Fermo we had remarked a deterioration in the indications of the social status of the population, as compared with that of the country we had been hitherto traversing. The cultivation of the fields was more slovenly, and the habitations of the cultivators worse and more sordid. We saw indeed several cottages scarcely better than those of a Buckinghamshire labourer!—a degree of misery of which Italy northward of the latitude in which we now were has few examples. And the interior of the city of Fermo, the capital of this district, seemed to bear the same relation to the cities we had been visiting, as its environs did to theirs.

But social arrangements, like those of Nature, have always their compensations. And there is one direction, in which a prospect of prosperity may be enjoyed at Fermo, which would doubtless be found on enlightened examination to be, as Nature's compensations are, strictly and accurately correlative to the depression and poverty which broods visibly over all the social system, with the exception of this favoured fleece of Gideon. The Church is prosperous at Fermo. If a poor city, it is a rich See. It is, indeed, I believe, the richest piece of preferment which the Holy Father has to bestow on the best deserving of his episcopal sons. And I find in a statistical return made to Pius the Ninth in 1846, and printed, it is to be understood, not for the peering of profane eyes,—though mine have chanced to obtain a peep at it,—but solely for the use of the various administrative departments of the Papal Government, a list of the ten largest owners of property in the delegation of Fermo, in which the first is the Cathedral Chapter, whose possessions are set down at the yearly value of 63,003 scudi and 26 bajocchi; and the second, the Archbishop, who figures for 54,557 scudi and 71 bajocchi! the first sum being equivalent to about £14,424; and the second to about £11,610. The total estimated yearly value in the delegation is only 3,606,757 scudi; and of the possessors of this, 10272 in number, 9529 stand for sums below a thousand crowns; and 6046 of these for sums below one hundred crowns. Truly, however dry the surrounding soil may be, the dew *has* descended on the fleece of Gideon and might be "wrung out, a bowl full of water." Perhaps it *may be wrung out* one of these days.

A traveller with the least tinge of romantic imagination about him, and duly up in the well-known scenic properties of Apennine adventure,—who knows at a glance the genuine slouched sugar-loaf brigand hat, and the true significance of velveteen breeches unbuttoned at the knee, would give himself up for lost on finding himself inside the low-browed cavernous arched doorway of the Fermo house of accommodation. Already his misgivings would have been aroused by the way to it, and the aspect of the street in which it is situated. We don't go down the black gulf, which yawns under Durham Street, Adelphi, to find the way to "Claridge's," or even to the "Golden Cross," Charing Cross. But even by comparison with the best parts of the city of Fermo, the way to the one inn there is hardly more re-assuring. A solitary bye-lane, dipping down from the main street with a descent so steep that it seems that the carriage must tumble over the horses' backs, and losing itself a few paces beyond the inn door in a confused chaos of dust and dung-heaps, under the wall of the city, which has no gate at that point, seems a strangely chosen position for an hotel, which assuredly no stranger could find if he were not led to it. And then the appearance of the people who receive you in the gloomy cavern-kitchen of that grim hostelry! Shade of Mrs. Radcliffe! If that landlord be not the captain of a band of brigands, and that hostess be not the brigand's lady-love, there is no faith to be put in cross-gartering, or in dishevelled black locks, piercing black eyes, and gay coloured head-kerchiefs.

The unimaginative traveller, on the other hand, who has strong cockney prepossessions in favour of the "first-pair front," will be indignant at being conducted to his chamber at the top of the house. He little dreams that he is being taken to the best rooms and the place of honour. The farther from the dirt and the odour and the noise of the stable, the street, and the kitchen, the better the accommodation! This is the principle, in obedience to which the piercing-eyed free-limbed brigand's-wife landlady urges you to climb stair after stair. See, the upper regions become somewhat more decently clean and orderly as we mount; and here in the passage of the third floor, which is quite wide enough for the purpose, is a sleek priest, doubtless come to Fermo from his country cure to see his Bishop, sitting at table at dinner, who bows smilingly to the new comers as they pass to their rooms. Things are not so very bad after all! And if only that brigand host can be induced to stay his hand when adding the garlic to the lambs-fry *frittata*, and the brigand's wife be coaxed into putting clean sheets on the beds, we shall do well enough!

Part of this prayer was heard; the other part the gods dispersed in air, according to classical precedent. The clean sheets were at once accorded; but Jove himself had not the power to wipe from the mind of that brigand cook the lessons learned from infancy upwards, that meat ungarlicked is not fit food for man.

The first impression, it has been said, of the interior of Fermo is disappointing and unpromising; and it may be added, that this first impression does not become changed on a further acquaintance, always with the exception of the one prominent feature of the Cathedral and the rock on which it stands. The city is rather a large one, stretching its main street for a considerable way along the steep crest of the hill, and lapping over the sides of this crest by secondary streets steeper still. There is scattered through the city plenty of old-world building, with its usual accompaniment of picturesque corners, and fragments pleasing to an artistic eye, both from their form and their colour. But all seems mean, and though not so much depopulated as some other cities of Pope's land, poverty stricken and dirt-stricken. The streets are narrow, tortuous, and shabby. And that central heart of the city, the site of the "*Palazzo pubblico,*" and the *piazza*, almost always so full of picturesque interest in old Italian cities, though not wholly devoid of this at Fermo, have nothing very striking about them.

At the further and higher end of the long winding main-street,—the further end, that is to say, from that at which the traveller will have entered the town, from whichever point of the compass he may arrive, the hill suddenly rises into a high rock-sided platform, large enough to contain the Cathedral and a small space before the west front of it,—about as large perhaps as Lincoln's Inn Fields,—planted as a garden, and called the "*Girone.*" And this spot, with the Cathedral and the promenade in front of it, is the glory of Fermo. The church, like the great majority of the cathedrals of the Papal States, has been modernized within to the destruction of all interest or beauty. It is well, when a similar fate has not befallen the exterior also. At Fermo the mediæval exterior with its fine grey stone colouring, and a great part of its original rich ornamentation of door and window remains. But it is the grandeur of the position which makes the charm of the place. He must be an enthusiastic lover of church architecture indeed, who on coming up the steep slope, which leads from the rest of the city to this high platform, does not turn first to the magnificent view of the sea and coast northwards and southwards before applying himself to the interesting details of the building.

To this remarkably situated rock was doubtless

due the first formation of a city around and beneath it. Fermo was not, as the best authorities among the antiquaries declare,* a city of the ante-Roman inhabitants; but had its first existence as a Roman colony. The strength of its situation however made it a place of mark in every subsequent age. And the Lombard Chronicler, Luitprand, records that Agiltrude deemed herself nowhere else in Umbria or Picenum, neither at Camerino or at Spoleto, so safe as in this stronghold of Fermo, where she stood a siege.

So entirely was the fortress, which once occupied this lofty isolated platform, recognized as the strongest place in all the Marches, and as able to give the law to the entire province, that there was an old proverb of the Middle Ages, which playing on the name of the city, declared that

"Quando Fermo vuol fermare,
Tutta la Marca fa tremare."

"When Fermo chooses to stand *firm*,
She makes all the Marches tremble."

No great family succeeded in subjecting Fermo to its tyranny for a sufficient length of time to form a dynasty. But the city was during the centuries which followed the tenth, at divers times subjected to the violence of a variety of lawless nobles;—a Gentile di Mogliano,—a Rioraldo di Monte Verde, —a Ludovico Migliorati,—an Oleggio Visconti,— sundry of the Euffreducci,—and lastly the more noted Alessandro Sforza. Grown wise at length by the experience of some centuries of similar evils, the citizens had the rare good sense in the year 1447 to destroy deliberately their own castle with their own

* Brandimarte. Op. cit. p. 41.

hands, in order that it might no longer serve as a temptation, and a means to usurping tyrants. No vestige of the fortress, once the most formidable in all the Marches, remains to encumber the magnificent esplanade, which formed the site of it; and which assuredly has given to the inhabitants more gratification in its present condition, than it could have done as a fortress.

There is a rather unusual but not unique feature in the construction of this church on the hill at Fermo, consisting of a sort of porch or *pronaos* at the west end, crossing the entire width of the nave and aisles, and so placed that the west front wall instead of giving access to the church, is but the side wall of this adjunct to the building, which is entered through it by a door in that part of the north side of the church, which is the north end of the porch.

In this otherwise entirely empty chamber there are a few interesting sepulchral monuments; one of a high order of artistic merit, to a member of the Visconti family, which is important in the history of art, from furnishing the sole record by which the name of the sculptor who executed it has been preserved to us. "*Tura da Imola fecit hoc opus,*" as we are informed by the Gothic letters of an inscription on the base of it. And had it not been for that curt piece of information, the name of Tura or Bonaventura da Imola would have been with those of the " brave before Agamemnon."

There is another monument there to one of the Euffreducci family, whose members play an important part in the mediæval annals of Fermo. But the most noteworthy memorial of that race is the tomb of

Ludovico Euffreducci, sculptured by Sansovino in 1530, which has been engraved in Litta's magnificent work, the "*Famiglie Celebre Italiane*," to illustrate his history of the Euffreducci family; and which may be seen in the Church of St Francesco.

These Euffreducci, though they never succeeded in establishing themselves for any length of time as recognized tyrants of Fermo, strove hard to play the same part there which the Varani played at Camerino, the Chiavelli at Fabriano, the Malatesta at Rimini, and so many others in other cities. The greater number of these communities are instances of the successful attempt to establish a sovereign house. At Tolentino we saw an example of the attempt nipped in the bud, and put down at once. At Fermo we have an example in which the struggle was a longer one. In both the two latter cases, the fact is that the attempt was made rather too late in the day, when the Papal temporal power had become too great. But the story of the Euffreducci has become famous chiefly from the circumstance of one, the most notable ruffian of the family, having been selected by Macchiavelli as a model tyrant, in that chapter of his extraordinary work, "*Il Principe*," which treats "Of those who have raised themselves to power by their atrocities."

Oliverotto Euffreducci was born in the last quarter of the fifteenth century, the scion of an ancient family, who, originally bandit territorial nobles, had in the fourteenth century been compelled by the burghers of Fermo to become citizens. This was quite according to ordinary course in a hundred similar cases. But it is a singularity to find this noble family raised to wealth and distinction mainly by the renown and professional gains of one of its members, who was one of the most celebrated physicians of his day, Tommaso Euffreducci, who died in 1403. His decendants became the most powerful family in Fermo; and his son, grandson, and great-grandson appear to have deserved and enjoyed the respect and esteem of their fellow citizens. But in the generation next to these the old instincts of the race seem to have cropped out anew. And Oliverotto, the great-great-grandson of the celebrated physician, became Macchiavelli's type of a Prince, who has become such by his successful crimes.

Oliverotto, left an orphan in his infancy, was brought up by his maternal uncle Giovanni Fogliani, who sent him to study the art of war under Paoli Vitelli, one of the greatest of the mercenary captains of that day. Under this teacher of the art he became a celebrated leader, and his master's close friend and ally. Paoli Vitelli however, having been hung by the Government of Florence for treason, Oliverotto for a short time joined his fortunes with Vitellozzo Vitelli, and then took service for a while with Cesare Borgia, under whom he was eminently successful, and increased his military experience and power. It was in the January of 1502 that, having thus earned the reputation of being one of the most successful soldiers of his day, he returned to visit his native city. Before doing so he wrote to his uncle Fogliani announcing his intention, and telling him "that, as he had toiled only for the sake of honour, and as he should wish that the citizens might see that he had not laboured in vain, he was desirous of making his entry creditably, accompanied by an hundred horsemen of his friends and followers,"* and begging his uncle to dispose the citizens to receive him with that retinue. All this Fogliani did, and received his nephew in his palace, where he was entertained with every sort of distinction.

Oliverotto spent two or three days in feeling his ground and maturing his plans; and then at one of the festivals given in his honour, to which all the leading citizens of Fermo were invited, his soldiers suddenly burst into the banqueting hall and slew Fogliani, his son, and several other of the principal citizens. No sooner was the deed done than, mounting his horse, he put himself at the head of his men, and rode off to the "*Palazzo pubblico*," where he obliged the magistrates, who were terrorstruck at what had happened, to proclaim him Lord of Fermo. "And," continues Macchiavelli, "having put to death all those whose discontent might have given him trouble,—a definition which included many other citizens, and several children, one of whom he himself poignarded in the arms of its mother, who was a cousin of his own;—he strengthened himself in the government by means of new civil and military dispositions, so that for the space of a year, during which he held power, he was not only safe in the city of Fermo, but was formidable to all his neighbours." And it would have been exceedingly difficult, as the political secretary goes on to point out, to oust him from his position, had he not suffered himself to

* Il Principe. Cap. 8.

P

be ensnared by that master-scoundrel Cesare Borgia; by whom he was put to death a year afterwards, together with so many others, at that famous Sinigaglia banquet which has been the subject of so many tragedies, and histories, and operas.

And the author of "The Prince" proceeds to moralize the tale of Oliverotto's master-stroke of traitorous murder in this wise: "If we seek to know," he says, "why some cruel tyrants have, like this man, successfully based their power on their cruelty, while others have by no greater cruelty irritated their subjects into successful resistance, we shall find the cause in the following distinction. The different results will be found to follow from cruelties, judiciously or injudiciously employed. They may be said to be judiciously employed, if it is permissible in any case to call evil good, (and here we may figure to ourselves the decorous Secretary of the Florentine Republic stopping to cross himself, as he turns up the white of his eyes with a compunctious sigh,) when they are perpetrated suddenly from the necessity of securing one's own safety, and are not followed up by others, but are changed for a course of government as useful as may be towards the subject. Cruelties injudiciously used are those, which, although they may be less in amount at the beginning, are increased rather than put a stop to, as time goes on. Those who use the first method, may by the assistance of God, and of men, find some means of stability for their government, as did Agathocles the Sicilian. But it is impossible for those, who act in the other way to maintain themselves. It is to be noted, therefore, that in seizing upon a government, it behoves the usurper to reckon up all those offences which it is necessary for him to commit, and to perpetrate them all at a blow, so that he may not have to commit fresh violences every day, but may be able, by avoiding the repetition of them, to give his subjects a sense of security, and to gain their affections by benefiting them. He who acts otherwise, either from timidity or ill counsel, is compelled to keep the knife always in his hand, and can never establish himself securely in his seat, seeing that his subjects by reason of his continued and fresh injuries against them can never trust him. For injuries should be done all of a heap, in order that little time being allowed for savouring them, they may the less give offence. Benefits ought to be conferred little by little; in order that the flavour of them may last the longer."

So Oliverotto, the bloody tyrant of Fermo, has left a name to other times branded with infamy by a hundred writers, but owing his noted place in the page of history mainly to the extraordinary moralization of his conduct in the above remarkable exposition of scientific state-craft by the immortal Florentine Secretary.

There was one other Euffreducci whose name occupies a prominent place in the annals of Fermo. This was Ludovico, the nephew of Oliverotto. He was very young at the time of his uncle's murder by Borgia on the 31st of December, 1502, and was saved from the fury of the citizens of Fermo by his mother, who escaped with him to Perugia, where she took refuge with her own family, the Baglioni. There the young scion of the Euffreducci was educated; and became, under the tuition of his warlike kinsmen, almost as noted a leader of free lances as his uncle Oliverotto. In 1514 he contrived to return to Fermo, where the people were inclined to let bygones be bygones, and received him well. For a time he seemed inclined to merit their good opinion, and to be content with being rather the first citizen in the free State than its master. He defended the territory of the city valorously and successfully against the Duke of Urbino, who was attacking it, acting under the orders of the magistrates like a good citizen. But though mostly successful, he met with a defeat at Chiaravalle; and this was the beginning of his ruin. For the Baglioni, his own relatives, taking advantage of the confusion produced in the city by the news of this defeat, fell on Fermo and sacked the city. Ludovico Euffreducci was absent, and these Baglioni were his near kinsmen. It was suspicious; and the heads of the Brancadoro* family, the principal rivals in wealth and greatness of the Euffreducci in the city actively spread the calumny, that the sacking of the city was in truth the work of Ludovico. Hence arose a mortal feud between him and the Brancadori. And the city as usual was ravaged by both parties. *"Plectuntur Achivi."* The heads of both factions were summoned by Leo the Tenth to Rome. Euffreducci set forth, but stopped by the way in a castle belonging to his friends the Orsini. Sallying forth hence he waylaid and murdered Bartolommeo Brancadoro, who was on his way to Rome. When the news of this assassi-

* This family is still extant; and I find the name fourth in that list of the richest proprietors which I quoted before, as having the Chapter and the Archbishop at the head of it.

nation reached Fermo, the magistrates in public council on the 3rd of February, 1520, declared Ludovico an outlaw and enemy of his country. From that moment he seems to have become desperate. He gathered round him a large body of desperadoes and malefactors of all sorts, and returning thus escorted into the neighbourhood of the city, seized the castle of St. Benedetto on the shore of the Adriatic; and fortifying himself there, prepared for a life in which his hand should be against every man, and every man's hand against him.

But, as has been already remarked, it was rather too late in the world for this sort of thing. Leo the Tenth despatched a certain fighting Bishop, one Niccolo Bonafede of Chiusi, to Fermo, with a large force of regular troops, and stringent orders to knock all disturbers of the public peace on the head at once, and especially Ludovico Euffreducci. That once honoured and successful general would not wait to be baited like a badger in his lair, but sallied forth with his hordes, and tried the fortunes of battle. But his bandits were no match for the Pope's soldiers. They were routed with much slaughter, and Ludovico, fighting to the last with the broken staff of his lance, was knocked on the head, as the Vicar of Christ had directed.

His death scene affords a curious and characteristic sixteenth-century picture, full of the anomalies and contrasts of that day.

The fighting Bishop, victorious at the head of his troops, who were busy in pursuing and killing the routed enemy, was riding over the battle field, when he came upon the wretched Ludovico felled from his horse and dying. With a dying sinner unshriven and unabsolved at his feet, the fighting Bishop felt that it was time to appear in his other character. The warrior's work was done; that of the priest was needed. And Nicholas of Chiusi was equal to either post. Quickly dismounting, and flinging from him his fighting gear in a trice, with a "*Benedicite*" in the place of word of command, and a rapid "*Paternoster*" substituted for shouted encouragement to his troops to smite and spare not, the Bishop was every inch a Bishop in a twinkling. He knelt by the side of the dying man, heard his confession, absolved him in the lump for all the sins incidental to such a life as his,—doubtless with more of fellow feeling than a clerk of more clerkly habits could have done,—and received his last breath.

Such was the end of the last of the Euffreducci; —or if not absolutely the last, the last with whom history has any concern.

Too late in the world's history, I have said, it was for such a career as that of Ludovico Euffreducci to have been successful. The power of the Holy See was becoming too well consolidated and too decent in its habits. Law-abiding times were at hand. Deeds of lawless violence could no more be permitted to deluge the streets of peaceful cities with blood. How beneficent a change! How absolutely essential to the progress of civilization and prosperity! And yet, as has been said, civilization and prosperity did not progress under the quiet and peaceful rule of the Popes.

Possibly some light may be thrown on this social problem by one other page from the annals of Fermo, which I am going to lay before the reader. The illustrations of the social condition of these districts in the days of

> "The good old rule, the simple plan,
> That they should take who have the power,
> And they should keep who can,"

which have been given, show a very terrible state of things, utterly intolerable, as they must seem, to our notions, and impossible to live under. Now our illustration of the social state, which has been produced by upwards of three centuries of priestly rule, shall be taken from a very recent epoch. Of course such horrors of lawless violence, injustice, and wrong-doing cannot be expected to take place under the government of a class of rulers, who must, however much we may deem them un-enlightened and old-world in their notions, be supposed to be mild, mercifulminded old men, prone rather to weak lenity towards offenders, than to excess on the side of severity.

Here follows then a bit of Fermo history of the year 1854, which the reader may compare as an illustration of the social condition of that city, with the specimens he has had of its fifteenth and sixteenth century existence:—

One dark evening in February, 1849, Michele Corsi, Canon of the Cathedral, was murdered by the knife of an assassin or assassins in the streets of Fermo. Now Canon Corsi was an old man of irreproachable character, much respected and beloved by all classes in the city; by all classes and by all parties. For equally during the period of unbridled clerical ascendency under Gregory the Sixteenth, and under the first liberalism of Pius the Ninth, and again when that liberalism was changed for persecution of those who had been the dupes of it, the old man had taken no part whatever in politics, but was known to hold moderate opinions, and to lament the intemperances of either party. He had latterly rendered himself specially grateful to the liberals by forbearing, almost alone among the clergy of Fermo, from rejoicing over or approving the Encyclic published by the Pope in Gaeta, excommunicating all who should take a part in sending deputies to the Roman parliament.

An universal cry of horror and indignation ran through the city at the news of the murder; and numerous patrols of the civic guard turned out instantly, determined to leave nothing undone for the discovery of the criminals. Many persons of known bad character were arrested, and such as could not give a satisfactory account of themselves were preventively imprisoned. Among these were two men of the worst possible character, who had both been convicted on criminal charges before. Their names were Filippo Testori and Giambattista Smerilli. These men, not having been discharged were still in prison on this accusation, when the short-lived Republican Government came to an end in Fermo, and the Pontifical authorities were restored.

The old Canon died in a few days of his wounds; and his fate gave rise to an immense amount of puzzled speculation and astonishment. How and by whom, in a city where the clergy, long noted for their inordinate wealth and insolence, were particularly hated, could the one man among them who was a well-known exception to this inimical feeling, have been marked out for assassination! Strange suspicions arose in men's minds, and were whispered about, and were put down as incredible;—which the circumstances, that have to be told, seemed afterwards to render not so incredible.

When the Pontifical Government was restored, the reaction was furious and vindictive enough everywhere; but at Fermo it was especially so. The Cardinal Archbishop De Angelis, and the Pro-Delegato Morici, were among the most violent and blood-thirsty of the upholders of the old *régime*. There was not a man in Fermo, who had in any way given in his adherence to the liberal government who was not subjected to vengeance in some form. Some were turned out of their offices, some were imprisoned, some condemned to the galleys, and some to exile. But of some, whom the restored government feared as well as hated, it was determined to have their lives.

Among these were three men, Giuseppe Casellini, living on his means, Ignazio Rosettani, a tailor, and Enrico Venezia, a coffee-house keeper. These men had all been strong republicans; two of them had fought for the national cause at Venice; and they were violent politicians; but thoroughly believed by all their fellow-citizens to be wholly incapable of a deed of murder.

It was therefore with the utmost astonishment and dismay that the city saw these three men seized and thrown into prison on a charge of having been accomplices with the two miscreants, who have been mentioned, in the murder of Canon Corsi. Of these two, one especially, Filippo Testori, was a man of the vilest character, whose whole life had been a tissue of crimes and infamies, and who had recently been released from the galleys. To this wretch the agents of the police applied to "designate his accomplices in the murder," which had very satisfactorily been proved to have been committed by his hand. No sort of caressing and cajoling was spared to obtain the declaration desired. There were a hundred and thirty-six political prisoners in the prison of Fermo at that time; and all these were able to testify to the indulgences shown to Testori, to the extra rations, the supply of wine, of cigars in contravention of the rules of the prison, of good bed and bedding, to the frequent private interviews with the directors of the police to which he was called, and to his display of the money which he brought back with him from these visits. To all this was added the promise of a free pardon; and then the desired avowal was obtained. Testori confessed his guilt, and declared Giuseppe Casellini, Ignazio Rosettani, and Eurico Venezia his accomplices in the deed.

Nevertheless, though the determination of the Government was so abundantly transparent, though the unscrupulous ferocity of the priests, who were bent on taking these men's lives, was but too well known to all Fermo, and plenitude of power was in their hands, the citizens yet thought that it would be found impossible to venture on a judicial murder so monstrous, in the teeth of the clearest evidence. For it so happened that all three of the accused were able to adduce the most convincing proofs that they could not have been in any way concerned in the crime in question.

The defence of Casellini was the most completely triumphant. Ever since his campaign in Venice he had been a sufferer from intermittent fever. And he proved by the sworn testimony of the physician who attended him, of the apothecary who supplied the drugs ordered for him, of the maid-servant who waited on him, and of a friend who nursed him, that he was ill in bed, and utterly unable to leave it on the night of the murder, and for several days before and after it. It would seem to any one that it was wholly impossible for even a Government of Priests to attempt to attain their purpose in the face of such testimony. But such was far from being the case. The first step taken was to induce these witnesses to retract their testimony by promises and threats. The second, when the first failed, was to throw all four into prison on a charge of perjury, keep them in separate solitary cells and subject them to the utmost rigour. Under this discipline the physician gave way first, disavowed his previous testimony, and was rewarded with the special patronage of the priests, and such a load of infamy by all the rest of the city, that his subsequent life was almost a sufficient punishment for his wickedness. His name was Baronciani. The friend, Gioacchino Tarini, a husband and the father of three children, all condemned to utter ruin and misery by his persistence in the truth, next yielded, and declared he knew nothing of the circumstances. The maid-servant was pronounced guilty of perjury, and was kept in prison for several years. But the apothecary, an old man named Carlini, could not be shaken in his testimony. He sunk, however, under the hardships inflicted on him, and died in the prison hospital, maintaining with his last breath, and in his last confession, the truth of the evidence he had given. The police declared and published that he died mad!

The way having been thus cleared, sentence was pronounced on the 22nd of December 1854, by a Tribunal of reverend judges, with a Prelate, Monsignore Salvo Maria Sagretti, for president, and another Prelate for public prosecutor; and Casselini, Venezia, Rosettani, together with the two criminals Testori and Smerilli were condemned to death.

But Testori, who had done the work dictated to him of swearing away the lives of three innocent men, on condition of having his own spared, was not disposed to be cheated of his reward. When taken to the condemned cell with the others he could not be persuaded that he was really ordered for execution; and to all the instances of the Confessor appointed to attend the victims, continually replied that by virtue of the promises made to him, he was not to die. But when midnight came, and he saw all the preparations for his execution proceeded with, and the Confessor, a Jesuit named Castiglione, solemnly assured him that he was infallibly to be put to death, he caused to be called to him the Marchese Antonio Trevisani, an old man of seventy years of age, and one of the most respected citizens of Fermo, who was then in the prison in discharge of his duty as a member of the "Confraternity of Mercy," one of the functions of which is to comfort criminals in their last hours. And to this venerable old man, in the presence of the Jesuit Confessor, he declared that Casselini, Rosettani and Venezia had nothing whatever to do with the murder of Canon Corsi, and that he had been induced to swear to their guilt by being told that they were the persons who accused him of the crime.

The Marchese Trevisani, well knowing that no representation of his would be of any avail, for as a liberal he was in sufficiently bad odour with the Government, urged the Jesuit Confessor to bring the facts immediately to the knowledge of the Archbishop and the Delegate. But the Jesuit answered that he was there to hear confessions and not to repeat them.

And the three innocent men, as perfectly well known to be innocent by the Right Reverend Fathers in God, who put them to death, as by their own hearts, were led to death; and the Church had her vengeance and her triumph.*

And now that the reader has had my second passage from the Chronicles of Fermo, what does he think of the progress of civilization and social morality achieved during three hundred years of government by Heaven's Vicar on earth?—and specially what does he think of the heart and con-

* The whole of the details of this judicial murder, told at much greater length than in these pages, together with those of many an equally horrible tragedy, may be found together with the unimpeachable documents which vouch for their authenticity, in the Cavre. Achille Gennarelli's work, " Il Governo Pontificio, e Lo Stato Romano;" which consists mainly of documents found in the Governmental Archives after the flight of the Papal Government. —*See* Vol. II., p. 572.

science that lies under the purple of His Eminence the Cardinal Archbishop De Angelis?—whom I have seen recently named as the probable successor of the present Pontiff in the chair of St. Peter.

For my own part I would rather live under the rule of our friend Oliverotto, ten times over!

## CHAPTER XIV.

FROM FERMO TO LORETO—PORTO DI FERMO—WHY NO FISH ARE TO BE HAD AT FERMO—UNATTRACTIVE COAST SCENERY—SOIL BROUGHT DOWN BY THE RIVERS—RAILWAY WORKS—SITES OF ANCIENT CITIES—CUPRA MARITTIMA—CLUENTUM—POTENZA—ST. ELPIDIO—BRANDIMARTE'S WORK ON PICENUM—THE HILL OF LORETO—LEGEND OF THE SANTA CASA—DALMATIANS AT THE SHRINE OF LORETO—BELIEF IN THE LEGEND.

LEAVING Fermo by the same gate by which we had entered it, but quitting the road we had come by, immediately after leaving the walls of the city we descended a steepish hill for four miles to the "Porto di Fermo," on the Adriatic, which is no port at all. Nevertheless there were one or two wretched fishing boats on the beach; and there was more appearance of life and movement in the little hamlet which had gathered round the landing place, than we had seen in the city above.

The day before up in the town, finding ourselves in the capital of the district, and within four miles of the sea, we had asked for fish for our dinner, and had been told that there was none in Fermo. As it chanced to be Friday, a Friday in Lent too, and in the so recently Papal dominions, we had thought this strange. But the landlord had philosophically explained the fact, lying stretched the while at his length with a pipe in his mouth on the coping of a parapet wall in the sun, as he talked to us, by saying that years ago there used to be fish in the town; but that the fish finding they were caught, if they came to the Port of Fermo, had grown wiser by experience, and did not come to the shore any more to be caught. It did not enter into his philosophy of life, or into that of the fishermen below, to conceive the possibility of going out to sea after the fish, if they would not come to the shore to be caught. And when we looked at the boats and the fishermen, we did not wonder that they should take a different view of their profession from that of Mr. Kingsley's "Three Fishers out into the West."

On leaving Fermo we were bound for Loreto, a distance to the northward of about twenty-six miles. The road first descends, as has been said, to the coast, then follows it as far as the Porto di Recanati, and then turns at right angles inland to climb the hill, and reach Loreto at a distance of three or four miles from the shore.

The journey along this bit of the coast-line of the Adriatic, the shore of the ancient Picenum Suburbicarium, is full of interest in one point of view, but totally devoid of it in another. There is no delight for the eye. It is an essentially ugly coast, flat and sandy, and intersected every few miles by the broad, straggling, shallow, generally almost dry beds of the mountain torrents, which indemnify themselves for the restraint they have been obliged to submit to while finding their way amid the hills, by wantonly occupying a space ten times greater than their needs require, as soon as they find themselves in the flat and fertile strip of alluvial land which intervenes, varying in this part of the coast from three to ten or twelve miles in width, between the last slopes of the Apennines and the Adriatic. We may fancy however the river gods of these Apennine streams defending themselves against any remonstrances on the score of thus wantonly occupying a needless extent of land, by asserting, as they could with perfect truth, that they were but doing as they would with their own; the strip of land in question having been brought grain by grain, and deposited where it now is, from the flanks of far inland Appenine ranges by their own labours. Their godships might also complain that it was the more hard that men should grudge them a small space of the territory created by themselves to gambol in, inasmuch as they are still busily engaged in preparing fresh lands and pastures new for man's use, laying the foundations of cornfields in the Adriatic, which will in due time be handed over ready for his use to the universal proprietor.

It cannot be denied however that this manufacture, or rather flumenifacture of new land is an exception to the general law, that all the processes of Nature are beautiful. The present aspect of the coast bears much such a relation to the smiling cornlands and pastures which shall one day rejoice the eye here, as a brickfield does to the stately buildings which shall be formed from its rent and lacerated entrails.

The face of the country moreover is still further scarred and marred by those most unsightly of all the operations of industry, the first works of a line of railway. The undertaking is being pushed on busily; as busily, that is, as any work ever is pushed on by any men not of Anglo-Saxon breed; and it will be of infinite advantage—of truly incalculable advantage—to all this district. The section at present in course of construction is from Ancona, which as the reader probably knows, is already connected by rail with Turin, to the Tronto, which formed the frontier of the old Neapolitan kingdom.

No! the journey along this portion of the coast, cannot be said to have any of the attractions of beauty. Not even by keeping his eyes turned to the right as he journeys, towards the expanse of the Adriatic, can the traveller avoid ugliness. The Adriatic hereabouts is not a well-favoured sea! Instead of the bright blue or beautiful shadow-flecked green, bursting into the musical laughter of the πολυφλοισβοιο θαλασσης, as the coruscating breakers tumble on the shore, with lines of dark rock or golden sand mottled with thousand-hued seaweed, which makes up an Englishman's notions of sea-side sights and sounds; the almost voiceless waters of the Adriatic, in this part of the coast, lie puddle-like in a long and wide dull yellow strip, along the shore, very shallow, very motionless; very unlike "the sea, the sea, the open sea!" Putting out of the question the risk of being caught by the Fermo fishermen—a danger which I cannot but think any Turbot or Sole of spirit would laugh at—the Adriatic fish evidently know what they are about in giving this ugly coast, with its uninviting zone of yellow water, a wide berth.

This ugly drive however, along the coast from the Porto di Fermo to the Porto di Recanati, is, as I have said, rich in interest of another kind. A great number of passages from the ancient authors, poets as well as geographers and historians, might be adduced to show that "Picenum" was always held to be a rich and highly favoured district. And in no part of Italy are there the remains, or as in many cases the memorials only, of so large a number of ancient cities which perished during the darkest part of the dark ages. In several instances the modern cities occupy the ancient sites, under names sometimes slightly altered, sometimes wholly changed from their classical appellations. In some cases the sites of cities of which the names, some fragments of their history, and some fragments of their buildings, have been preserved, are well ascertained, and fixed beyond all reasonable doubt. In other cases, the unmistakable traces of destroyed towns are to be seen, and the antiquaries fight unending and delightful battles over the insoluble question of which among the ancient names, hitherto unprovided with a local habitation, should be assigned to them. In other instances again, the mere *nominis umbra* of some once important *municipium* still extant, perhaps in one sole passage of Pliny, wanders like a disconsolate ghost over the land, bandied hither and thither by the learned, and unable to find the place that once knew it so well. Suasa, Calle,* Ostra, Pitulo, Sentino, Attidia, Tadino, Plenina, Cupra Montana, Cupra Marittima, Matilica,† Capra, Camerio,‡ Veregra,

---

\* Now Cagli.  † Now Matelica.  ‡ Now Camerino.

Auximum,* Pausulæ, Recina, Numana, Potenza, Cluentum, Falerio, Novana, afford examples of all these various categories. And several of these ancient sites lie on or near to the route of the journey in question.

Cupra Marittima, one of the most interesting of these sites, seems to have been fixed with tolerable certainty at a spot on the coast a little to the southward of Porto di Fermo, and therefore not necessarily passed by the traveller on his way to the northward; and it may be more conveniently visited from Fermo.

The antiquity of Cupra is anti-Roman. "Here," says Strabo, "was *Cypræ fanum conditum, dictatumque ab Hetruscis, qui Junonem Cupram vocant.*" And Silius Italicus speaks of the spot where "*littoreæ fumant altaria Cupræ.*"

There can be little doubt however that the Goddess worshipped under this name was Venus. It would seem that this was the great sanctuary of the Picenian nation; and that, as Livy† tells us that the grand council of Etruria was held at the shrine of Voltumna, and that of the Latin peoples at the grove of Ferentinæ;‡ so that of the Picenian nation was held here. Great numbers of bronze articles have been found here, as in most of the sites of Etruscan cities; especially a great number of rings of considerable weight,—three or four pounds,—some of which may be seen in the house-doors of the hill village of Lapidona, itself a place of great antiquity, probably of eastern origin, a short distance to the south of Fermo, and well worth a visit.

* Now Osimo.  † Lib. 4, c. 23.  ‡ Lib. 7, c. 25.

Cluentum was situated on the coast, probably a little to the southwards of the mouth of the Chienti; Potenza at the mouth of the river still bearing the same name, and Numana yet a little further to the northwards. Further inland the traveller sees from the road a succession of towns perched on their lofty hill-tops, many of which were the sites of ancient cities;—St. Elpidio, most picturesquely situated, built as Brandimarte* thinks from the ruins of the ancient Novana; Civitanuova, high above the road at the point where the mountains approach most nearly to the coast, and unquestionably the usurper of an older city's seat; Monte Cosaro behind it; and Monte Lupone and Montesanto overlooking the estuary of the Potenza.

The best guide to the antiquities of all this region will be found to be the work of Brandimarte, which I have frequently cited, entitled "*Plinio Seniore illustrato nella Decrizione del Piceno,*" a small 4to, published at Rome in 1815. It is not a very rare book, though probably nearly if not wholly unknown in England. It should be considered an indispensable companion in a ramble through the district of which it treats.

In going up from among the memorials and names of classical sites and times to the world-celebrated shrine of Loreto, the traveller passes at once into a widely-distant age of the world's history. A thousand years lie between Cluentum and Loreto. We are suddenly plunged into the atmosphere of a thoroughly different system of ideas, a different antiquity, and above all a different mode of examining and learning

* Op. cit., p. 38.

the lessons of that antiquity. Neither ancient Rome, nor ancient Etruria, nor ancient Umbria knew anything of Loreto. The place is wholly and solely the creation of Mariolatry;—lives, is rich, and has its being, uniquely by and for that alone, and embodies probably on the whole the *most* impudent, and *most* monstrous of all the impudent and monstrous impostures of the Marian religion.

The town,—I beg its pardon, the city, for it is such by special Papal grace;*—the city of Loreto is a neat little town, tacked on to an enormous church and proportionate subsidiary ecclesiastical establishments, on a pleasant hill, not above five or six hundred feet above the level of the sea, nor above three miles or so distant from it, and approached by an admirably wide, well-made, and handsome road, which seems to warn the traveller to put his mind into an attitude of respect, and to remind him that he is approaching a place worthy of far other regards and administrative care, than may suffice for the centres of mere worldly commerce and industry.

The following is a succinct statement of the legend of the Santa Casa, as propounded by the Church for the edification of the faithful:—

In the Pontificate of Celestine the Fifth, at two o'clock in the morning of the 10th of December in the year 1291, " the venerable dwelling appeared on the shore of the Adriatic, and advancing a small space inland stopped in the thick recesses of an ancient grove, the owner of which was a rich and

---

* Of Sixtus Fifth.

pious lady of Recanati, named Laureta."* In this house, we are told, the Virgin had been born; and, as she was the only child of her parents, she inherited it. It was the scene of the Annunciation, of the miraculous Conception, and of that period of the Saviour's childhood which is recorded to have been passed with his parents. When the Empress Helena visited in pilgrimage the holy places of Palestine, she went to Nazareth, and there amid the ruins of the destroyed town found this sacred building untouched, and "by the poor naked walls, by the small hearth, by the few articles of household use, by the poor array of domestic furniture, but much more by a certain sacred awe which that august precinct inspires, knew it to be the true house of Mary, and as such humbly venerated it." The Empress, we are told, left the house in its primitive simple condition, but erected over it a magnificent temple, whither, in the subsequent ages, a long succession of Saints and personages of renown, among others St. Louis of France, thronged to worship. On the western wall of the house there may still be discerned remains of paintings, in which St. Louis is represented kneeling before the Virgin. "Nor must it be imagined that this painting is of any age nearer to our own, for it was seen as it now is from the moment in which the Holy House halted for the first time in Dalmatia." The visit of St. Louis, thus recorded, took place in 1252. But in the year 1291, " Kalil, Sultan of the

* Authorized "Historical Relation of the Prodigious Translation of the Holy House of Nazareth." 22nd Edition. Loreto. 1858.

Saracens and King of Egypt," made himself master of the whole of Galilee, put to death 25,000 Christians, enslaved 200,000 others, took the fortress of Ptolemaïs, now St. Jean D'Acre, and utterly extirpated Christianity in the Holy Land. "But lo! at the same time God Almighty, in order to save the house of His divine Mother, puts His hand to one of His most stupendous and unheard-of miracles, severing the dwelling from its foundations (which, in proof of the great prodigy remain still visible), and transporting it successfully (*felicemente*) through vast tracks of air and sea towards the coasts of Dalmatia, where it remained deposited for some time." The precise epoch of its arrival in Dalmatia was the 10th of May, 1291; and the precise place was between Tersatto and Fiume in a little valley called Dolaz, where no house or cottage had ever been before. At the same time the Virgin appeared to Alessandro di Giorgio, the priest of the place, who was dangerously ill in bed, informed him of the arrival of her house, and restored him to perfect health. The Dalmatians, overjoyed at the special favour shown to them, nevertheless to verify the fact to the utmost, sent a deputation of three of their most respected and trustworthy citizens, of whom the above priest was one, to Nazareth to see if the Holy House had really departed thence. "The worthy explorers went on their mission; returned; and with extreme jubilation unanimously deposed that the birth-house of the Virgin no longer existed in Nazareth of Galilee; that having been conducted to the spot where it had stood [those Saracens who had just slain 25,000 Christians and enslaved 200,000 others were strangely civil to this Christian deputation], and having examined the foundations still visible, and the cement, and the stones, all without the slightest shadow of difference corresponded with the measures which they had taken with them."

The Dalmatians lost no time in paying honour in every way to the new arrival. They built around it a temple of wood, after the manner of the country; they enriched it with magnificent gifts, and flocked from far and wide to visit the favoured spot. And this continued for three years and seven months.

The compiler of the authorized account of the legend, from which these notices are taken, has fallen into a strange inconsistency here. He states that the house arrived in Dalmatia in May, 1291, remained there three years and seven months, and arrived in Italy in December, 1291. In the atmosphere of transcendental miracle however in which we are moving, a little matter of this sort, more or less, is of small importance.

All of a sudden, at the end of these three years and seven months, without the slightest warning, the house "was lifted again by angels in the air, disappeared thence, and, having passed the Adriatic, was seen placed in the midst of a wood not far from the fortunate hill where it is now venerated."

"The dismay and astonishment of the Dalmatians at their sudden loss is not to be described," says the author, whose account I am abridging. Nor are they yet consoled for it. Since after five centuries have passed (his "Manual for Pilgrims to Loretto" seems to have been written in 1791), numbers of Dalmatians still come to Loreto, and are seen "dragging themselves into the church on their knees, licking the pavement with their tongues, remaining for entire nights before the closed doors of the church on their knees, praying with devout hymns to the great Virgin Mother, and exclaiming in their native language amid sobs, "Return! return to us, O Maria! Return to Tersatto, Maria! . . . . Maria! . . . . Maria!' . . . . Oh! what a grand testimony such lamentátions and sad tender emotions render to this admirable sanctuary!"

"Shepherds watching their flocks by night" were the first to discover the house in the wood, attracted to it by a miraculous light. But in the same night the Virgin appeared to two saints, St. Nicholas of Tolentino, and one Frà Paolo, a hermit of those parts, and told them of the arrival of her house from Dalmatia. Forthwith enormous crowds of devotees from all the neighbouring cities thronged to the grove and filled it day and night. "But the common invidious enemy of the human race, shuddering at the infinite benefit thus offered to mankind, turned all his efforts to prevent this piety and devotion and concourse to the holy spot." With this view he induced certain wicked men to lie in ambush for the pilgrims, and assassinate several of them;—which seems strange, as the entire wood was so full of people day and night that there was no room, and the sound of prayer and hymns filled the whole region. The result however was, that the devout were frightened, and the Holy House became quite deserted. And the consequence was that eight months after its first arrival, it took another flight from the wood of Laureta to a pleasant hill not far from Recanati, a spot which belonged to two brothers.

This time the migration does not seem to have caused much astonishment; for use lessens marvel. But the two brothers began to quarrel for the profits to be derived from the piety of the pilgrims, and came near to desecrating the sacred house with fratricidal blood. And the result of this was that the house, very properly, once again changed its quarters, and permanently settled down about a bow-shot off, beyond the limits of the domain of these unworthy brothers; and this time took up its position in the middle of the high road, in the spot which it has from that day forward occupied.

Such is the history which the faithful are required to believe, which hundreds of thousands have believed with the most entire and implicit faith, and which a long list of the great and powerful of the world have deemed it prudent to pretend to believe, and to honour with a vast quantity of costly gifts!

# CHAPTER XV.

COMMENCEMENT OF THE RELIGION OF THE SANTA CASA — ST. FRANCIS DI ASSISI AT LORETO — ST. CARLO BORROMEO AT LORETO—FIRST CHURCH BUILT THERE—SECOND CHURCH—THIRD CHURCH BUILT BY GIULIANO DA MAIANO—ALTERED BY PICCIONI DA ST. GALLO—LITTLE TO ADMIRE IN THE CHURCH AS IT NOW IS, EXCEPT THE SCULPTURES ENCLOSING THE SANTA CASA ITSELF—MEASURES OF THE SANTA CASA—DESCRIPTION OF THE INTERIOR—MODE OF BLESSING ARTICLES —SANTA SCODELLA—THE OFFICIATING PRIEST—THE TREASURY —ROBBERY OF IT BY THE FRENCH—ITS PRESENT CONTENTS —MAJOLICA VASES—MAIN INDUSTRY OF THE TOWN OF LORETO —AN ESPRIT FORT—BATTLE OF CASTEL FIDARDO — TOOK PLACE UNDER THE EYES OF THE CANONS OF LORETO.

Of course a church was forthwith raised over the little building; accommodations for the expected concourse of pilgrims was added; and no means were neglected to accredit the newly invented superstition, and establish it as a source of power and revenue to its inventors. None of the extraordinarily numerous inventions of the Catholic priesthood has ever answered better than this. Very many, of which the world has heard little, and hears nothing, having failed "to take," have remained in provincial obscurity, and though perhaps still recorded by the anniversary of some village festival, have never been greatly remunerative to their ingenuous authors. A curious subject of inquiry might be found in an examination of the characteristics of the most successful, and the non-successful superstitions, which have been proposed to the world by Rome's priesthood. At first sight it would really seem as if the success of such inventions were proportioned to the monstrosity and grossness of them. There is the celebrated case of the blood of St. Januarius, and that other not less celebrated tale of the eleven thousand virgins, which has been equally profitable in its time, though from its locality destined to be less durable in its fruitful operation. And this story of the holy house, perhaps the most audaciously outrageous of all, has from the very outset been one of the most successful of all.

It started well from the first. Both the time and the place were well chosen. Italy was convulsed and sore troubled; her provinces were isolated; communications were scanty; and the distance of a few score miles produced a greater effect of hazy uncertainty and difficulty of verification than would at this day be caused by the interposition of the entire globe. Trouble, sorrow, violence, injustice, wrong of all sorts were rife, and all men save the strongest and boldest, and all women without exception, seeing small hope or comfort in the natural life around them, were prone to turn to the consolations offered to them by the supernatural. The locality was well adapted to the purpose;—neither so remote as to make pilgrimage to the favoured spot too difficult, nor so near to the great centres of population as to be too much under the supervision of what little honest intelligence existed in the world in the thirteenth century.

The new superstition started at once, accordingly, with a display of miracles on the most liberal scale. They were the events of every day. "Numbers possessed by devils (*i. e.* liable to epileptic and cataleptic seizures), were cured, the lame were made to walk, the blind received their sight, the sick were healed; the most abandoned and perverse sinners were converted. Not a few heretics, Jews, and infidels saw here shining the friendly celestial light descend to dissipate the darkness of their unbelief." A great number of Saints have visited and testified their belief in and devotion to the Holy House; among others St. Ignatius Loyola, St. Francis di Sales, St. Francis Xavier, the Apostle of the Indies, St. Francis di Paolo, St. Alphonzo de' Liguori, and many others, with names less known beyond the Alps. As for St. Francis di Assisi, it is true that he died before the translation of the Holy House. But the seraphic patriarch, when he was at the convent of Sirolo in the neighbourhood, which was founded by him in 1215, "turning towards the hill of Loreto, which was then a solitary and uninhabited desert, surrounded by woods, and moved by the spirit of prophecy, saluted the said hill of Loreto in a divine transport, as a place favoured by God, and which would be honoured by Him towards the end of the century by an extraordinary miracle concerning one of the greatest sanctuaries venerated by mankind; thus alluding to the Translation of the Holy House of Nazareth to Loreto." Lastly, in comparatively modern times, St. Carlo Borromeo came twenty miles on foot to Loreto, insisted on administering the Communion to the vast crowd of pilgrims assembled there on the day of the Nativity of the Virgin, dined with the Chapter, and concluded by begging to be allowed to pass the night shut up in the Holy House, which he accordingly did.

These facts, which are unquestionably true, will appear to many minds about the most noticeable and extraordinary of any recorded in the annals of the holy house. Did Cardinal Borromeo believe in the miracle of the translation? Bearing in mind the really high and noble nature of the man, it can hardly be doubted that he did so. Nothing made it in any way necessary for him to enact the above rehearsed comedy, if he did not. And yet how wonderful, how fearful, how humiliating to think, that it should have been possible for such a man in the latter half of the sixteenth century, to give credit to such a fable. The fact is a most striking evidence of the extreme difficulty with which even a highly gifted mind can free itself from the influences of the intellectual atmosphere in which it has lived from infancy, and from which it has drawn all its own increment.

Of course a church was very speedily erected over the little building, in the spot on which it finally settled itself. This first fabric was erected about the year 1300, in the pontificate of Boniface the Eighth. A larger and handsomer one was erected within the first half of the fourteenth century. But it was not till the second half of the fifteenth, under the pontificate of Paul the Second that the present structure was raised by the Florentine architect, Giuliano da Maiano. But it was not left by him at all as we now see it. The character of Giuliano's church was entirely Gothic. The present building has no trace in any part of that style. The fact is that in Clement the Seventh's time, probably in consequence of some movement of the soil of the hill, which even to the present day does not appear to be very reassuringly firm, the beautiful work of Giuliano gave alarming symptoms of instability. Clement sent the Florentine architect, Antonio Piccioni da S. Gallo, to examine the building, and do what was necessary for its preservation. Vasari has given us a minute account of the measures adopted by Piccioni, who gave the church the form it now wears, which is purely that of a building of the *renaissance;* "propping up the arches," says Vasari, "and fortifying the whole with most resolute courage, as a judicious architect should, he refounded the entire church, re-enforcing the walls and the pilasters within and without."

The church thus modernized, with dome, portico, round ends to nave and transept, and cream-coloured stone, after the exact semblance of so many in the Pontifical States, makes an imposing appearance from its size and fine position on the brow of the hill, overlooking the Adriatic. But it has little of beauty and less of interest. Before the west front, which is ornamented in correct Palladian guise with a fine portico and enormous columns, there is a very large square, surrounded on two sides by colonnaded ranges of buildings, containing the dwellings of the numerous clergy belonging to the church, and the lately Apostolic, now Royal residence, for the reception of the Sovereign, when he comes to visit the city of pilgrimage.

## MEASUREMENT OF THE HOUSE.

In the interior, the church, handsome for its spaciousness, has nothing to distinguish it from all the others, built on the same monotonous and well-known model, save the Holy House itself. This is situated in the middle of the church, under the dome, just in the position the huge bronze canopy over the pontifical altar occupies in St. Peter's.

The erection is about thirty or forty feet long, by about fifteen feet wide, and as much in height. The exact measurement of the wall of the Holy House is as follows:—

|  |  |  |
|---|---|---|
| Height | 19 palmi,* | 4 oncic. |
| Length | 42 „ | 10 „ |
| Width | 18 „ | 4 „ |
| Thickness of walls | 4 „ | 7 „ |

But the building which meets the eye of the spectator is a good deal larger than this, because the walls of the house have been encased in a series of sculptures by the greatest masters of the best period of art. The entire height of the walls is divided into two series of subjects in *basso relievo*, separated perpendicularly by full length statues of prophets, patriarchs, and sibyls, all good, and some among them of very striking majesty and beauty. It is needless to particularize here the subjects and the authors of them; for all this will be found minutely done both in the general and local guide-books. The general design is by Bramante. The work was commenced under the pontificate of Leo the Tenth, continued during that of Clement the Seventh, and completed by Paul the Third. Taken as a whole,

* The Roman palmi is $8\frac{35}{100}$ inches. The oncia the 12th part thereof.

R

this casing of the *Santa Casa* is perhaps the most remarkable assemblage of Cinque-cento sculpture extant. Almost all the great names of that spring-tide of art are represented there,—Sansovino, Giovanni di Bologna, Girolamo Lombardo, Guglielmo della Porta, Baccio Bandinelli, Sangallo, Raffaelle da Montelupo, and other less known names. It is recorded that the cost of this unique work was sixty thousand crowns, and that it would have been much more, had not many of the artists and workmen given their labour gratis, out of devotion. And in truth the sum named seems a small one for the production of such a result.

The fireplace of the *Santa Casa* is in the wall of that end of it which, as the building now stands, is the nearest to the east end of the church. In front of this fireplace, and so close to it as to leave only a narrow space of some three feet in width, an altar has been erected, enclosing the original one placed in the house, according to the legend, by the Empress Helena, which stretches across the entire width of the house, in such sort that access to the space between it and the fireplace can only be had by a small door opening into it from the church on the south side. The larger space of the house, in front of the altar, is entered by two doors, one on the north and one on the south in the walls of the house near its western end. Over the fireplace, in a niche in the eastern wall, so high that it can be seen over the altar, is the celebrated figure of the Virgin and Child, carved by St. Luke. Nothing can be conceived more hideous, more vile, more fetish-like, than this black figure, swathed in a bell-shaped dress, all tinsel and gold, and hung about with gems of an enormous amount of value. The figure of a black doll hanging above the door of a dealer in "marine stores," is a work of high art in comparison with this effort of the Apostle's chisel.

It so chanced that I had a walking-stick in my hand when I approached one of the doors leading into the sacred enclosure. It was courteously taken from me by an attendant, who whispered low (for the exceeding sanctity of the place seemed to press with a weight of awe on all near it), that persons having been led to poke out fragments of mortar from the holy walls, it was now forbidden to enter with any sort of stick or other implement. At either of the two doors, the position of which has been described, stood a soldier of the line, mounting guard,—a precaution against, it is almost difficult to say what,—which is never dispensed with, from the opening of the church in the morning, which takes place, both in summer and winter, at 4 A.M., to its closing, a little after sunset.

We entered; and gazed, as well as the very feeble light would permit, with no little curiosity. In front of us was the altar all ablaze with gems, and gold, and lamps, and precious stones. On the three other sides the space was enclosed by the bare brick walls of the *Santa Casa* in all their primitive nakedness. They are of dark-red bricks, about the size of, but somewhat thinner than our ordinary brick, blackened by age, and smoothed by rubbing. They are coarsely and unskilfully put together, having a considerable thickness of mortar between the courses, which in the lapse of ages either by the natural operation of crumbling, or from having been picked out by devotees anxious to carry away with them some morsel of the sacred material, has been removed from the surface of the wall, in such sort as to produce little channels between brick and brick, and to give the wall the appearance of being greatly in need of the process called by bricklayers pointing. I suppose that the desire to carry away some fragment, however minute, of the substance of the building, is a common one; for I noticed an air of suspicious and alert vigilance on the part of the two sentries, which appeared explicable only by such a supposition.

Such a practice on the part of visitors is the more unjustifiable in that a legitimate means of gratifying devout wishes of the sort has been provided, and that gratuitously. Prints of the figure of the Virgin carved by St. Luke, of various degrees of quality and price, little brass stamped representations of the same, rosaries, crucifixes, may be bought for a very few halfpence in the town, and any one or more of such articles is on demand subjected by an attendant priest to a process which communicates to it the virtues of the holy walls and the sacred idol. The process observed is as follows:—The object to be impregnated with supernatural virtues is first rubbed against the wall of the house, and is then placed for a short space in the "*Santa scodélla*,"—the holy porringer, or soup-dish. Two of these porringers are kept in the "*Sacro armadio*,"—the holy cupboard,—which is in the house, and seem, together with a third, which is used as just mentioned, to be the only extant pieces of the household utensils said to have arrived with the house. All three of these were handsomely mounted in settings of gold, till the French tore the gold from two of them and cracked the dishes in doing so. They were afterwards sent to Rome, and were subsequently sent back to Loreto by Pius the Seventh, newly set in gilt copper mountings. The third *scodélla* by some chance escaped the rapacity of the French robbers, and that is the one now used for the purpose above described. Besides the two processes mentioned, if the article is a print, a small strip of black crape which has been placed against the figure of the Virgin is affixed over the picture of the figure by a wafer.

Close outside the small door opening from the church into the narrow space between the fireplace and the back of the altar, a priest is always sitting at a sort of counter. His duty it is to perform the above ceremonies, to bless the articles, and to deliver a written attestation that the sanctifying process has been duly and veritably performed. There he is to be found at his post, winter and summer, from four o'clock in the morning till dusk (relieved by colleagues, it is to be presumed), ready to rub the things anybody may bring to him against the wall, lay them in the soup-dish, stick the bits of crape on the prints, and attest the same,—all gratis!

We took a print and a little bit of brass stamped with a rude representation of St. Luke's carving, value about twopence, and presented them for consecration, for the sake of seeing the process. It was rather dusk at the time, except in the full light of the lamp; and I observed that the priest looked closely at the bit of brass, to make sure that it was duly stamped; from which I conjecture that profane persons have tricked him into operating upon improper objects.

No fault however was to be found with our presentation, and the ceremony was duly proceeded with. The priest, who sitting at his counter, where he is entrusted with the further duty of receiving all alms and offerings made to the *Santa Casa*, and all payments for masses ordered, etc., seemed a sharp, business-like sort of man, either had a profound belief in the virtues of the mummeries he was practising, or he acted his part consummately well. The awe-struck air with which he put the things into the porringer, waited awhile as if they were soaking, and then took them out gingerly with his finger and thumb, lifting them out, and touching their extremities against the rim of the vessel, as he did so, in the way one touches anything dripping with liquid, to remove the adhering drops, was a sight to see!

The *Santa scodélla* is a small shallow dish of very coarse earthenware, about eight inches in diameter, not so deep as an ordinary soup-plate, and ornamented with some coarsely daubed design, very much resembling, as it seemed to me, the style of ornamentation to be seen on some of the most ordinary specimens of the fifteenth century majolica ware. I saw it very closely; for there was barely room for the priest, my companion and myself to enter the narrow place behind the altar, where this part of the ceremony was performed, partly occupied as it was previously by the kneeling figure of an old man, who with his head thrust into the opening of the holy chimney, was to all appearance absorbed in prayer. I saw the *scodella* therefore very closely; but the light was imperfect.

The following day we returned to visit the treasury, containing all the precious gifts that have been presented to the *Santa Casa*; with the exception of such jewels as are used to adorn the altar, and the idol above it.

The hall in which these possessions are kept is a truly magnificent chamber, admirably proportioned, some eighty feet in length I should think, the ceiling very finely painted with subjects from the life of the Madonna, and single figures of sibyls, and prophets; and the walls entirely lined with a series of closed walnut-wood cupboards below, to the height of four feet or so, and above them of cases fitted up with shelves, and enclosed with glass doors. The amount of wealth, the harvest of the superstition of five centuries, which was contained in these cupboards and cases up to the close of the last century, was something enormous and wonderful. But then came the French,—those same "eldest sons" of the Church, whose tender religious feelings will not now permit them to allow Italy to withdraw her neck from the fatal yoke of the Papal Government,—and made very nearly a clear sweep of all the gatherings amassed from the conscience money of princes and peasants in five hundred years! Terrible was the wail that arose from the bereaved bees, when the hive was thus rifled; and it has not yet wholly subsided. The busy creatures, with the instinct of acquisitive garnering-up strong in them, forthwith recommenced their hoarding; and have in truth accomplished wonders towards refilling their shelves and cupboards.

"But," as the author of one of the many manuals sold here, pathetically observes, "what can be expected from the result of fifty years, as contrasted with those of five centuries!"

The results of fifty years' practice on the credulity of mankind however has done wonders. The cupboards below, the beggarly account of empty shelves in which is concealed by solid doors, are, as the old sacristan admitted with a sigh, for the most part empty. But the glass cases are decked out with a multiplicity of objects of the most heterogeneous kinds, and make a goodly show. The intrinsic value of the articles however is very little in comparison with what it was, before the treasury was robbed by the pioneers of European civilization. There are coloured glass and paste where precious stones should be, and copper gilt in the place of massive gold. After one or two questions had drawn forth humiliating replies, I forebore to ask any further as to the genuineness of the articles exposed to view, so painful did the confession of poverty appear to be.

Respecting one treasure however, which we knew to be still at Loreto, we made special inquiries; I mean the celebrated set of pharmacy vases of choice majolica, the work of Fontana and Franco, after designs by Raphael, Giulio Romano, and others. The set consisted of upwards of three hundred pieces, and was presented to the *Santa Casa* by Francesco Maria, the second Duke of Urbino. We knew that these celebrated vases were no longer in the *Spezieria*, or Pharmacy; and had supposed that the "two rooms" in which the latest edition of Murray's Guide-book says that they are kept, were attached to the treasury of the church. We were told however in the town, that the vases had been removed to a room in the apostolic palace for safe keeping. This was repeated to us by several persons, and was evidently the general belief among the townsfolk. In reply to every inquiry we could make however at the palace, we were assured that no vases were there, or ever had been there. The keepers of the palace knew nothing upon the subject.

Now among the various articles on the shelves in the glass cases around the treasury room, we saw a few small vases, of a shape very common among the majolica ware, which was manufactured in great quantities for the apothecaries. And we closely questioned the sacristans and the guide who accompanied us, as to the whereabouts of the remainder of the celebrated set, if indeed those we saw had ever formed a part of it. The latter knew nothing of the matter. The former maintained that the vases we saw constituted the entire set; and that the *Santa Casa* had never possessed any others. This we knew to be untrue, and we soon showed the old sacristan, that we were well informed as to the nature and extent of the collection. He then said that the few, small, and by no means extraordinarily fine vases on the shelves before us, were all that remained of the entire set,—that the rest had been lost, stolen, broken,—how should he know! I knew that the vases had been seen at Loreto, within a very few years; and did not believe it possible that such a wholesale destruction could have taken place since that time. So I begged to speak to the *Padre Guardiano*, to whose care the treasury is entrusted, and who is responsible for its contents; and when he had been called from the neighbouring sacristy, I asked him with many apologies for troubling him, whether I had his authority for stating publicly, that the whole of the celebrated collection of vases of majolica had been lost or destroyed, with the exception of the few small ones visible around the room?

*Che! Che!* Lost or destroyed! Nothing had been lost or destroyed that had ever been entrusted to his care! The vases were safe enough; but he wished they were further! What business had the *benedetto* (to be understood as meaning the exact reverse) Government to send the *benedetti* vases to *him* to be taken care of? They made no part of the church treasury!

With much expression of sympathy for the wrong put upon him, we inquired where in point of fact at that time of speaking, the vases in question were?

"There they are, in those cupboards," said he, pointing to some of the range which has been mentioned, as running round the entire room, below the glass cases.

"Then no doubt you will kindly allow us to look at them?"

Oh no! we must excuse him! it was impossible, out of the question; they were not prepared for being seen. They could not be seen *in* the cupboards, and might be broken in being taken *out;* and he was responsible for them! And he wished they were at Jericho!

By dint of coaxing however, and joining in his abuse of the authorities who had sent the vases to *him* for custody, we succeeded in inducing him to draw from his pocket a key, which two minutes before he had sworn was put away, lost, not in his possession, left at home, and open the cupboards in question. And there in truth were the vases, not ranged on shelves, but literally stacked one on another, higgledy-piggledy, top upwards, bottom upwards, side upwards, as it might chance. Well might the *Padre Guardiano* say, that they could not be taken out without a risk of breaking them, tumbled one upon another as they were!

Nevertheless, having once yielded to our importunity he became very gracious, and with much care and trouble, and rating of the sacristan who assisted in the operation, he *did* draw forth several of the largest of the pieces, and brush the thick-lying dust off them. I was rather disappointed in them, my expectations having been pitched too high. I have seen many much finer majolica vases, both as regards form, and brilliancy of colouring, and perfection of glazing; perhaps not as regards the design and drawing of the subjects represented on them. The immense number too of the collection, is unrivalled.

But of the larger and finer vases by far the greater number are more or less broken. Some had lost their feet, many of them their ornamental handles, many of them pieces out of their rims. They must have been kept for years with the most abominable carelessness, of which the manner in which they are now stowed away is but a specimen. The *Padre Guardiano* declared that out of the entire series there were only eighteen pieces completely whole!

The town of Loreto is but an appendage to the

church, existing by it, and for it. There is a **comfortable** little inn outside the gate, at the further end of the town from the church, well exposed to the fresh breeze from the Adriatic. The inn inside the walls, which I suppose would be considered the **first** in point of dignity, inasmuch as it has attached to it the posting establishment, looks far less inviting, and is at all events much inferior in desirableness of position.

The whole of the little town is full of the main industry of the place, the sale of prints, carved figures, rosaries, manuals of devotion, little medals, and stamped representations of the carved figure by St. Luke, of all sorts and at all prices. And as you walk down the main street, the proprietors of these magazines of *tromperie* (one is but too strongly reminded of the etymology of our word trumpery;) sally forth from their doors, and entreat you to come in and examine their stock. That any human being should come to Loreto, and not want to make the acquisition of an assortment of such good things, is not considered to be upon the cards.

Even in the inn the same trade was carried on. In the "*sala da mangiáre*" there was a large handsome glass case full of wares of the same description. When we sat down to dinner in this room, being the only occupants of it at the time, a very pretty girl came to wait on us; and we took the opportunity of questioning her about the "*tromperie*" in this case. Some of the articles contained in it were ready blessed, and had been rubbed on the holy wall, and immersed in the holy "*scodella*," with the attestations to the fact in due form.

We asked her how much more these cost than similar articles that had not been so operated on.

"Don't you think," she said, with a quick sly glance of her laughing black eyes, "that they ought to cost at least double? Well, you shall have that print, blessing and all, for exactly the same price as the unblessed one!"

"And what sort do you patronize for your own especial use?" I said. "I'll be bound that you have some blessed bit of brass or ivory hanging round your neck at this minute, if one could only see through your handkerchief."

"*Che! vi pare?*"\* she said, tearing open the neck of her dress as she spoke, and showing—that assuredly there was no "*tromperie*" there. "Confectioners," she added, "do not eat much pastry; they prefer bread."

It was clear that the pretty maid of the inn was an *esprit fort*. So I ventured to ask if the people of the country really believed in the holiness and efficacy of these amulets and talismans.

The *contadini* (peasantry), she said, did perhaps; but hardly the people of the town, and certainly nobody of any education. Not that I think her testimony is quite to be depended on in this matter, it may be observed.

I asked her, if so, what was the use of keeping a case of such goods in that room, which certainly was not frequented by the peasantry.

"Oh! many strangers," she said, "might like to carry away with them some such memorial of the

\* "Pooh! Do you think it likely?"

place, although they had no belief in the virtue of such things. And then," she added, rather inconsistently with what she had said before, "many of you gentlemen, who do not believe, have wives who do; and may like to take them a souvenir. Is it not so?"

"How comes it then that you don't believe?"

"Oh! I! That is different! *Ne ho visto troppe!*"* With which words she turned and tripped out of the room.

The houses of the Canons of the Church of the *Santa Casa* occupy the first floor of the fine range of buildings which has been already spoken of as forming one side of the *piazza* in front of the church. The windows at the back of this long line of comfortable dwellings look away from the Adriatic, and command a fine view over the surrounding country, comprising the cities of Recanati and Osimo on their neighbouring hills, *and of the still nearer town of Castel Fidardo*. The town, bearing this henceforward celebrated name, stands, like all the others in this part of the country, on a hill, not more than three miles from Loreto, on the opposite side of a valley watered by a little stream called the Musone. The hill of Castel Fidardo, steep immediately below the walls of the town, falls in its lower part to the level of the stream in a long gentle slope; and on this slope to the south-east of the town, the celebrated battle to which it has given its name was fought. Rarely can it have happened that people looking from their own windows can have commanded so

* " I have seen too much of it."

perfect a view of a battle-field as the Canons of the *Santa Casa* did of that of the fight of Castel Fidardo. If it had been a spectacle got up for their amusement, instead of a fateful fight in which their fate and fortunes were hanging in the balance, it could not have taken place more entirely under their eyes. And I was told by more than one informant at Loreto, that in point of fact, nearly the whole of the reverend Chapter were at their windows looking on at the action, respecting the favourable issue of which to their cause and that of the Papacy, I was assured that they felt no misgivings. The progress of the fight however must have very soon changed their views upon this point; for the upshot did not remain long doubtful even to reverend eyes. The sight of their champion Lamoriciere's utter and ignominious rout must have been very bitter to them; and if they really believed all that they professed to believe of the atrocities that the Piedmontese would assuredly commit if they should be victorious, no small amount of personal anxiety must have mingled in their hopes and fears as they watched the defeat of the Papal army.

Then was the moment for their Madonna to have helped them and her own cause! Why did they not bring out the miraculous figure, as the Church so often does with its idols on less momentous occasions, and with such signal effect? The heroes of the cause of the Church might have seen the holy figure from the battle-field, and surely something might have been hoped from such a display!

The Canons of the *Santa Casa* saw the sun go down on the defeat of the Papal troops, and of the Papal hopes; and then withdrew from their windows into their comfortable rooms, and rose the next morning to do their wonted functions, and draw, when dividend-day came round, their undiminished revenues. Nor did the value of their life-interest in the same sink in any perceptible degree as the fortune of the fight went in favour of Italian liberty and regeneration. But the value of the advowson of a canonry in that richly endowed church, I think, must have fallen very considerably during those fateful hours. And I fear that the wail, which is raised by Catholic Europe, over the waning temporal power of the Papacy, is both more sincere and more correct in its anticipations than the assurances of the liberals of Europe, that the destruction of it will in no degree endanger the existing ecclesiastical establishment. For my own part, I entirely sympathize with those cardinals, bishops, and canons, who invincibly object to the dependence of ecclesiastical revenues on the will of a lay House of Commons.

## CHAPTER XVI.

RECANATI—ITS SITUATION AND FORM—A MAD GALLOP THITHER—APPEARANCE OF RECANATI WITHIN THE WALLS—CURIOUS ANCIENT LAW—FORMER HISTORY AND POLITICAL CONSTITUTION—MONTEFANO, AND ITS DIRECT SUBJECTION TO THE HOLY SEE—UGHELLI'S LIBEL ON RECANATI — TYPOGRAPHICAL ENTERPRIZE AT RECANATI IN THESE DAYS—THE "GREAT REBELLION" AT RECANATI—SPECIMEN OF A PAPAL BULL IN THE FIFTEENTH CENTURY—REMARKABLE CHARGE OF IDOLATRY—FRIAR ANDREW AND HIS FORTUNES—CRUSADE AGAINST RECANATI—TERRIBLE FATE OF THE CITY—RETURN TO LORETO.

THE City of Recanati, which has been already mentioned as claiming, in all probability with justice, to have sprung from the ruins of the destroyed city of Ricina, is not more than five miles from Loreto, to the south-west. It stands on the top of a much higher hill than that of Loreto, the site of the city being one thousand and six Parisian feet above the level of the sea; and it makes a very striking object in the landscape for many miles around, and from the walls of all the neighbouring towns. Its form is different from all the many others of these hill cities. Instead of being clustered clump-like round the top of a round or conical hill, as most of them are, it stretches in a long crescent-shaped line along the crest of a sharp mountain ridge, and thus makes a greater show than it would otherwise do.

We purposed visiting it from Loreto, returning thither to our comfortable quarters to sleep. In making this arrangement there had been a question of the length of time required to traverse the five miles, all composed of steep ascent and descent as they were; and there had been a competition between two candidates for the job of taking us thither; one a young lad, who was just starting in business, with a very light sort of little spring waggon, and one tall raw-boned steed, who looked as if he had seen better days, and had been a right good horse in his time; the other, an elderly man, with a carriage and pair, who pooh-poohed the boy's asseveration, that he would do the five miles in forty-five minutes, with the scorn of infinite superiority, and asserted that two horses were absolutely necessary for the trip, and besides that it was not respectable for Signori, like our Excellencies, to travel with less than two horses. This last argument decided the matter in the boy's favour, and we committed our respectability to his ram-shackle waggon and tall gaunt single horse, and started in the midst of a volley of prophecies that we should tumble head over heels in going down the hill, and stick fast in our attempt to go up the opposite one.

Stung by these jeers from the elders of his profession, the young Jehu started with a stern determination to show the world the injustice of them; and really began his journey in a style, that made me think the first evil prophecy would assuredly be accomplished.

The road from the one neighbouring city to the other is an excellent one, broad, straight, hard as a brickbat, and white as a ball-court, down one steep hill and up the other in face of it, very much like many a bit of road among our south downs, over which I have been whirled at twelve miles an hour, by "Telegraph," or "Quicksilver Mail," in the good old days—"*Consule Planco*,"—when such pleasant things were. Nor do I remember that any sensation of nervousness ever mixed with the pleasure of the box seat by the side of some crack whip, though we *were* top-heavy with eight or nine great sacks of letters on the roof, and "she" rocked a little in the bottom before steadying as she mounted the hill. But Plancus is Consul no more! It is a very long time since he was in office! And what with those circumstances and the small confidence I had in the skill of our ambitious charioteer, or the soundness of his old horse, I was right glad when we got to the bottom of the hill! Down we went at a *ventre-à-terre* gallop, while the light waggon bounded and pitched in such a lively fashion, that if the question had been put to any one, what they would take to sit in it, the most judicious reply would have been that of the sailor, who was asked what he would take to go to the mast-head in a storm, and who answered, "Fast hold!" As for our youthful Jehu, he was in some sort tied down to his little cushionless bench in front of us, by the cord of what he called the "*mantenica*,"—a corruption from "*martinica*," which is a corruption from the French "*mechanique*," *i. e.* the drag. For this "*mantenica*," on which all our hopes depended, instead of being worked with a screw as in vehicles of higher pretensions, was of a very simple construction. A rope passing through a couple of pulleys under the body of the waggon, was so adjusted as to press, when pulled, a couple of bits of wood against the tires of the two hind-wheels with the force of a powerful lever. But as there was no means of fixing the cord when pulled tight, it behoved the driver not to relax his tug on it. And in order to maintain this, the boy having drawn it tight with all his strength, passed it over his thighs, and round the narrow bench on which he was sitting, and held the end in one hand, while the other was busily engaged in unceasingly flogging his horse, and cracking his whip. As for the reins, they played a very small and subordinate part in the business; and no notion of " holding up" a horse seemed to form any part of the traditions of Picenian charioteership.

"*Audaces fortuna juvat!*" We got safe to the bottom of the hill, and proceeded to climb the long ascent to Recanati at a more sober pace.

At the first aspect the impression which Recanati makes on a visitor is a pleasing one. It is in the first place a clean town; and indeed, as long as Heaven sends water from the skies, can hardly be otherwise. For the ridge of mountain on which the long line of city is built is so narrow and so steep, that every shower must needs wash it almost as completely as it washes the roof of a house. It is, partly from the same cause, a remarkably healthy place; for every blast that blows from the higher regions of the Apennine to the Adriatic, or from the latter comes still fresh and salt on its way to the mountains, must needs sweep Recanati in its course, and from the narrow shape of the city must sweep it thoroughly. The winters are much more severe there than in any part of the neighbouring district. The long line of walls, utterly useless now, if ever they were otherwise, for any purpose of defence, but admirable as a promenade for the citizens, encircle the city a little below the crest of the ridge, the last bit of which rises within them to the watershed line, so steeply as to make the little narrow lanes which climb from the different gates up to the main street almost impracticable for wheeled carriages. This main street runs along the highest crest of the ridge, and of itself constitutes nearly the entire city. The ancient town-hall stands at about the centre of its long extent, and by the dignity of its presence constitutes the immediate neighbourhood the heart and centre of the city. I was amused by lighting upon a curious indication of the degree in which this was felt to be the case in the olden time, and of the mania for exceptional legislation and privilege, which was a main characteristic of all ancient codes, in turning over a volume of the statutes by which Recanati governed herself in the Middle Ages. A certain amount of punishment, chiefly fine, having been enacted against assault, the code goes on to direct that double the aforesaid punishment shall be inflicted on whosoever shall commit an assault within the limits of a carefully defined part of the main street, comprising a short distance to the right, and as much to the left of the "*Palazzo pubblico.*"

Recanati seems to have maintained itself as a free self-governed community till it fell, gradually rather than by any violent revolution, under the government of the Popes. It never was ruled by any native "tyrant" or usurper, and doubtless was in a great degree enabled to escape that fate, by the consistent profession of Guelph principles, and fidelity to the suzerainty of the Popes. The little State was a strict and close oligarchy, without being an aristocracy— a singular constitution. The legislative power was vested in a council of two hundred citizens, the right of sitting in which was hereditary. But ninety-seven only of these hereditary legislators were nobles. The executive officers were by the form of the constitution to be chosen exclusively from among these. And it is very curious that the same constitution, which secured that privilege to the nobles, should also have secured to the plebeians a majority in the council. Curious also to observe that the quarrels and jealousies which were sure to arise from such provisions, cropped out to the surface and developed themselves into a violent struggle just when a similar struggle was raging in richer, larger, and more prosperous Florence. It is an instance of the epidemic nature of ideas. Similar thoughts, persuasions, desires, seem to take possession of widely sundered communities at the same time, as if the contagion of them were carried by the air, which alone is common to all of them. It is interesting too to observe that the struggle for political power between the nobles and non-nobles in this miniature little State was carried on, at least for a long time, not by extra-legal violence, but within the forms of the constitution, the two parties legislating against each other, as the nearly balanced majority in the council wavered to one side or the other.

During a great portion however of the many generations, during which Recanati lived under the above described constitution, practically self-governed, it was, and admitted itself to be subject to the Popes; and it is difficult to understand with any satisfactory degree of accuracy, what was the nature, and what the limits of their sovereign authority. There is, however, an interesting passage in the Recanati chronicles, which at all events proves that it was deemed highly desirable to be subjected directly to the Papal Court, and not to any secondary and nearer feudal superior.

The city of Osimo, about ten miles to the north of Recanati, on the top of a high hill, like all the rest of these numerous towns, was, unlike the latter, continually rebelling against the Popes.

On the accession of Innocent the Eighth, in 1484, Osimo seized the opportunity of withdrawing itself from the Papal authority; and when the Cardinal Giuliano della Rovere was sent from Rome to reduce it to obedience, the people of Recanati, glad to curry favour, and eager to help in oppressing a rival city, hated with an intensity accurately proportioned to the nearness of it, supplied the Cardinal with a number of troops. Now there is a small town called Montefano about ten miles to the west of Recanati, and as nearly as possible equidistant from Osimo, so that the three stand at the points of an equilateral triangle. This town had been subject to and ruled by Osimo. But in punishment for the rebellion of the latter city, and in reward for the assistance of Recanati, the Pope promised that Montefano should be taken from Osimo and given to Recanati. When the Cardinal della Rovere however had been set at defiance by the inhabitants of Osimo, who shut their gates in his face, he retired to Montefano, "where he was received," says the historian Calcagni,* "with such refinement of flattery and affection," that the inhabitants succeeded in persuading him to use his influence with the Pope, to the end that their town might be taken from Osimo but not given to Recanati;—that it might be immediately subjected instead to the Holy See. The Recanatesi however did not trust implicitly to Papal gratitude, nor the Montefanesi to Cardinalitial promises. Both parties sent ambassadors to Rome, and both instructed their representatives to have recourse to bribery. Little Montefano offered the Apostolic Chamber 1300 crowns for a bull subjecting it directly to the Holy See and to no other jurisdiction. Recanati told her men to offer 1600 crowns in the first instance, and to go higher if needs were. Nevertheless the remembrance in the Cardinal's mind of the "refined obsequiousness" of the Montefanesi prevailed; and after the matter had remained in suspense for five years, and the Apostolic Chamber had doubtless received the bribes from both parties, a bull was issued in 1489 granting the wishes of Montefano.

Notwithstanding the general fidelity of Recanati to the Holy See, the citizens of that self-governed little community occasionally gave the Popes a good deal of trouble. And Ughelli, the author of that great storehouse of Italian ecclesiastical history, the "Italia Sacra," more impressed, it would seem, by

* "Memorie Istoriche delle Città di Recanati." 1 vol. fol. Messina. 1711. p. 77.

these exceptional outbreaks, than by the more normal condition of relations between the city and the Roman See, has written some hard words about the fickle-mindedness and turbulence of the men of Recanati. This has grievously riled the local historians; and it is amusing to observe the eagerness with which they strive to show that their city merited no such reproaches. The best of these writers is Giuseppe Antonio Vogel, a Canon of the Cathedral of Recanati, who wrote a History of its Bishops, at the beginning of this century, which has just been published for the first time at Recanati, in two volumes in imperial quarto, in a style as regards typography, paper, and general getting up, that would do credit to the press of any capital city; and which truly astonished me, as the product of this little mountain town, not only as a specimen of the work which its presses could turn out, but as showing the amount of capital that could be risked on such a work, and the circulation for a book of the kind that could be reckoned on to return such an outlay. The price of the two handsome volumes on large paper, is ten dollars, equivalent to about two guineas.* The work takes the form of a chronological history of the Series of Bishops. But in communities, in which the civil and ecclesiastical affairs are mixed up together as they are in the cities of the Papal States, and in which the latter power is constantly encroaching on, and over-riding the former, a History of the Bishops is in fact a general history of the city to quite as

* The title of the work is "De Ecclesiis Recanatensi et Lauretana carumque Episcopis, Commentarius Historicus Josephi Antonio Vogel.—Recanati, 1859.—Badaloni.

great or to a greater degree, than a History of the French Kings is a History of France. And the only fault that can be found with Canon Vogel's History of Recanati is, that it is written in detestable Latin, comfortably intelligible only to him who is familiar with Ducange, instead of in good Italian. And this circumstance makes the recent publication of the book still more remarkable as an indication of the very noteworthy amount of attention and study which is now being bestowed in Italy on the sources of Italian history. It may very safely be asserted, that no London publisher of the present day would undertake the speculation of publishing an erudite historical work in Latin on the annals of any provincial city of England, of the bulk and pretensions of that which Signor Badaloni has printed wholly at his own risk, in this little remote highland city.

Among the occasional insurrections of the citizens of Recanati against the Popes which Canon Vogel honestly relates despite his anxiety to show that the city was mainly faithful to the Holy See, there is one, of which it is worth while to mention some of the leading circumstances, because they resulted in the most signal calamity that ever befel the city, and because they afford a vivid notion of the conditions under which society existed in those cities in the Middle Ages.

It was the year 1313; and John the Twenty-third was then "*Servus Servorum.*" One Frederick, "the son of Nicholas, and the grandson of John" *had been elected* Bishop by his fellow citizens and confirmed by the previous Pope, Boniface the Eighth. The Guelph and Ghibelline quarrel, as everybody knows, was then running high in Italy; and in an unfortunate hour a Ghibelline faction in Recanati succeeded in ejecting the Bishop and the Guelph party out of the city. And the leaders of the victorious faction, in the city, among whom I observe that one Percivallus and several of his family were among the most active, went in the month of April with arms in their hands to the Bishop's house, and plundered it, " carrying off 425 loads of wine, and bread, and other goods; and driving out his farmers from his lands, seizing whatever they could find of grain, olives, vine, &c., and cutting down the vineyards and the trees.*" Not content with this, they destroyed in the following month five houses belonging to the Bishop; "yea, and to such a pitch of audacity did they arrive," that in the month of August they went to the Church of the Blessed Virgin, and carried off all the money " *quæ erat in trunco dictæ Ecclesiæ*," and stole all the oblations, " *et omnes tortitios et faculas*†" and all the images of wax and of silver; and what was worse taking from the image of the Virgin Mary, " *et de Cona‡ ejus*," and from the image of our Lord Jesus Christ, " *quæ erat in dicta Cona* " all the garlands of silver " *cum pernis et sine pernis*" (pearls) and the headbands and veils of silk, " et omnes tobaleas di sirico et sine sirico," —(all the napkins of silk and not of silk.)

For which enormities they were sentenced by the

* Vogel. Op. cit. Vil. p. 108.
† Torches and tapers.
‡ Vogel, who cites these words from the sentence pronounced against the perpetrators of these deeds by the Apostolic court, explains "Cona" by the word "Statua." It must be a corruption of "Icona.."

criminal Judge of the March of Ancona to make good the damage done, *and* forfeit all their property to the Apostolic Chamber. But it was easier to pronounce this sentence than to enforce it. Pope John therefore makes Amelius the Rector of the March a present of these fines, leaving him to get them as best he may. Amelius sends his cousin Pontius Arnaldi who was Marshal of the March with a body of soldiers, who take possession of a suburb of the city; and issue thence a proclamation declaring that they have not come to do harm to any man, but to restore peace; and therefore invite "all those who for their crimes had been condemned to exile and confiscation of their goods to come and receive pardon for their offences." But as this gentle and courteous invitation sounded in the ears of the offenders very like the "Ducky, Ducky, come and be killed" of the nursery rhyme, they declined to profit by the Marshals kind suggestion. "*Quid tum illi? Arma arripiunt!*" writes the ecclesiastical historian, who of course is all on the side of authority and the higher powers. James and Bernard Percivalle, Zarolo, Leone, and Zanolo of the Leoni family, several of the Mazoleni family, other branches of the Percivalle family, together with Thomas the priest, all of them nobles of Recanati, league themselves with certain men from Ancona, who were then in the city, and secretly introduce into it a gang of noted rebels and desperadoes from neighbouring Osimo. No blacker nor more damnable deed than this, could a fourteenth century citizen be guilty of! To cut a few throats, and sack a few houses, *á titre de revanche*, as the French say, all among themselves, within their own walls, would have been nothing to it! But to bring in "foreigners" from the town on the opposite hill there, desperate fellows from that reprobate and accursed Osimo, the nest of rebellion and Ghibellinism, from out of which no good thing was ever known to come, —to admit the "natural enemies" of one's country into the gates! This indeed was an excess of atrocity which shewed that the authors of it had broken with the world and the world's law, and were ready for anything. And the truth is, that in all probability these Recanati nobles would have had recourse to no such desperate step, had it not been for those popular encroachments in the Council, before alluded to, which excluding the nobles, not only from that monopoly of the government, which they had formerly enjoyed, but from any share in it whatever, had made Recanati, as we may suppose those exasperated nobles to have phrased it, "no longer a place for a gentleman to live in;" and had driven them to think that there was no alternative left for them save making a successful dash for obtaining definitively the upper hand and power in the city, or, should the attempt fail, becoming desperate and outlawed men.

Well did the envious men of Osimo know that night, as they watched the band of desperadoes from their own city walls steal across the valley, up the opposite hill side, and under the shadow of the battlements of the betrayed city, that that night would be a dreadful and memorable one in Recanati!

As soon as the foreigners were in the city, a sudden onslaught was made on the Marshal's men, and on all the citizens, who took part with him. Three hundred of the latter were put to death. They were dragged through the streets by their feet. Many more were buried alive beneath the ruins of their houses levelled to the ground. Corpses dangling from gibbets, and headless trunks were seen on all sides. Infants were not spared, but were dashed to death on the stones. Women married as well as single, and what was much worse, holy nuns, were submitted to every outrage. Abbesses were turned out of their convents, and other women installed in their places. And worst of all, the Bishop's palace was levelled with the ground.

When the news of these doings in Recanati reached the ears of Pope John the Twenty-third at Rome, he instantly issued a bull, which is a curiosity of fourteenth century ecclesiastical invective eloquence* and reminds one of the style of the Ingoldsby "*Vir nequissime! quissime!! issime!!!*"

"Our Marshal of the Marches came to your city," the instrument recites, "with the mildest and most pacific intentions. All past offences were to be pardoned. But you, children of ingratitude and eternal malediction, as you are, returning evil for good, nor remembering with fear that you and the men of Osimo's pestiferous progenitors of damnable memory, fell, from the immensity of their demerits, into the ignominy of such ruin,"† that they were

---

\* It is to be found at length in the second vol. of Vogel's History, which consists entirely of documents.—P. 77.

† Sed vos, sicut ingratitudinis et perpetuæ maledictionis alumni, mala retribuentes pro bonis nec verentes, quod damnatæ memoriæ vestri et Auximani progenitores pestiferi ex ingentibus demeritis eorundem, in illius confusionis ignominiam corruerunt.

held up to the scorn and contempt of other cities by being deprived of their bishops, you have done abominations—recited in a sentence occupying an entire folio page. " Your iniquity has absorbed your intellect; pride has overturned your reason; and wickedness has thrown down your understanding, your malice depriving you of right judgment."*

The statement of the evidence on which the charges rest is curious: *" Sane vulgaris fama denuntiat, et veritas notio publica manifestat, ipsamque transgressio injuriosa notariat..."* "You murdered," the document goes on to say " even fellow citizens, *qui caro de carne vestra, et os de ossibus vestris extiterant."* And, what "exceeds every excess of impiety," you murdered infant chilcen, despite the custom, which hath often been observed in war, "*ut faciem, quam pubertas non noverat gladium bellatorum non læderet.*"

It is notable that the perpetrators of all the recited atrocities are accused among other charges, which the bull continues reiterating, enlarging on, ringing the changes on, with " miserably rushing deeply down into the abyss of infidelity."† And subsequently as a justification for the severity of the punishment inflicted on Recanati, we find the " Marchio," or Lord of the Marches, who acted for the Church, "*imponendo eis vitium idolatriæ.*" And the historian tells us that an idol was found,

* " Absorbnit intellectum vestrum iniquitas; consilium evertit elatio; et precipitavit in vobis nequitia rationem, rectum judicium malitia depravante."

* "In infidelitatis profundam voraginem miserabiliter corruendo."

which some of the rebel leaders " were said" to have worshipped. It is curious to observe that a priest in his anger always rushes to an accusation of unorthodox *belief*, however little the real matter in hand may have to do with any question of creed.

The exuberant indignation, however, in the Papal bull, ends in what seems, considering the real gravity of the offence, a weak and feeble conclusion. The criminals are told to return to their allegiance, and do so no more, under pain, if they do remain impenitent, "*quod absit!*" of excommunication and interdict.

Far from repenting, the rebels fortified themselves in the city now wholly in their hands. Pope John launched his interdict against it; and every priest obeyed save Friar Andrew, the Prior of the Augustine Convent, who said his mass, and rung his bells, he alone in the whole city; and served the rebels, it may be supposed as Friar Tuck served Robin Hood and his men, and "absolved all their sins," as the case might require." This Friar Andrew who thus snapped his fingers at·the Pope and his interdict, was imprisoned for his disobedience, as soon as the Church got the upper hand again in Recanati. But there was another turn in the wheel for him after that. For when shortly afterwards the Antipope, Clement the Eighth, caused a schism in the Church, Friar Andrew of course took his side, and was made by him Bishop of Recanati!

To return however to the story of the rebellion, when the Pope found that his threats and his scolding produced no effect, he sent some troops under Bernard Varani of Camerino to reduce Recanati to obedience. But on the 15th of September, 1320, the Recanati Ghibellines coming down from their hill into the valley beneath Castel Fidardo defeated the Varani and his troops with great slaughter;—thus beating *Servus Servorum* for the first time on ground, that was afterwards to be so fatal to him.

Upon that occasion however the Pope had a resource which no longer remains to him. He sent Laurentius de Mondaino, the inquisitor, to make a few inquiries into the particulars of the creed of these stubborn rebels, and that sharp-scented heresy-hunter very soon nosed such a pestilential odour of infidelity and idolatry, that his master found himself compelled to call on the faithful of all the neighbouring countries to make a Crusade against these corruptors of the Faith. At that word a vast number of fighting men from the Romagna, from Tuscany, Lombardy, and other parts of Italy assembled and marched against the doomed little city on its lofty hill. Of course resistance to such an array, coming against them on such a pretext, was not to be thought of by the Recanatesi. The terrified city rose against the leaders in the late disturbances, turned them out of the walls, sent ambassadors to offer the keys of their gates in the most humble manner to the Lord "Marchio," pulled down the gateways themselves that the standards of the Church might not have to be lowered, as they said, to pass under them; and in short they did everything in their power to appease his anger, and moderate the storm that was about to burst on them.

But the nephew of the "Marchio" had been traitorously killed at Recanati, though not by the citizens who were now seeking to appease his kinsman, as the "Marchio" knew perfectly well.

And according to the terrible "solidarity," which universally in those ages made kinsmen responsible for the deeds of those of their blood, and cities for the acts done within their walls, Recanati had to abide the vengeance due to the deed. The "Marchio" grimly answered to their supplications that they had been found to be idolaters, and that their city must undergo the fate reserved for the towns of the infidels.

So the town was fired in several places; and any one who has stood on these breezy walls, may judge how the flames devoured it. Almost the whole of it was destroyed; and the sight of the blazing city, visible as it must have been from the opposite coast of Dalmatia, and from many and many a town and city of the district around, must have been felt as a terrible manifestation of Papal vengeance. "It was," says an ancient writer, "a deed of too great cruelty on the part of the Lord "Marchio," but on the part of God a just judgment on the great crimes of the city."

For a long time afterwards deeds and legal instruments, and records of all sorts continued to be dated in Recanati from the epoch of this terrible calamity; "*a tempore combustionis civitatis Recanati,*" and documents are recited, "*quæ combusta fuerunt tempore quo tota civitas combusta fuit.*"

Our return from Recanati to Loreto was performed in the same mad style, in which we had left the latter city; and it was so much the worse, as the hill to be come down from Recanati is much higher than that of Loreto. The rays of the setting sun were streaming full on Castel Fidardo just in front of us, as we descended the hill, and gilded the reddish little town into an object of positive beauty, as it was seen against the background of Monte Conero, an isolated hill, rising suddenly from the coast, and hiding Ancona behind it.

It was by certain by-paths round the base of this mountain known only to the peasants of the district, that General Lamoricière escaped into Ancona after the defeat of Castel Fidardo.

## CHAPTER XVII.

FROM LORETO TO OSIMO—POSITION OF OSIMO—CLASSICAL AUTHORS WHO MENTION IT—BESIEGED BY BELISARIUS—MAINTAINED ITS INDEPENDENCE—ITS RESISTANCE TO THE POPES—SUCCEEDS IN CAUSING ITS FORTRESS TO BE DESTROYED—THE CITIZENS TAKE COGNIZANCE OF THE DISORDERS OF A NUNNERY, AND SUCCEED IN HAVING IT ABOLISHED—THE CATHEDRAL OF OSIMO—REMARKABLE SERIES OF PORTRAITS—STORM OF WIND AT OSIMO—WALK ROUND THE WALLS—FROM OSIMO TO ANCONA—MONTE CONERO—POSITION OF ANCONA—APPARENT DISCREPANCY BETWEEN STRABO AND POMPONIUS MELA—ENTRANCE TO ANCONA—FIRST IMPRESSIONS MADE BY THE CITY—CONTRAST BETWEEN IT AND THE CITIES AROUND IT—INCONVENIENCE OF THE "FREE PORT"—MEMORIAL OF ANTIQUITY—THE CATHEDRAL—ITS SITUATION—ITS DANGERS FROM THE ENCROACHMENTS OF THE SEA—MILITARY STRENGTH OF ANCONA—THE PORT.

THE drive from Loreto to Osimo, though the distance is not above ten miles, was an affair of some two hours and a half. For we had not our daredevil boy with his raw-boned, long-legged old charger, and jingling rattletrap of a waggon, but a carriage and pair "respectable" and proportionably slow; and the hill up to Osimo is a long one, although less so than that of Recanati, the latter being 1034 Parisian feet above the level of the sea, while Osimo is only 871. Nor does the city make nearly so fine an appearance from the outside. Within, however, there is much more that is picturesque and characteristic.

It is a city of more undoubted antiquity than most others of this part of Italy, and possesses a greater number of ancient inscriptions than any other. It was a Roman colony, dating from the close of the sixth century after the building of Rome, and is mentioned by Cæsar, Plutarch, Velleius Paterculus, Lucan, Strabo, and Procopins. "*Est Auximum,*" says the last, "*urbium Piceni princeps, quam Romani Metropolim nationis vocare solent, . . . . . . excelso in colle sita nullum habet in plane aditum; quo fit, ut hostibus omnino sit inaccessa.*" According to the same writer Belisarius besieged it in person, to recover it from the Goths who had taken possession of it. He succeeded in making himself master of it by means of poisoning the wells, after a siege, as another chronicler reports, of six months; and after having had a narrow escape of his life, threatened by an arrow from the walls, and turned aside by one of those close to him, at the cost of his own hand.

The history of this little town, in which the spirit of independence seems long to have run high, affords another example of a community which succeeded, or very nearly succeeded, in preventing itself from falling into the power of any tyrant, and the hated "*governo di uno solo.*" I say very nearly, because one or two tentatives which were made, did keep the city in subjection for a short period, but failed to establish themselves. And the story of these attempts illustrates very clearly the sort of dangers to which these little mediæval communities were exposed, and the small circumstances on the turn of which their republicanism or subjection depended. In the case of Recanati, we have a community which maintained its freedom from the tyranny of any lord, by a fidelity, constant, with a few and short exceptions, to the Church. The general political sentiment there was always Guelph. In Osimo the task of preserving their freedom was a more difficult one; for the city was often in a state of rebellion against the Church.

But we find several little indications in the course of the history of Osimo of the spirit, sense, and independence of the plucky little community. In the year 1500 we find the town insisting on the demolition of the fortress, which had been erected for the usual purpose a long time before. And six years later they obtained that which Perugia has at length in these days achieved. It is true the men of Osimo had a pretext of a very curious kind, which had the fortunate effect of placing the clergy of the city on their side. The very ancient Cathedral occupies the extreme summit of the hill, a kind of peak rising to an elevation above the rest of the city. This spot offered the only position adapted for the erection of a fortress intended to dominate the city. But the space thus rising above the rest of the top of the hill is very small, and was not enough to accommodate conveniently both the Cathedral and the fortress; so that Church and State could not on this occasion walk together as lovingly as they were wont to do in this part of the world. The consequence was, as usual, that the successor of St. Peter did not hesitate an instant to sacrifice his spiritual to his temporal interests; and built his fortress all round the church, so as absolutely to block up the main door of the Cathedral, in such sort that the Bishop and Canons were compelled to perform their services in another church;—to the great indignation of the inhabitants, who never rested, till the obnoxious building was levelled to the ground.

Again the city succeeded by the energy of its proceeding in achieving another object, which at a later day baffled all the power of the celebrated Ricci, the reforming Bishop of Pistoia, and of his patron Peter Leopold, the reforming Grand Duke of Tuscany. The extremely interesting story of their endeavours, —principally of the Bishop's—to reform one or two nunneries of notoriously ill fame in the diocese of Pistoia, is not so well known as it deserves to be, because De Potter, the historian of it, has given the details of the atrocities committed by the offending communities with such fulness of detail, and unveiled nakedness of phrase, as to make his book an absolutely unreadable one to a great part of the world of readers. The upshot of the matter was that the active opposition of the Jesuits, and the passive "*non possumus*" resistance of the Court of Rome foiled all attempts at reformation, and well-nigh broke the Bishop's heart.

The Osimo men were more energetic, or more fortunate, or better favoured by the complexion of the times. We find the Council of the town again debating what was to be done with the nuns of a certain convent of the Order of St. Clare, who were found to be incorrigible, "*eo quod ipsum monasterium a longo tempore malam et inhonestam vitam continuando, ad maximam apud dictos cives in-*

*famiam ac nauseam pervenerit, ita ut experientiâ evidentissimâ edocente, fuerit sæpius per cives dictos ac prelatos incorrigibile judicatum et insanabile;"* * "to such a pitch, that the said monastery, continuing for a long time past an evil and dishonest life, has become to the greatest degree infamous and revolting to the said citizens, so that by the teaching of the most evident experience, it has been again and again judged by the said citizens and prelates to be incorrigible and irremediable." For some time the steps taken appear to have been attended with no result. But the Council returns again and again to the charge; and in 1510 succeeds in causing the nunnery to be shut up and abolished. It is a remarkable instance of a body of lay citizens exercising a supervision of the kind over an ecclesiastical corporation, especially so close and secret a one as a nunnery; remarkable too that in 1510 there should have existed in Osimo a tone of public feeling, which made the irregularities and scandals of the nuns of St. Clare revolting to the lay morality of the city. These Osimo nuns must have been bad indeed, if their conduct was more scandalous than that of certain communities composed of the most noble ladies in Florence, and perfectly well tolerated by the public feeling of that refined and polished city. But public feeling, and the tone of morality in Florence was, at the period in question, the result of a social system under the rule of a Medicis; at little highland Osimo that of a society self governed as a republic.

* "Memorie Istorico-critiche della Chiesa, e de' Vescavi di Osimo Raccolte ed illustrate da Monsignor Pompeo Compagnoni, Vescovo di della Città. 5 vols 4to. Roma. 1782." Vol. III.,p. 117.

The Cathedral of Osimo, freed, as we have seen from the encumberment of the fortress, is an interesting building, of which some portions are of great antiquity. The door on the north side of the nave, which is the principal entrance, is with its deep and ample porch curiously ornamented. The moulding around the doorway is formed of two snakes, whose heads meet at the summit of the arch, and hold an apple between them, half of which is in the jaws of either reptile; while three or four coils of their tails are so disposed as to form the bases from which the door-mouldings rise. The interior of the church is remarkable for a series of portraits of the Bishops of Osimo from the time when the city was raised to the dignity of an Episcopal See to the present day. They form a series uniform in size and shape, being ovals of some four feet in the long, and three or so in the short diameter, each in a handsomely moulded frame of yellow marble. They occupy as may be imagined, by far the greater part of the surface of the walls of the church, and produce a very singular effect.

The deep and ample porch before the door of the Cathedral is at Osimo an object of necessity quite as much as of ornament. For the city on its isolated hill is exposed to such winds as the neighbouring country knows nothing of. The day we passed there was a perfectly fine one, with a brilliant sun shining in a deep-blue cloudless sky. But such a wind was blowing through the streets of the little town, that it was without exaggeration at times as much as I could do to walk against it. It was market-day there, and the dealers had erected their stalls and tables in the picturesque *piazza* immediately below the Cathedral, with the old *Palazza della Comunità* on one side and the more recent home of the Papal Government on the other. But they were obliged to take them down in all haste, or they would assuredly have been very shortly blown away over the city walls into the valley below.

Here also, as at most of these hill-built Picenian towns, the walk around the outside of the walls is charming; more especially that part of the circuit of them which surrounds the space on which the fortress stood, and which is now occupied by the Bishop's garden. But there are certain angles in the wall, which it really was almost a service of danger to turn, while the wind was singing such a dirge, as it did, among the cypresses of the Bishop's garden.

Like its old rival and enemy, Recanati, Osimo has the air and appearance of a particularly clean and healthy city. With the washing it must get from every shower, and the sweeping from every wind, it could perhaps hardly be otherwise. In the *piazza* from which the wind had swept every particle of dust, and in which the market people were busy in securing their goods and stalls, the national guard of Osimo were drawn up in front of the *Palazzo pubblico*, and were going through their exercise amid a great deal of laughter at the difficulties of the task in such a tempest; and mutual quizzing between the soldiers and the equally embarrassed market people.

From Osimo our route took us to Ancona, a drive of about twelve miles, behind, or on the inland side of that isolated mass of Monte Conero, which has been before mentioned. From Fermo to the Porto di Recanati below Loreto the coast is entirely flat, and the road accordingly follows the shore. From Ancona to Pesaro it is the same, although the mountains at this part of the coast press much more closely on the shore. But between these two tracts of coast, from the Porto di Recanati, that is to say, to Ancona, the way is barred by Monte Conero, the seaward cliffs of which descend sheer into the water. The Viâ Flaminia therefore was,—the present post-road is,—and the railroad will be, obliged to dip inland and pass behind it  This isolated position of Monte Conero, and its sudden rise from out of a soil formed of horizontal strata, and of an entirely different system, has rendered it an object of much interest to geologists. The Italian geologists consider it part of an Anti-Apennine chain, or secondary range running parallel to the main chain, which being of no great elevation, remains for long spaces buried beneath the tertiary formation, and here and there thrusting itself up through it, with the upper chalk formation of the Apeninnes. The height of Monte Conero is only 1812 Parisian feet above the level of the sea; but it completely shuts out Ancona and all the coast to the northward from the landscape as seen from the walls of Osimo or its neighbour towns.

This chalk formation gives an appearance to the scenery of the road to Ancona, as it winds up and down the minor hills around the base of Monte Conero very English in character. There are parts of the South Downs of which it strongly reminded me; but the beauty of the exquisitely fine turf of our breezy downs is wanting. The country more resembles some of the light soil districts of arable-land, which the road passes through between Basingstoke and Winchester, with their stony fields and turnip-strewed sheep-pens.

Nothing is seen of Ancona, till the traveller is close upon it. The first sign of its vicinity is the huge fortress, which crowns the peak in which Monte Conero ends, and round the base of which the road winds. The mountain, which, as has been said, rises so immediately from the sea as to leave no space for a road from the southward along the shore, first juts out from the line of coast in that bold headland, from which the Greek founders of the city called it "Ancon," and then receding so as to leave a space barely sufficient, or rather not sufficient for the city, advances again in a perpendicular cliff so close to the shore, as to leave only just room for the gate of the city. The position of Ancona is thus one of very great military strength. It would be still stronger, and would be walled around with a natural barrier of cliff on all sides were it not that, at that part of the mountain which recedes the farthest from the shore, thus leaving a small space for the city to occupy,—a depression of the hill, not sufficient to be called a valley, occurs which divides the mountain into two heads, and allows a road to descend from the higher ground, and access to be had to the city at that point. The two headlands thus divided are called, the one Monte Guasco, and the other Monte Astagno, or Capodimonte. But they are both parts of one and the same mountain mass, Monte Conero, which name should be understood to inclnde the whole of the high region encircled by a line drawn from the coast a little to the north of Porto di Recanati, following the course of the road behind the mountain, and coming down to the coast again just outside the gate of Ancona. And the interest of these topographical details lies in the fact, that they put an end to one of those difficulties so dear to erudite antiquaries, which has arisen from an apparent discrepancy between the statements of Strabo and Pomponius Mela. The first says that Ancona is situated on a promontory, which bending towards the north encloses it in its curve. And the description is as accurate as it could well be. Mela speaks of the city as "placed in the narrow bay of two promontories converging from different directions, in the form of a bent elbow, and thence by the Greeks called, 'Ancon,' which is also a very intelligible description of the locality. And the whole of the discrepancy between the two accounts consists in the one writer having considered the two headlands, partially divided, as above described, as two mountains; while the other more correctly looking upon the entire mass of Monte Conero as one and the same mountain, speaks of it as such.

Coming round the base of the hill topped by the fort above mentioned,—by which is not to be understood a mediæval fortress, picturesque and useless, but a huge mass of modern fortifications not picturesque at all, but hideous with lumpy earthworks and long straight lines of white wall in excellent repair, and bristling with cannon and sentries;—the road descends in a direct line to the beach, at a spot where the railway terminus now is; and then turning at a right angle to the right hand,—back again southwards, that is,—enters the city by a narrow causeway having the sea on the left hand, and the precipitous face of the white cliff on the other, and by the same gate through which passes all the traffic going northwards. So that the traveller from the south has encircled the entire city before entering it.

Having once entered the city by winning one's way through this narrow pass, which is not altogether an easy task, as nearly all the communication between Ancona and the rest of the world has to pass by it, and the difficulty is increased by the Custom-house impediments arising from the fact that Ancona is a free port; and having admired the natural strength of the position due to the remarkable relative situation of the cliff, the sea, and the city, one begins, as one struggles through the dirty and over-encumbered street to *the* Hotel, "La Pace," in the centre of it, to perceive that Ancona is not a pleasing city to the eye, nor indeed to the nose, nor the ear.

There is much indeed that should make it pleasing to the mind's eye of the political economist. There are signs of prosperity; although much less than from the natural advantages of the place there ought to be, and much less than there will very shortly be. But the changed world in which the traveller suddenly finds himself as soon as he has turned the corner of Monte Conero, and made his way through the waggon and omnibus, and *dogana* choked gateway, is startling enough. It is like coming out of a past century into the present.

Behind him he has left the quiet little old-world

cities, each remote on its lofty hill, though in sight of each other, with their great uninhabited or half-inhabited palaces, their dreamy streets and breezy crumbling battlements, their ever-open and long-disused city gates, their lazy easy-going inns with abundant space, if sometimes somewhat restricted larders, their leisurely strongly localized inhabitants, always with plenty of time on their hands and plenty of inclination for a chat anent their glories and the histories and particularities of their respective towns, their storied cathedrals, and their picturesque town-halls.

He turns the shoulder of Monte Conero, struggles through the gateway of Ancona, and suddenly finds himself amid a jabbering population of jostling brokers, polyglot commissioners, money-dealing Jews, and cosmopolitan bagmen. He has to go up no end of stairs, to find a little closet of a bedroom, and be thankful to get it; he dines at a *table d' hôte* by the side of a ringed and curled individual with very dirty hands and a magnificent diamond pin in his smart shirt-front, who talks fluently in rather queer English, and who turns out to be a Wallachian diamond merchant; instead of having a pretty girl to wait on him, anxious to do the utmost to please him which the limited resources of the house will permit, and very willing to chatter for half an hour together, while the dawdling meal is in progress, he is served by a perspiring waiter with a greasy cloth under his arm, who in his hot haste dashes a plateful of food before him, and is gone before he can decline it; he is nearly run over in the narrow streets by carts, barrows, trucks, waggons laden with barrels, sacks, cases, and drawn some by horses, some by men nearly as naked as their quadruped fellow-labourers; he is challenged by sentries for walking through some gateway, or approaching some fortification, or setting foot on some glacis in contravention of the rules; he is considered by everybody who sees him, to be anxious to go on board some steamboat, or to catch some railway train; and before long he discovers, that not being so anxious, and not having any bills to discount, no samples of goods to offer for sale, nor any intention of purchasing such, nor baggage to "clear" in or out, he has plainly no business at Ancona, and that there is no room for him there.

No! Ancona is not a pleasant city in its outward physiognomy. It has all the annoyances and disagreeables of a sea port, without any of the agreeables that should belong to the coast. There is no possibility of pleasant rambles along the shore; all exit to the southward being absolutely forbidden not only by the cliff itself, but by fortresses and walls, and sentries, *ad infinitum*; and exit to the north leading only to the crowded mile or so of causeway between the city and the railway station, and beyond that to a flat and very ugly shore, cut up by little creeks, and hedged in by the railway. There is no shipping of any interest in the offing. There is not even any fish to eat,—or none that is worth eating. Then there are all the inconveniences and botherations of that stupidest and most illusory of all institutions a so-called "free port,"—the whole advantage and scope of which might be attained without any of the infinite trouble which arises from the present arrangement, by a system of bonded warehouses. The present plan converts the entire city into a sort of huge and cunningly contrived douane-trap, into which whoever enters the place finds that he has been inveigled. "*Facilis descensus! Sed revocare gradum!*" You go into Ancona freely enough,—not easily indeed, for the narrow way is blocked by the troubles, sorrows and labours of the crowd, who are striving to escape from the " free port ;" but that getting out, while the railway whistle of the train which is to carry you away is warning you that you have not a minute to lose, and the *doganieri* are as impassively unconscious of any reason for accelerating their operations, as if time were indeed only made for more vulgar souls than they,—that is a "*revocare gradum*" which may well make one repent of having entered the trap.

Not that Ancona is without interesting memorials and monuments of its past history, and of an antiquity which is second in its pretensions to those of no other city in the Peninsula. Fragments of mediæval architecture are abundant; memorials of the period of Roman domination not rare; nor are traces of the civilization of a yet earlier epoch wanting. You may admire the fine old arched entrance, noble staircase, and richly moulded door-cases of a house, up the filthy stairs of which you are making your way to get a note changed by a Jew banker,—(the Jew element in the population is remarkably strong in Ancona,)—and you may find on inquiry, that the building in question was once a commandery of the Templars. You may be making your way among obstructions of all sorts to the little bit of a quay, which forms the Harbour of Ancona, in the hope of getting a mouthful of fresh sea-breeze from the Adriatic, and stepping briskly out of the way of a troop of galley-slaves, clanking along in their chains in the custody of a file of soldiers with loaded muskets, and may find yourself standing under a celebrated Roman arch, the work of Trajan, which formed the ancient sea-gate of the city.

There is one thing however to be seen at Ancona, which it must be admitted is alone worth a visit to the city, including the trouble of getting out of it again. It is the Cathedral—not so much for the sake of the building itself, though it is not without points of interest, as for the magnificence and grandeur of its site. It is unquestionably, as far as my experience goes, the most finely situated church in Europe.

A part of the mass of Monte Conero, as has been said, juts out into the sea, before receding so as to leave space for the town, and thus forms the *ancona* which has given the place its name, and the harbour which gives it its value. On the topmost headland of this jutting promontory, which protrudes from the coast line, with an inclination towards the north, far enough out into the sea to be washed at its base on both sides, and to command a twofold seaview from its summit, the Cathedral stands on the spot where stood the

"Domus Veneris quam Dorica sustinet Ancon"

of Juvenal's Fourth Satire.

The position of the Cathedral, perhaps in consequence of the disposition of the foundations of the ancient temple which preceded it, is not in accordance with the usual rule. For the west front, or rather that which should be the west front, with its fine red marble porch and columns, stands facing the opposite coast of Dalmatia, from which with a good glass it must be visible. The whole city and its port are close beneath the eye, which may wander away along the coast-line to the northwards as far as Pesaro, but is prevented from scanning the numerous city crowned hills of Picenum to the south by the intervening mass of Monte Conero.

The building on this magnificent site, first as a Temple to Venus, and then as one of the earliest of Christian Cathedrals,—for Ancona boasts that it was the first city in Italy to receive the Gospel,—has stood there exposed to every storm of the " Improbus Hadria" for, it would be rash to say how many centuries. But it is to be feared that it will not stand there much longer. For the sea has within the memory of man been making very serious encroachments on the back or inner side of the promontory. The east, or altar end, of the church, stands immediately above the cliff on this side;— almost close now to the edge of the utterly precipitous face of it. But the danger consists in the fact that within the memory of man, a considerable space intervened between the walls and the precipice. And it is very easy to calculate that, if the cliff continues to be eaten away at the same rate as has been the case latterly, a few more decades will close the long life of this celebrated fane.

From the brow of the cliff, on the outward side of the promontory, looking towards the coast of Dalmatia that is to say, a complete view may be had of the new works which the present Government are executing for the further strengthening of the place as a naval and military station. And it is easy for the least instructed eye to see that the natural disposition of the ground has done so much towards fortifying the town, that it needs but a helping hand from art to become one of the strongest positions,— probably the strongest on all the coast of Italy.

As a port, it does not seem to me that Ancona has the possibilities requisite for becoming a very important one. The Italians of the Pontifical States used to think very much otherwise, as is indicated by the old popular saying:

> "Unus Petrus in Roma,
> Una turris in Cremona,
> Unus portus in Ancona!"

But then to the inhabitants of the Adriatic side of the Peninsula, Ancona is their little all in this respect.

## CHAPTER XVIII.

FROM ANCONA TO RIMINI BY RAIL—RIMINI TO SAN MARINO—DIFFICULTY OF THE JOURNEY—POSITION OF THE TOWN—ITS ELEVATION—MEANS OF REACHING IT—APPEARANCE OF THE TOWN ON APPROACHING IT—LIFE AT SAN MARINO—POSTAL ARRANGEMENTS—TERRITORY OF THE REPUBLIC—THE "BORGO"—ASCENT THENCE TO THE CITY—MANUFACTURE OF GUNPOWDER—OF PLAYING CARDS—SOLITUDE OF THE TOWN—ITS ASPECT—CHURCH—WATER SUPPLY—THE FORTRESS—ITS GUARDIAN—ITS POSITION—ANCIENT NAME OF SAN MARINO—VIEW FROM THE FORTRESS—INMATES OF IT—ADMINISTRATION OF JUSTICE—MEETING OF THE COUNCIL—SUNRISE VISIT TO THE CASTLE—KNOCKING UP THE CITY—SUNRISE FROM THE CASTLE BATTLEMENTS—COAST OF DALMATIA—PRESERVATION OF ITS INDEPENDENCE BY SAN MARINO—RETURN TO RIMINI—THENCE TO FLORENCE—CONCLUSION.

HAVING thus suddenly plunged at Ancona into the midst of nineteenth century ways and associations, we were prepared for leaving it by rail, and rushing blindfold, as it were, through a wide tract of country, which separated us from one other remote nook, as rarely visited by, and as little known to travellers as any perhaps in Italy, with which we intended to conclude for the present our Lenten ramble through the by-ways.

It was not that there is any lack of interest in the cities we thus dashed past, unheedingly. The country, indeed, of this part of the Adriatic coast, though aboundingly rich and fertile, is not picturesque; for it is too monotonous in its magnificent extent of never-ending cornfields to delight other eyes, as it does those of its owners. But the thick-set and populous cities, which dot this fertile and wealthy district, and which have every one of them important and interesting independent histories of their own, Sinigaglia, Fano, Pesaro, La Cattolica, Rimini, are all well worthy of being studied in their present appearance, and still more in their past history. But there is the railway! They may any one, or all of them, be reached with the utmost readiness; they lie in the traveller's beaten path; and therefore not in that of the journey described in this volume.

The one remaining neglected nook, which we purposed on this occasion exploring, lies indeed only about twelve miles off this line of rail; and yet, as has been said, it is as little known a spot as any in Italy. But then the twelve miles which lead from Rimini to San Marino are twelve such miles *comme il y en a peu*. "*Non cuivis curru contingit adire*" San Marino!

And when even curious travellers, with ideas of thirty miles an hour in their heads as the normal average rate of locomotion, are told that five hours must be spent in achieving the twelve miles that separate them from the little highland town, which they can descry perched on its eagle's nest away in the horizon, they abandon the enterprize, thinking that the proposed game will not be found to be worth so large an expenditure of candle.

They are wrong! And those who will take my

advice, and perform the pilgrimage will not, I venture to say, think that their time and labour have been ill spent.

There is something curious, something exciting to the imagination in visiting this the smallest and the oldest of the social bodies in Europe, this virgin Republic of eight hundred years' duration, which has never wished, and does not wish to change its lot;—this only spot of Italian ground which does not aspire to unite itself to the dominions of the King of Italy, and which the Italian nation has no desire to possess.* But the physical aspect and peculiarities of the place are yet more calculated to repay a traveller for the trouble of visiting them. The situation of the town of San Marino is one of the most remarkable and extraordinary in Europe.

The only road by which it is approachable is that from Rimini, to the south-west of which it is situated, in such a position, that a line drawn from that point at right angles to the coast-line of the Adriatic would very nearly, if not exactly touch the little town. Its elevation above the level of the sea is no less than 2366 Parisian feet.

When on inquiry at Rimini a small covered carriage with one horse was proposed to us for the excursion, we suggested the desirability of a lighter carriage and two horses; but were told in answer that it would make no difference at all;—that no horse or horses could draw us up the mountain;—that that work must be done by oxen, which would do the

* Since the above was written, a treaty has been signed in due form, regularizing the relations between the Kingdom of Italy and the Republic of San Marino.

journey in the regular time, neither more nor less, whether the carriage were a little lighter or a little heavier!

So we bowed to experience, and set off in the direction of the mountains, the first few miles of the road taking us across the rich alluvial flat in which Rimini is situated.

By the time we came to the commencement of the ascent, we could see somewhat more accurately the shape of the hill rising in the clear atmosphere before us. Gradually the white line of buildings could be discerned high up on the mountain, but considerably below its top; and I feared that we had been deceived by the statement, that the town was placed absolutely on the summit of the peak. Immediately above this line of buildings a black face of apparently precipitous rock rose to a very considerable height. In truth, we said to each other, it would be absurd to suppose that the town could be on the top of that wall of crag! Neither oxen nor any other quadrupeds could scale that rock! and faith, it looks sufficiently inaccessible to bipeds!

But before going much further, we could distinguish the outline of so sharply defined and square-looking a projection on the very highest peak of the outline of the crag, that we thought it surely must be a building of some sort. Gradually the eye became certain that a sharp irregular line, which gave the precipice the appearance of being topped with battlements, must be composed of the outlines of buildings. And in fact, almost incredible as it seemed, an illuminating sunbeam just then falling full on the face of the rock and the crest of it, showed beyond all dispute, that the first object we had made out on the topmost peak, was in truth a castle keep, and that the battle-mented angular line was composed of the tops of the houses of the town of San Marino!

Some small pilgrimage-chapel piled up by the enthusiasm of a faith, that deemed the painful transport of each sweat-bedewed stone the purchase money of so much exemption from purgatorial torture, I have seen in positions almost as inaccessible. But a town in such a position! A community of men and women, needing bakers and butchers, needing doctors! being born and being buried up there on the top of that precipice among the eagles' nests! Eagles' nests in truth there are none. For the bird is not sociable in his habits; and ubiquitous man has taken possession of the storm-beaten peaks, that seem fitted only for his solitary residence. But the eagles assuredly would live there if San Marino the Dalmatian soldier, turned Christian quarryman, had not taken the place from them.

Butchers! Bakers! Doctors! Why the Post goes up there! The very notion seemed absurd! As well expect a daily delivery on the summit of Mont Blanc! But there *is* a daily post, man, boy, and donkey, communicating between that widespread smiling sunny world of cities and towns down there below, and this stern and storm-swept eyrie. The arrivals are not very regular to be sure; and in winter often not at all, the postboy and his donkey wisely declining to tempt the stormy crag that day. And this uncertainty, together with the considerations of a wise economy of the resources of the State, has given rise to a novel mode of serving the San Marino public with their correspondence. In order to avoid the expensive necessity of keeping a post-office open for the inhabitants to seek their letters when they please, or the yet more expensive plan of sending them round to the several houses, the manner is to ring the great town bell, when the donkey from the world below arrives. Then San Marino expects that every man, who wants his letters, shall hasten to be present at the opening of the bag. Should he fail to be so, he must wait for his correspondence till the next day.

But this is anticipating information acquired at a subsequent period of our excursion.

Very shortly after we began to ascend the first slopes of the hill, a little bridge over a streamlet was pointed out to us as the boundary of the territory of the Republic. This consists of the mountain itself and a certain portion of the surrounding valleys, to the extent of a circuit about eight miles in the longest and five in the shortest diameter. The inhabitants of this district are about 8000 in number.

We could not help observing as we advanced into the territory of the Republic that there was a notable deterioration in the appearance of the agriculture. But it is probable that this is to be attributed wholly to the far greater poverty of the soil, which as might be expected becomes lighter and poorer as the hill is ascended. After long hours of wearily creeping upwards, at the monotonous unvarying and wonderfully slow pace of the oxen, who move with a machine-like regularity, apparently utterly unaffected by the greater or lesser weight of the load behind them, we at length reached that white line under the precipitous cliff, which we had first perceived; and were told that that was the "*Borgo*" of San Marino; that the task of the oxen was ended here; that he who would go to the city on the rock above must do so by means of his own legs, or in the saddle. To go up the face of the rock to the city, which we could see peering over the edge of the precipice some five hundred feet above us, is as impossible either to man or horse as to go up the side of St. Paul's. The rock is absolutely perpendicular, though the face of it is sufficiently varied by fissures and little ledges to admit of a great portion of it being richly enamelled with a very various growth of wild-flowers. This face of the rock is turned towards the north-north west, and is therefore much covered with mosses and lichens, which could not live there, if the exposition were to the south. The same circumstances of position cause the "*Borgo*," which is closely nestled in at the foot of the precipice to be totally without sun during all the winter, and to have but a few hours of it even in the height of the summer.

The only inn, we were told, was down here in the Borgo. There was a private house, where beds might be had up in the city. But there was one "*forestiere*," a gentleman from Rimini, up there already. And the resources of the place would not furnish two other beds. So we took possession of some very tolerable quarters in the lower town; and then set forth on foot to scale the height above us. We found a very sufficient bridle-path cut in the side of the mountain, a little to the northward, where, though steep enough to make the zigzags of the path too abrupt for wheels, the face of the rock was not absolutely vertical as in the part immediately fronting Rimini and the Adriatic.

By the side of the road on the way up, and very near the top,—just outside the city gates,—I saw a large quantity of gunpowder,—several barrels full,—spread out on a sheet to dry in the sun, without any protection or precaution, save such, was secured by the presence of a lad, who was lying half asleep on the turf, by the side of his dangerous charge. I could not but think of the result of a spark from the cigar of any passenger! For there was nothing whatever to prevent any one from passing close by the mass of gunpowder either smoking, or carrying fire in any other shape. The manufacture of gunpowder, which is a Government monopoly in all the rest of Italy, is an important branch of free industry at San Marino.

And another curious industry of the San Marinesi, arising from the same exemption from the fiscal laws of the world around them, is the manufacture of playing cards; not intended, exclusively, it need hardly be said, for the use of their own citizens.

At length, not without sundry pauses to recover breath and gaze with panting sides the while at the wide-spread world below us, we reach the gate of the city, most picturesquely placed at an angle in the wall, at the edge of the precipice. We passed up the main street of the town from end to end without meeting with a single living thing! It was about four o'clock in the afternoon; and the utter absence of all appearance of life produced a strange effect, and added to the air of stern and grim severity occasioned by the dark colour of the buildings, the paucity of windows, the entire absence of shops, and the rigorously closed doors. Later in the afternoon there was a little more movement in the town, and we saw a few small shops in other parts of it. But still the severe, prim, almost monastic aspect of the streets, composed, for the most part, of very good and solid houses, and, in some parts of large and handsome though perfectly plain palaces, is very remarkable.

This main street rises very considerably, as it approaches that part of the hill in which the fortress stands; and at the further end of it (from the gate at which we had entered) an almost stair-like ascent leads to a higher platform, on which the principal church, (not Cathedral, for San Marino is not a Bishop's See) is situated. It is an entirely new building and has no features of any interest whatever. There is just below it an open *piazza*, from which there is a very wide view over the country landwards, and the whole of which forms the roof of a vast cistern for the preservation of rain water. San Marino has no other sources of supply. But the means for the collection and preservation of it are so abundant and well contrived, that I was assured that the supply of water was never deficient either in quantity or quality.

From the church, a steep path, first finding its devious way amid houses and attempts at little gardens, disposed not in streets but in the utterly disorderly arrangement dictated by the inequalities of the rocky ground, and then leaving the houses altogether, and emerging on the ragged and craggy brow of the perpendicular precipice, but still within the walls of the town, leads by a continuous steep ascent to the castle; which occupies the highest peak of the mountain. Crossing the open down-like space of mingled grey rock and green turf, we found ourselves before a small closed door in a grey tower, with a bell handle hanging by its side. We rang once, twice, thrice; and were turning away in despair of getting any answer to our summons, when the door was at length opened by a little girl, who instantly took to her heels on seeing us, calling loudly on " Babbo, Babbo!"* as she ran. She left the door open however; and following her in, we found ourselves in a little garden, or rather potato ground, enclosed by lofty battlemented walls, on the sides furthest from the precipice, and by the main keep of the fortress on the other. In a minute or two, "down the lord of the castle came," and first carefully shutting the door which his daughter had left open, announced himself as captain and garrison of the fortress of San Marino, town gaoler, and shoemaker in the leisure left by weightier cares. He very courteously offered to show us all his domain; and if it did not comprise within itself any thing very beautiful or wonderful, that which might be seen from it was truly both.

 The castle is perched at the very edge of the wall of rock, so that from its battlements you look sheer down on the Borgo below, a height of some five or six hundred feet. The landward view, that towards the higher Apennines, that is to say, over the world of hills, composing a district, of which it is

* " Daddy! daddy!"

no exaggeration to say that it looks like the battle-field of a discomfited army of Titans, strewn with the wreck of their fight against Heaven, is a most singular and striking one.

The ancient name of the mountain of San Marino was Monte Titano; and the antiquarians have suggested a variety of origins, each more absurd than the other for the appellation. Melchiore Delfico, in his excellent book on San Marino,* sensibly enough remarks that it is far more probable, that the name was suggested by the general appearance of the district. And it is impossible to look over the view from the castle tower without being struck by the probability of the theory, and the appropriateness of the name.

The view towards the Adriatic is scarcely less varied; for the immense sweep of sea, which despite its monotony, always constitutes so strangely fascinating an object for the eye to rest on, occupies but the distance of the immense panorama. In front of it, and more immediately beneath the eye is all the coast of Picenum, with its legion of storied cities and castle-crowned hills.

The *custode* assured me that the coast of Dalmatia was sometimes very plainly visible, but rarely at that hour. The best time, he said, was a minute or two before sun-rise; and he strongly advised me to pay him a visit at that hour on the following morning. To do so would involve getting up more than an hour

* "Memorie Storiche della Republica di San Marino, raccolte del Cavre. Melchiore Delfico Cittadino della medesima." 1 vol. 4to, Milano, 1804. Also Capolago, 1 Vol. small 8vo. 1842. This edition does not contain the documents. This well-known work is one of the best local histories Italy possesses.

before sun-rise, as I was to sleep six hundred feet below there, down in the Borgo. But I determined to accept his invitation, not so much for the sake of seeing Dalmatia, as for the hope of seeing the sun rise out of the Adriatic and gradually light up one after another all the world of hill-tops with their towns and castles around and beneath me.

For the purpose of ascending the tower of the castle, we had to pass through the captain-gaoler's private room; and there we saw sitting a most repulsive and disreputable looking priest. The gaoler pointed him out to our notice with much eagerness, evidently considering him the great point of interest in his establishment; and as soon as we had passed through the room, informed us that he was a prisoner for forgery;—that he had three other prisoners under his care who were locked up in separate cells;—but that his reverence, for the sake of his cloth, was allowed to have the liberty of the whole castle, including a little chapel on the further side of the garden, where he had the advantage of saying daily mass! On our way to the gate we saw the shock heads and villainous faces of the three other state prisoners of San Marino thrust out through as many square holes cut in the doors of their cells. One of these, the gaoler told us, had been in the prison for the last six months, on a charge of homicide, and had not yet been brought to trial. A fresh judge, he said, had just been appointed; and was to arrive at San Marino on the morrow; and it was to be hoped that the accused man would now at last be tried. It struck me that if similar facts are of frequent occurrence at San Marino, it might occur in these our days, that the Republic itself, despite its eight hundred years of existence, might find itself put on its trial.

Before parting with us at the threshold of his domain, the *custode* told us that we were very fortunate in the day of our arrival, for that we should that evening hear the great bell of San Marino, which was under his charge, ring out in warning to the members of the great Council, which under the title of "*Il Principe*," the prince, is the ruling power of the Republic, that there was a meeting of the Council appointed for the next day. And in fact, soon after we had descended to the Borgo, we did enjoy that honour and satisfaction; and were led by it to grave suspicions as to the soundness of the venerable bell in question.

The next morning I was punctual to my appointment, being at the castle door about a quarter of an hour before sun-rise. I had found the city gate shut, and feared that the purpose of my early walk would be frustrated. But there was a huge rusty knocker on the worm-eaten old gate, which I should think had not been used for many a day; and with this I struck three mighty strokes, that seemed to echo through the whole silent town, and frightened me with the responsibility I was taking on myself of knocking up the whole city, that I might pass on my way to see the sun rise. My summons however brought out the gatekeeper, evidently in a state of the most unmitigated astonishment; which was in no degree lessened by my reply to his demand where I was going and what I wanted, that I was going to the castle to see the sun rise! He held the wicket

x

open as he spoke, and waiting for no further permission I stepped in, and walked up the solitary street, waking a legion of echoes with every footfall. The gatekeeper had said no word more; but turning my head to look when I was a good bit up the street, I saw him still standing with the wicket open in his hand, staring after me in speechless wonderment.

The *custode* of the castle was also punctual, and was expecting me. There was a very fresh breeze blowing in from the Adriatic; and my walk up from the Borgo had done more than warm me. So I was very glad to accept the Warder's offer of a cloak to throw over my shoulders, as I stood by his side on the battlements waiting for the beginning of the great spectacle.

Just a minute or two before the first limb of the sun peeped above the sea horizon, the *custode* told me to bring my eye to a level with the coping stone of a certain point in the battlement wall, and look steadily in the direction of the line formed by its edge. I followed his directions, and did most unmistakably see the outline of a mountain on the opposite coast. I could therefore say, as he remarked,—and do hereby say accordingly, that I have seen across the Adriatic from one coast to the other with the naked eye.

But the truly magnificent part of the spectacle was yet to come. In about two minutes more it did come; and few such sun-rises, I think, are to be witnessed from any spot in Europe. First came the gradually kindling path of fire athwart the cold deep blue of the Adriatic. Then one after another the mountain tops were waked up to the new day.

The Ancona promontory was the first to catch the

ray; then the higher of the tops further inland, and lastly the lowlands and the distant city of Rimini, which, by comparison, seemed close beneath our gaze.

Let no one whose love of seeing has induced them to climb the hill of San Marino, leave it without having stood on the castle battlements at sun-rise.

Of course the extraordinary phenomenon of this little community having maintained through the chances and changes of eight centuries its freedom, independence, and republican form of government in the midst of a number of comparatively powerful and often unscrupulous neighbours, who hated all these things, is to be explained chiefly by the peculiarity of its position and its extraordinary isolation and inaccessibility. But doubtless also much wisdom and moderation, and consistent prudence has been necessary to secure that immunity from the troubles that have vexed every other community in Italy. The main part and chief rule of this prudence has consisted in the most cautious abstention from aught that could give umbrage to the powers around it. And it can hardly be denied that this prudence has been sometimes pushed to an extreme of caution somewhat humiliating, and almost amounting to a consent *"propter* libertatem libertatis *perdere causas,"* as when the Republic forbade the existence of any printing press in its dominions, for fear matter offensive to the despot governments around it might be printed there. Doubtless the probability is, that had the little free State not stooped to such concessions, it would not have been permitted to exist.

Of course the *"facilis descensus"* is strongly exemplified in the case of an expedition to San Marino.

The return to Rimini may be accomplished in a quarter of the time which it required to reach the highland city thence. We ran down in time to catch a train which brought us to Bologna the same evening, and found there a courier's carriage, which carried us to Florence within twenty-four hours from the time that I had been standing to see the sun rise on the top of the peak of San Marino!

AND SO ENDED OUR LENTEN JOURNEY.

FINIS.